£11-50

S10

James Lumby —

Oxford 1995.

A QUEEN ON TRIAL

'Queen Caroline. Britain's best hope!! England's Sheet-Anchor!!!' (19 October 1820)

A QUEEN ON TRIAL

The Affair of Queen Caroline

E . A . SMITH

ALAN SUTTON

First published in the United Kingdom in 1993 by
Alan Sutton Publishing Limited
Phoenix Mill · Far Thrupp · Stroud · Gloucestershire

First published in the United States of America in 1993 by
Alan Sutton Publishing Inc · 83 Washington Street · Dover · NH 03820

Copyright © E.A. Smith 1993

British Library Cataloguing in Publication Data

Smith, E.A.
  Queen on Trial: Affair of Queen Caroline
  I. Title
  941.074092

  ISBN 0-7509-0383-X

Library of Congress Cataloging in Publication Data

Smith, E.A.
  A queen on trial : the affair of Queen Caroline. 1820–21 / E.A. Smith.
  Smith.
     p. cm.
  Includes bibliographical references and index.
  ISBN 0-7509-0383-X
  1. Caroline Amelia Elizabeth, Queen, consort of George IV, King of
Great Britain, 1768–1821. 2. Adultery—Great Britain—Public
opinion—History—19th century. 3. Scandals—Great Britain—
History—19th century. 4. Queens—Great Britain—Biography.
  I. Title
DA 538.A22S63 1993
941.07'4'092—dc20
[B]   93–26288
                                                                CIP

Typeset in 10/12 Plantin.
Typesetting and origination by
Alan Sutton Publishing Limited.
Printed in Great Britain by
The Bath Press, Avon.

Contents

List of Illustrations

Acknowledgements

I am grateful to the following owners of copyright for permission to include extracts from the works specified in this book:

The Cambridge University Press for *The Letters of T.B. Macaulay*, ed. T. Pinney, vol. 1, 1974; The Macmillan Press Ltd for *The Journal of Mrs Arbuthnot 1820–1832*, ed. F. Bamford and the Duke of Wellington, vol. 1, 1950; John Murray (Publishers) for *The Letters of Lady Palmerston*, ed. Tresham Lever, 1957, and *Private Letters of Princess Lieven to Prince Metternich 1820–1826*, ed. P. Quennell 1937.

I am also grateful to Mrs Elizabeth Berry for her unfailingly efficient and heroic secretarial services. Above all, I am as always indebted to my wife Virginia for the inspiration, encouragement, and criticism which have done so much to bring this book into being. Her contribution to its origins and its final shape has been immeasurable, and has added greatly to my enjoyment in writing it.

Illustration nos 3, 4 and 5 are reproduced from the Royal Collection, by gracious permission of HM the Queen; 1, 6, 11, 12, 13, 15, 17, 18, 20, 21, 24, 25, 27, 31, 32, 34 and 35 by courtesy of the Public Record Office (Treasury Solicitor's papers); 2, 8, 22, 23, 26, 33, 36, 37, 38, 39 and 40 by courtesy of the University of Reading; 7 by courtesy of the British Museum; 9, 10 and 19 by courtesy of the National Portrait Gallery; 14 by courtesy of the Royal Pavilion, Art Gallery and Museum, Brighton; 16 and 30 by courtesy of Dr P.J. Jupp. Nos 28 and 29 are from prints in the author's collection.

Preface

King George IV's abortive attempt to divorce his wife, Caroline, in the summer and autumn of 1820 is one of the best-known and most scandalous chapters in the history of the British throne. Whether or not she was in fact guilty of adultery with her Italian chamberlain and servant Pergami (or Bergami) was never precisely proved, though the evidence against her was circumstantially strong. It is also a strong possibility that she had lovers in England after her separation from her husband, then the Prince of Wales, which took place only a short time after their marriage in 1795. George Canning and Sir Thomas Lawrence were among those named and suspected at the time. During the twenty-five years of their separation she and the Prince lived separate lives and went their own ways. The Prince himself was known to have had several mistresses, and indeed had married Maria Fitzherbert ten years before his wedding to Caroline, though that previous marriage was regarded as unlawful because it infringed the Royal Marriage Act. As Mrs Fitzherbert was a Roman Catholic it would, if avowed, have endangered the Prince's right of succession to the throne, so it was always kept a secret from the world at large. Bigamy was not the Prince's only iniquity; he consorted with a succession of mistresses and was generally considered to be no better, morally, than his legal wife. Together with his selfish extravagance with public money and the responsibility which, as Prince Regent, he bore for the distressed state of the country after the end of the Napoleonic Wars in 1815, this made him for a time the most despised and unpopular of Britain's rulers. He hardly dared to go out into the streets of his own capital for fear of insult from his subjects, and he was pilloried by the Press and in innumerable cartoons and caricatures, often of the most obscene kind.

It was no wonder, then, that when he became king in January 1820 and immediately tried to deny his wife the title and status of queen, the people at large, and especially in London, adopted her as their heroine, as a persecuted woman who, if not entirely innocent, was certainly no worse than he was. Her appearance in England in June sparked off a series of demonstrations, addresses, cartoons and other manifestations of popular feeling that even seemed to endanger the stability of the throne and the peace of the country. Only a few weeks before, a group of conspirators had plotted to murder the entire Cabinet at dinner – the 'Cato Street conspiracy' – and the political radicals who had been vociferous since before the end of the war were clamouring for measures to end the distress of the people by reducing taxes and conceding parliamentary reform. Queen Caroline provided them with a symbol of persecuted innocence and an instrument to use against an unpopular regime. She was adopted by the Radicals in London, led by men such as Alderman Matthew Wood, a former Lord Mayor, William Cobbett the popular journalist, and other leading figures. Her so-called 'trial', the proceedings in the House of Lords on the bill to divorce her which the King forced on his ministers, became the centre of the Radicals' campaign to discredit the monarchy and the government. It marked the apogee of the success of the early nineteenth-century Radical movement: never was it so popular as when personified by the picture of an injured woman, the victim of a worthless monarch and a corrupt government. It also engendered a new, if temporary, phenomenon, of feminist agitation, for the Queen's plight highlighted the male-dominated nature of society and the injustice of the law towards women's rights. In all these respects the affair of Queen Caroline was a crucial episode in English history, and if in the end it all came to nothing it had raised issues and aroused passions which could never entirely be hidden away again.

This book is modelled on the format of my work *Reform or Revolution? A Diary of Reform in England, 1830–32*, published by Alan Sutton in 1992. It tells the story of the tumultuous months of the second half of 1820 through the experiences and recollections of those who took part in or witnessed the events and scenes of the time. It thus provides an immediacy of view which helps us to understand the reaction of the people of the time and to appreciate how events appeared as they unfolded and without knowledge of how it was to end. The final revelation that, despite it all, the monarchy and the constitution survived, proving stronger than the effects of temporary crisis, may also have a lesson for the present day in showing that the historic institutions of Britain are more firmly and deeply rooted in popular affection than the passing moment sometimes suggests.

CHAPTER ONE

An Unsuitable Bride

Caroline Amelia Elizabeth of Brunswick-Wolfenbüttel was born on 17 May 1768, the second daughter of Duke Charles William Ferdinand of Brunswick-Wolfenbüttel and his wife Princess Augusta, daughter of Frederick, Prince of Wales and sister to King George III of England. Brought up in a minor German princely court, she lacked and never acquired the refined social graces and manners of the highest society of Paris or London. The Brunswick-Wolfenbüttel court was described as 'one of the gayest in Germany' with little of the 'stiff etiquette' characteristic of the other north German courts. At the age of fourteen Caroline was described as 'a lively, pretty child with light coloured hair hanging in curls on her neck, with rosebud lips from which it seemed that none but sweet words could flow, and always simply and modestly dressed'. By her twenties, however, she had a reputation as something of a flirt and was notorious for her unbridled and sometimes indecent conversation in public company. It was said that her parents forbade her to speak to anyone but her governess lest she should shock those about her, and that her generally 'indecent conduct' had led to a ban on all amusements. Whether because of this reputation or not, by the age of twenty-six she was still unmarried, nor was she even attached to any suitor. Her person was not particularly attractive. It was said that neither she nor her underclothes were often washed. As one English historian baldly put it, 'she swore like an ostler and smelt like a farmyard'.

No less suitable bride could be imagined for the fastidious, fashionable and cultivated George Augustus Frederick, Prince of Wales, eldest son of George III and leader of the *beau monde* – 'the first gentleman of Europe'. Yet on the evening of Wednesday 8 April 1795 they were married in the Chapel Royal at St James's at a glittering ceremony, the bride dressed in white silver tissue, richly ornamented with jewels, with a coronet and a royal robe of crimson velvet bordered with ermine. Her bridesmaids wore white satin, with head-dresses of ostrich feathers. The King, Queen and other members of the numerous royal family were present, and Caroline chatted animatedly to those around her. Yet, as Lady Maria Stuart, who was present at the drawing-room which followed, remarked, it was 'an odd wedding'. The bridegroom, in fact, appeared to be the worse for drink and had to be supported by his two groomsmen, the Dukes of Bedford and Roxburghe. He 'looked like death', Lord Malmesbury commented, and 'had manifestly had recourse to wine or spirits'. His eyes were not upon his bride but on Lady Jersey, his mistress of the moment – not that he was capable of any more than glancing at any woman, for, according to his wife's later account, after taking a great deal more liquor at the supper which was held at Buckingham House, he arrived with his bride at his residence, Carlton House in Pall Mall, in a state of alcoholic helplessness, collapsed on the floor of the bridal bedchamber and spent the wedding night insensible.

The reasons for the Prince's unforgivable – and ever afterwards unforgiven – conduct lay in his own disreputable past. As a youth he was wayward and undisciplined, attracted to women of all kinds and to every dissipation that London could offer, with companions as notorious as he became. In reaction against the strict upbringing he endured in the oppressive and moralistic court of his parents he and his brothers pursued pleasure without restraint. At the age of eighteen, Horace Walpole wrote, he and his brother the Duke of York 'drank hard, swore, & passed every night in brothels. Such was the fruit of his being locked up in the Palace of Piety. . . . He passed the nights in the lowest debaucheries, at the same time bragging of intrigues with women of quality, whom he named publicly.' In his 'teens his father had to buy off 'Perdita' Robinson, the celebrated actress, to whom the Prince had written some indiscreet letters, but nothing restrained his son's continued dissipations.

Despite these debauched tastes and habits, the Prince showed a passion for the fashionable arts, and became a devotee of every new style in architecture and decoration. He spent hundreds of thousands of pounds in restoring and furnishing his princely residence at Carlton House and later in remodelling in the oriental taste the modest farmhouse which he acquired at Brighton and which was named The Pavilion. Heedless of expense and of his father's warnings to practise economy – deliberately reacting against his parents' parsimony and his father's deep sense of responsibility to the public purse – he spent money like water and was soon head over ears in debt. By 1786 his debts were estimated at no less than a quarter of a million pounds.

The biggest imbroglio of all, however, was his clandestine and (strictly speaking) illegal marriage in 1785 to a respectable Roman Catholic lady, six years his senior and twice widowed, named Maria Fitzherbert. The Prince had pursued her with extravagant ardour almost from the time they first met, but she was a woman of devout principles and she refused to follow the path trodden by so many before her and become his mistress. Yet a marriage to a commoner would never have been permitted by the Prince's father, and without his consent no marriage would have been legal under the Royal Marriage Act. Even worse, marriage to a Catholic would have excluded the Prince from the succession to the throne under the Act of Settlement.

However, the prince's infatuation was so desperate that he declared he could not live without Maria. He staged a fake suicide by cutting himself with a sword, and swore to tear off his bandages and bleed to death unless she gave in. Finally, she agreed to a clandestine marriage carried out by an Anglican clergyman bailed from the Fleet prison for the occasion who was promised a bishopric when the Prince became King. Unfortunately, or perhaps fortunately, he died before that promise could be redeemed. However, in the eyes of both Anglican and Catholic churches, if not in secular law, it was a valid marriage. It was never publicly admitted, but it was widely suspected and when in 1787 the House of Commons was asked for additional funds to pay off George's debts veiled threats were made of disclosure. The Prince added to his infamies by persuading his crony Charles James Fox, who did not know the secret, to deny the marriage in the House. When Fox and his political friends discovered the truth they abandoned him for two years. Parliament nevertheless paid off his debts, but his extravagance continued. Five years later his debts had reached £400,000.

In the eyes of the law and of his parents the Prince was still a bachelor, and by 1794, when he was thirty-two years of age, it was high time he was settled into a royal marriage. A Protestant princess, preferably German in accordance with the Hanoverian family's own ancestry, was the necessary goal, and the Prince's choice settled on Caroline, who was his first cousin. She believed that his brother the Duke of Clarence, who had met her, recommended her to the Prince, but in truth George cared little who she might be. 'One damned German Frau is as good as another,' he is said to have muttered. Lady Salisbury later asserted that Lady Jersey encouraged the match in order to destroy Mrs Fitzherbert's influence over him 'and place her on the same footing as his other loves'. The real inducement to marry, however, was the King's promise to pay his outstanding debts and the prospect of a substantial increase in his allowance from the civil list. The fact that he had never met or even seen his intended bride was not unusual in European royal marriages, which were always arranged for dynastic or diplomatic ends. It was not expected, or required, that the parties should be in love, or even acquainted with each other. The royal marriage market was rather akin to the breeding of pedigree cattle: the purpose was to provide heirs to the thrones of Europe of the requisite stock.

★ ★ ★

In the autumn of 1794 James Harris, Lord Malmesbury, a friend of the Prince of Wales, was sent on a diplomatic mission to Brunswick-Wolfenbüttel. Part of his task was to discuss future operations in north Germany against Revolutionary France, but the main purpose of his mission was to demand the hand of Caroline, the daughter of the Duke, as a bride for the Prince of Wales. In his diary he recorded his impressions of the future Princess from their first meeting until their arrival in England over four months later, their journey having been delayed by bad weather and by military operations during the war. His concern about the bride's unsuitability as a partner for the Prince led him to try to educate her in the manners, conduct, and hygiene which would be expected of a young woman in high society and which might make her acceptable to the Prince. She seemed a willing pupil, but her habits were too deeply rooted and her character too frivolous to adopt new ways. Malmesbury's worst fears were to be realized when she met her future husband for the first time.

Lord Malmesbury's diary, 1794

Thursday, Nov. 28 [sc. 20th] – . . . The Princess Caroline (Princess of Wales) much embarrassed on my first being presented to her – pretty face – not expressive of softness – her figure not graceful – fine eyes – good hand – tolerable teeth, but going – fair hair and light eyebrows, good bust – short, with what the French call 'des épaules impertinentes'. Vastly happy with her future expectations . . .

Sunday, Dec. 7. – . . . Another long conversation with the Duke about his daughter: he extremely anxious about her doing right; said he had been with her for two hours in the morning – that he wished to make her feel that the high situation in which she was going to be placed was not simply one of amusement and enjoyment; that it had

'The lover's dream,' J. Gillray (24 January 1795). The Prince of Wales hugs a bolster and dreams of his future bride and of the increased income of £150,000 a year promised by his father. On the left, Lady Jersey, Mrs Fitzherbert and Charles James Fox and R.B. Sheridan, his old Whig cronies, flee into oblivion

its duties, and those perhaps difficult and hard to fulfil. He again earnestly entreated me to be her adviser – not to forsake her when in England; that he was more afraid of what would happen there than here; that he dreaded the Prince's habits. . . . Sat next Princess Caroline at supper; I advise her to avoid familiarity, to have no *confidantes*, to avoid giving any opinion; to approve, but not to admire excessively; to be perfectly silent on politics and party; to be very attentive and respectful to the Queen; to endeavour, at all events, to be well with her. She takes all this well; she was at times in tears, but on account of having taken leave of some of her old acquaintance. . . .

Tuesday, Dec. 9. . . . She asked me about Lady [Jersey], appeared to suppose her an *intriguante*, but not to know of any partiality or connection between her and the Prince. . . . She said of her own accord, 'I am determined never to appear jealous. I know the Prince is *léger*, and am prepared on this point.' I said I did not believe she would have any occasion to exercise this very wise resolution, which I commended highly; and entreated her if she saw any symptoms of a *goût* in the Prince, or if any of the women about her should, under the love of fishing in troubled waters, endeavour to excite a jealousy in her mind, on no account to allow it to manifest itself; that reproaches and sourness never reclaimed anybody; that it only served as an advantageous contrast to the contrary qualities in the rival; and that the surest way of recovering a tottering affection was softness, enduring and caresses; that I knew enough of the Prince to be quite sure he could not withstand such a conduct, while a contrary one would *probably* make him disagreeable and peevish, and certainly force him to be false and dissembling.

Tuesday, Dec. 16. – . . . At dinner next Princess Caroline . . . She [Caroline] has no *fond*, no fixed character, a light and flighty mind, but meaning well, and well-disposed; and my eternal theme to her is *to think before she speaks, to recollect herself.* She says she wishes to be *loved* by the people; this, I assure her, can only be obtained by making herself respected and *rare* – that the sentiment of being *loved* by the people is a mistaken one – that sentiment can only be given to a few, to a narrow circle of those we see every day – that a nation at large can only respect and honour a great Princess, and it is, in fact, these feelings that are falsely denominated *the love of a nation*: they are not to be procured as the goodwill of individuals is, by pleasant openness and free communication, but by a strict attention to appearances – by never going below the high rank in which a Princess is placed, either in language or manners – by mixing dignity with affability, which, without it, becomes familiarity, and levels all distinction.

Saturday, Dec. 20. – Walk with Sir B. Boothby. We regret the apparent facility of the Princess Caroline's character – her want of reflection and *substance* – agree that with a *steady* man she would do vastly well, but with one of a different description there are great risks. . . .

Sunday, Dec. 28. . . . At dinner I found the Duchess and Princess alarmed, agitated, and uneasy at an anonymous letter from England, abusing the Prince, and warning them in the most exaggerated terms against Lady —, who is represented as the worst and most dangerous of profligate women. The Duchess, with her usual indiscretion, had shown this to the Princess, and mentioned it to everybody. . . . Princess Caroline shows me the anonymous letter about Lady —, evidently written by some disappointed milliner or angry maid-servant, and deserving no attention. . . . I told her Lady — would be more cautious than to risk such an audacious measure; and that, besides, it was *death* to presume to approach a Princess of Wales, and no man would be daring enough to think of it. She asked me whether I was in earnest. I said such was our law; that anybody who presumed to *love* her was guilty of *high treason*, and punished with *death*, if she was weak enough to listen to him; so also would *she*. This startled her.

. . . On summing up Princess Caroline's character today, it came out to my mind to be, that she has quick parts, without a sound or distinguishing understanding; that she has a ready conception but no judgment; caught by the first impression, led by the first impulse; turned away by appearances or *enjouement*; loving to talk, and prone to confide and make missish friendships that last twenty-four hours. Some natural, but no acquired morality, and no strong innate notions of its value and necessity; warm feelings and nothing to counterbalance them; great good-humour and much good-nature – no appearance of caprice – rather quick and *vive*, but not a grain of rancour. From her habits, from the life she was allowed and even compelled to live, forced to dissemble; fond of gossiping, and this strengthened greatly by the example of her good mother, who is all curiosity and inquisitiveness, and who has no notion of not gratifying this desire at any price. In short, the Princess in the hands of a steady and sensible man would probably turn out well, but where it is likely she will find faults perfectly analagous to her own, she will fail. She has no governing powers, although her mind is *physically* strong. She has her father's courage, but it is to her (as to him) of no avail. *He* wants mental decision; *she* character and *tact*.

Sunday, Jan. 18 [Osnabruck] . . . Queen's birthday – gala – great dinner . . . Princess Caroline very *missish* at supper. I much fear these habits are irrevocably rooted in her; she is naturally curious, and a gossip – she is quick and observing, and she has a silly pride of finding out everything – she thinks herself particularly acute in discovering *likings*, and this leads her at times to the most improper remarks and conversation. I am determined to take an opportunity of correcting her, *coute qu'il coute*.

Wednesday, Feb. 18. – . . . Argument with the Princess about her toilette. She piques herself on dressing quick; I disapprove this. She maintains her point; I however desire Madame Busche to explain to her that the Prince is very delicate, and that he expects a long and very careful *toilette de propreté*, of which she has no idea. On the contrary, she neglects it sadly, and is offensive from this neglect. Madame Busche executes her commission well, and the Princess comes out the next day well washed *all over*.

March 6. . . . I had two conversations with Princess Caroline. One on the toilette, on cleanliness, and on delicacy of speaking. On these points I endeavoured, as far as was possible for a *man*, to inculcate the necessity of great and nice attention to every part of dress, as well as to what was hid, as to what was seen. (I knew she wore coarse petticoats, coarse shifts, and thread stockings, and these never well washed, or changed often enough). I observed that a long toilette was necessary, and gave her no credit for boasting that hers was a 'short' one. What I could not say myself on this point, I got said through women; through Madame Busche, and afterwards through Mrs Harcourt. It is remarkable how amazingly on this point her education has been neglected, and how much her mother, although an Englishwoman, was inattentive to it. . . . The Princess felt all this, and it made a temporary impression; but in this as on all other subjects, I have had but too many opportunities to observe that her heart is very, *very* light, unsusceptible of strong or lasting feelings. In some respects this may make her happier, but certainly not better.

Sunday, April 5. . . . we arrived and were set down at St James's (the Duke of Cumberland's apartments, Cleveland Row) about half-past two.
    I immediately notified the arrival to the King and Prince of Wales; the last came immediately. I, according to the established etiquette, introduced (no one else being in the room) the Princess Caroline to him. She very properly, in consequence of my saying to her it was the right mode of proceeding, attempted to kneel to him. He raised her (gracefully enough) and embraced her, said barely one word, turned round, returned to a distant part of the apartment, and calling me to him, said, 'Harris, I am not well; pray get me a glass of brandy.' I said, 'Sir, had you not better have a glass of water?' – upon which he, much out of humour, said with an oath, '*No*; I will go directly to the Queen;' and away he went. The Princess, left during this short moment alone, was in a state of astonishment; and, on my joining her, said, '*Mon Dieu! est ce que le Prince est toujours comme cela? Je le trouve très gros, et nullement aussi beau que son portrait.*' I said His Royal Highness was naturally a good deal affected and flurried at this first interview, but she certainly would find him different at dinner. She was disposed to further criticizing on this occasion, which would have

Princess Caroline of Brunswick (Dupont after Gainsborough)

embarrassed me very much to answer, if luckily the King had not ordered me to attend him.

The drawing-room was just over. His Majesty's conversation turned wholly on Prussian and French politics; and the only question about the Princess was, 'Is she good-humoured?' I said, and very truly, that in very trying moments, I had never seen her otherwise. The King said, 'I am glad of it;' and it was manifest, from his silence, he had seen the Queen *since* she had seen the Prince, and that the Prince had made a very unfavourable report of the Princess to her. At dinner . . . I was far from satisfied with the Princess's behaviour; it was flippant, rattling, affecting raillery and wit, and throwing out coarse vulgar hints about Lady [Jersey], who was present, and though mute, *le diable n'en perdait rien.* The Prince was evidently disgusted; and this unfortunate dinner fixed his dislike, which, when left to herself, the Princess had not the talent to remove; but, by still observing the same giddy manners and attempts at cleverness and coarse sarcasm, increased till it became positive hatred. . . .

The marriage ceremony on 8 April passed off without undue incident, though it was noticed that the Archbishop of Canterbury paused meaningfully at the passage concerning the disclosure of 'any lawful impediment' and twice repeated the passage which abjured the Prince 'to live from that time in nuptial fidelity with his consort'. The wedding night was hardly even an anti-climax: rather it was a fitting prelude to the honeymoon, in which the Prince openly neglected his wife. She later alleged that during their stay at a rented house near Basingstoke the only other woman present was Lady Jersey and that the rest of the

The wedding of the Prince of Wales and Princess Caroline (Henry Singleton)

party were all 'very blackguard companions of the Prince's, who were constantly drunk and filthy, sleeping & snoring in bouts on the sofas . . . & the whole resembled a bad brothel much more than a palace'.

The Prince had, however, managed to perform one duty. By the time they moved to Brighton two months after the ceremony the Princess was pregnant – rather to her surprise, for she hinted to Malmesbury that she thought him incapable. Their child, christened Charlotte after the Queen, was born in January 1796 – nine months to the day after their wedding – to the joy and satisfaction of the Prince's parents. The Prince himself, however, was unreconciled to his wife and two days after Charlotte was born, in a state of almost nervous hysteria, he wrote out a long, rambling will leaving all his personal property to his 'beloved & adored Maria Fitzherbert', his only true and adored wife, and demanding that Caroline should in no way be concerned with the education, care, or upbringing of their daughter: even his wife's jewels, given to her by him, were to be passed to Charlotte while to Caroline herself, 'her who is call'd the Princess of Wales I leave one shilling'.

After further quarrels and humiliations, Caroline confronted her husband at Carlton House in December 1797 and declared that she would no longer obey him – she had not truly been his wife for nearly two and a half years – and she retired to a rented house at Blackheath, leaving her daughter in the Prince's care. They never lived under the same roof again, and in 1799 he persuaded Maria Fitzherbert to resume their relationship.

Caroline did not retire from society after her separation from the Prince. She set up almost an alternative court at Blackheath, where she resided for sixteen years. She entertained lavishly, being visited by a variety of 'remarkable persons', as one lord remarked, notable in the arts and sciences, politics and the law. She entertained men from both sides of the political world, from Pitt and Canning to Charles Grey, and some of them were rumoured to be her lovers. In the case of Canning in particular that seems to have been true, which was to be an embarrassment to him in 1820 when he was a member of the government which brought in the bill to divorce her on the grounds of her alleged immoralities. Rumours about her sexual conduct quickly spread, and in 1802 she was alleged to be pregnant again; indeed, she herself foolishly pretended to be so, and her friend Lady Douglas was to allege that a boy child named William was born to the Queen early in 1803. The child seems in fact to have been abandoned by his real mother, a Mrs Austin, a poor woman from Deptford, and adopted by Caroline as a focus for her thwarted motherly instincts. When, however, Caroline quarrelled with the Douglases, they sought to blackmail her by making allegations about the child, which they fed to the Prince and to London society in the winter of 1805–6. The outcome was the so-called and rather inappropriately named 'Delicate Investigation' by a commission of Cabinet ministers who dredged through the scandals and allegations of everything from adultery with men such as Thomas Lawrence, the painter, Admiral Sir Sidney Smith, and Captain Thomas Manby RN, to lesbianism. The commission concluded that the story about the Princess's illegitimate child was false, that there was no evidence of actual adultery, but that her conduct in general 'must . . . give occasion to very unfavourable interpretations'. The Cabinet recommended that, while the King might continue to receive her at court, he should warn her about her general conduct. The Prince was furious, for he had been hoping for evidence which would allow him to divorce her. She had obviously been sexually promiscuous, but there was no firm proof.

In addition, Caroline's affairs now became a source of political contention. Her defence was taken up by the opposition, led by Spencer Perceval and Canning; after the change of government in 1807, they were replaced as the Princess's defenders by the former ministers, now in opposition, who had investigated her conduct the previous year. Caroline's full defence against the allegations was composed by Perceval in 1806 under the title of 'The Book', though the change of ministry prevented its publication. Nevertheless, the affair redounded to the discredit of both the Princess and her apparently cuckolded husband, who, however, had an even stronger track record of immoral conduct. The general opinion was that, though Caroline was no better than she should be, she had been scurvily treated by her dissolute and selfish husband and as his popularity waned, hers correspondingly advanced. The foundations were being laid for the public reaction in her favour and against George IV in the affair of 1820.

In the meantime, the upbringing and education of Princess Charlotte added further tensions between her parents. The Prince insisted on full control of his daughter and the total exclusion of her mother, from whose bad influence she was to be protected. His dictatorial attitude, however, alienated Charlotte, who was naturally fond of her mother and equally headstrong and volatile in temperament. She resented the barriers raised between her and her mother, and in 1812–13 when the Prince again attempted to expose Caroline's conduct and 'The Book' was published to provide full details of her alleged crimes, Charlotte was angry with her father. It was also feared that the Prince's renewed campaign was intended to lead to divorce, remarriage, and possibly the birth of a legitimate son who would take Charlotte's place as heir apparent. George's attempt to marry Charlotte off to the Prince of Orange and to send her to live in

Holland was seen as further evidence of a desire to remove her from rival political influence at home. Charlotte refused to marry her father's choice of suitor and demanded an independent establishment; but her prospects were diminished when Caroline decided in 1814 to leave England and travel to the continent, where she spent the next six years in, it was to be alleged, a series of immoral liaisons with menial servants in a kind of exotic travelling circus of pretended oriental splendour. Charlotte's death in 1817 meanwhile increased the pressure on the Prince and his royal brothers to produce another heir to the throne. Caroline's conduct was accordingly the subject of another ministerial enquiry in 1818, when a special commission (known as the Milan Commission) investigated rumours about her alleged immoralities in Italy. No conclusive evidence was found but George continued to press his ministers on the subject and in the summer of 1819 the following exchanges took place.

Minute of Cabinet, 17 June 1819

Your Royal Highness's confidential servants having fully considered the paper which your Royal Highness has been graciously pleased to refer to them, beg leave humbly to submit it as their opinion that it appears to them to be quite clear that a divorce between your Royal Highness and the Princess of Wales never could be accomplished by arrangement, nor obtained except upon proof of adultery, to be substantiated by evidence before some tribunal in this country; and such a proceeding could not, in the judgment of your Royal Highness's servants, be instituted without serious hazard to the interests and peace of the kingdom.

On the other hand, the separation which already exists between your Royal Highness and the Princess of Wales might be rendered complete, the scandal in the eyes of Europe effectually removed, and other eventual inconveniences obviated, by some arrangement upon the principles suggested in the paper referred to by them. But your Royal Highness's servants cannot advise your Royal Highness to entertain such an arrangement unless the proposition, and the terms of it, were distinctly stated to originate on the part of the Princess of Wales, and to be sanctioned by her authority.

The Prince Regent to the Prime Minister, the Earl of Liverpool

Carlton House, Tuesday night, June 22nd, 1819

Most private and confidential

The Prince Regent finds it necessary to remark upon the Minute of the Cabinet of the 17th inst. that his observation in the note delivered to the Earl of Liverpool has been misunderstood.

In stating that it appeared to the Prince Regent that it might be useful to the public interests that the ultimate purpose of divorce should be effected rather by arrangement than by adverse proceeding, the Prince Regent was fully aware that the divorce never could be accomplished except upon satisfactory proof of adultery.

The Prince Regent, for the purpose of the communication in question, did assume (as the party from whom the communication proceeded might be inferred to have assumed) that the evidence collected would afford such satisfactory proof, and the Prince Regent considered that the offence to public decency and public morals which belonged to the nature of that evidence might more certainly be avoided if the ultimate purpose of divorce were submitted to by arrangement, than if the case were left exposed to the clamour of hostile feeling, however little supported by the public sentiment.

The commissioners employed to collect that evidence are in the course of preparing their report, and when such report is concluded, the Prince Regent will cause the same, together with the evidence annexed to it, to be laid before his confidential servants.

The Prince Regent will then have to call their attention to a vast mass of testimony collected under their own immediate sanction, with more than ordinary caution and ability, and which, in the opinion of those who have collected it, affords the clearest and most decisive proof of guilt.

The Prince Regent is sensible that the policy of any proceeding in the present case may be influenced by other considerations; but it is obvious that the weight and character of the evidence are circumstances of the utmost importance with respect to the public feeling.

The Prince Regent, concurring in the opinion that a divorce could never be effected by arrangement without satisfactory proof of adultery, cannot but entertain great doubt whether the sort of separation referred to in the communication could be effected by arrangement without the same proof of adultery.

It is presumed that without proof of crime the Legislature could not be brought to deprive the Princess of Wales of her high station, and of the rights, present and future, which may belong it it. But the sort of separation referred to does deprive the Princess of Wales of that station, and of all its rights present and future. It is equally irreconcileable [*sic*] with the notion of innocence; and as to her, it differs only from divorce in maintaining a fetter which can be of no advantage to her, and which is not likely to be sought by her.

The Prince Regent therefore desires that it may be well considered whether, for the purpose of arrangement, there is any essential difference between divorce and the sort of separation referred to, and whether the party who would propose the one would not accept the other, and whether the aiming at separation instead of divorce would not be an unnecessary sacrifice of important public interests, as well as of the personal feelings of the Prince Regent.

Minute of Cabinet, 24 July 1819

Your Royal Highness's confidential servants have attentively considered the several papers your Royal Highness has been graciously pleased to refer to them, relative to the conduct of her Royal Highness the Princess of Wales.

Your Royal Highness's servants thought it their duty in the first instance to desire the opinion of the King's Advocate, and of his Majesty's Attorney and Solicitor-General, on several points arising out of the information contained in these papers, and they have annexed copies of the questions so put, and of the answers which have been returned to them.

According to these opinions your Royal Highness's servants are led to believe that the facts stated in the papers which have been referred to them would furnish sufficient proof of the crime of adultery, provided they were established by credible witnesses; but it is at the same time the opinion of your Royal Highness's confidential servants, in which they are supported by what has passed in personal communication with the law officers of the Crown, that, considering the manner in which a great part of this testimony has unavoidably been obtained, and the circumstance that the persons who have afforded it are foreigners, many of whom appear to be in a low station of life, it would not be possible to advise your Royal Highness to institute any legal proceeding upon such evidence, without further

George IV as Prince of Wales, 1792 (George Hoppner)

enquiry as to the characters and circumstances of the witnesses by whom it is to be supported; and it is further material to observe, that the law officers are of opinion that the papers do not furnish the means of stating in a proceeding in the Ecclesiastical courts, with the proper precision and accuracy, the facts to which those papers relate. . . .

With regard to . . . a direct application to Parliament, the difficulties in the way of a proceeding of this description will naturally have presented themselves to your Royal Highness's mind.

A legislative proceeding upon a judicial case which does not rest in the first instance upon the judgment of some regular and competent tribunal, must be in principle liable to very serious objections.

Your confidential servants are not prepared to say that no case could exist which would warrant such a proceeding, but they are satisfied that evidence which in a common case, and before the ordinary tribunals, would be deemed fully sufficient to establish the fact of adultery, would, in a proceeding of this kind, be received with the greatest suspicion, particularly where the witnesses happened to be foreigners; and they doubt the success of any application to Parliament upon such a transaction, except in a case in which the testimony was so unexceptionable, clear, and distinct, as to be subject to no reasonable doubt. . . .

Meanwhile, Henry Brougham MP, an ambitious and none too scrupulous Whig lawyer who had been appointed the Princess's legal representative, was attempting to resolve the difficulty in his own way. He offered to mediate between his client and the government, suggesting that the offer of an increased allowance, on condition that she did not return to England to claim the position and title of Queen on her husband's accession, might keep her quiet. He writes in his memoirs of the preliminary negotiations whose breakdown led to the Queen's determination to come to England.

. . . While she remained abroad, many rumours, of course, reached this country; but I had accounts which I could better rely upon from those in her suite, and there was great ground for alarm at the carelessness with which she suffered strangers to make her acquaintance, and of her gaiety and love of amusement leading her into the society of foreigners, and thus exposing her to the constant risk of false reports being conveyed to England by the spies set about her. Nothing, however, was done until the Princess Charlotte's death removed one of her steady friends, with whom it was not thought convenient to renew a quarrel that had proved injurious to all but herself. When she no longer remained to take her mother's part, the Commission was sent to Milan, and then it was quite manifest that measures were prepared to attack her. My correspondence with some friends of the Princess, on whom I could entirely depend – as Sir William Gell, the Miss Berrys, Lady Charlotte Lindsay, and Lady Glenbervie – made it quite clear that, after her daughter's death, she had given up all wish to return; but that the vexation of the constant spies she was beset by, and all the mean contrivances to lower her in the eyes of whatever court she came near, had made her existence intolerable under this endless annoyance of every kind, and that she would be most happy if any arrangement could be made for her entire freedom from all vexation. Her wish was to take some royal title in the family, and, having her income secured, to be recognized by our foreign ministers at whatever court she might choose for a time to have her residence. . . . I have little or no doubt that if the proposal had been at once accepted by the Regent and his advisers she would have been glad to remain abroad. . . .

Brougham's attempt to buy off the Princess is detailed in a letter to the Prime Minister's representative, Lord Hutchinson.

Henry Brougham to Lord Hutchinson

London, June 14th, 1819

In the expectation that proceedings are to be instituted which may call the attention of Parliament to questions concerning the Princess of Wales, and with a view of avoiding the consequences, unpleasant to all parties and hurtful to the country, which may arise from the renewal of such discussions, I am desirous of stating through your Lordship, that upon a mature consideration of the whole subject I am disposed to advise the Princess to accede to an arrangement grounded on some such basis as the following: That she shall agree to a formal separation, to be ratified by Act of Parliament, if such a proceeding can be accomplished; that she shall renounce the right to be crowned in the event of a demise of the Crown, and shall from thenceforth take some other style and title, as that of Duchess of Cornwall; that she shall renounce the jointure to which she is entitled in the event of her surviving the Prince Regent, and that her present annuity shall be granted for her life instead of ceasing on the demise of the Crown. My firm belief is that, although the Princess can have nothing to dread from the result of any proceedings, she will be more comfortable after such an arrangement, since the Princess Charlotte's death has in all probability removed any desire of returning to England; and I am quite sure that if it prevents the manifold evils of a public enquiry into the most delicate matters connected with the royal family, it will be highly beneficial to the country.

I remain, &c.
H. BROUGHAM

Nevertheless, the Prince remained obdurate and no agreement had been reached when he inherited the throne in January 1820.

CHAPTER TWO

Caroline Claims her Rights

King George III died on 29 January 1820. The new King George IV was proclaimed on the 31st, the 30th being the anniversary of the execution of Charles I, and he at once determined to exclude his estranged wife from the position of Queen, demanded that her name be left out of the Anglican liturgy, and indicated his determination to seek a divorce. He refused to listen to his ministers' protests and even appeared to be ready to dismiss them if they did not do as he wished.

Charles Greville, Clerk to the Privy Council, recorded these events in his diary.

February 4th – . . . On Sunday last arrived the news of the King's death. The new King has been desperately ill. He had a bad cold at Brighton, for which he lost eighty ounces of blood; yet he afterwards had a severe oppression, amounting almost to suffocation, on his chest. . . . Yesterday afternoon he was materially better for the first time. . . .

February 14th – The Cabinet sat till past two o'clock this morning. The King refused several times to order the Queen to be prayed for in the alteration which was made in the Liturgy. The Ministers wished him to suffer it to be done, but he peremptorily refused, and said nothing should induce him to consent, whoever might ask him. . . .

February 20th – The Ministers had resigned last week because the King would not hear reason on the subject of the Princess. It is said that he treated Lord Liverpool very coarsely, and ordered him out of the room. The King, they say, asked him 'if he knew to whom he was speaking'. He replied, 'Sir, I know that I am speaking to my Sovereign, and I believe I am addressing him as it becomes a loyal subject to do.' To the Chancellor he said, 'My Lord, I know your conscience always interferes except where your interest is concerned.' The King afterwards sent for Lord Liverpool, who refused at first to go; but afterwards, on the message being reiterated, he went, and the King said, 'We have both been too hasty.' This is probably all false, but it is very true that they offered to resign.

John Wilson Croker, a Tory Member of Parliament, also kept a diary:

Jan. 31st – The hurry and agitation of all these great affairs has made the King worse. He was proclaimed exactly at 12 o'clock at Carlton House inside the screen, with a good deal of applause of the people, but more of the soldiers. A very fine day.

Feb. 5th – The King would be better but that his anxiety about the Queen agitates him terribly.

Feb. 6th Sunday – The King was better, but unluckily last night he recollected that the prayers to be used today were not yet altered. He immediately ordered up all the Prayer-books in the House of old and new dates, and spent the evening in very serious agitation on this subject, which has taken a wonderful hold of his mind. In some churches I understand the clergy prayed for 'our most gracious Queen'; in others and I believe in general, they prayed for 'all the Royal Family'.

'Reflection – to be or not to be?' I.R. Cruikshank (11 February 1820). George IV looks in the mirror and sees the spectre of his wife, wearing a crown, looking over his shoulder

Feb. 10th – Came in [to town] to breakfast with Lowther[1] We talked over the difficulty about praying for the Queen. It struck me that if she is to be prayed for, it will be, in fact, a final settlement of all questions in her favour. If she is fit to be introduced to the Almighty, she is fit to be received by men, and if we are to *pray* for her in Church we may surely bow to her at Court. The praying for her will throw a sanctity round her which the good and pious people of this country will never afterwards bear to have withdrawn. Lowther said that in all the discussions he had never heard the matter argued from this religious point of view, and he advised me to communicate my opinions to the King. We accordingly went over to Carlton House, and saw Blomfield [*sic*],[2] and, strange to say, this view of the subject was as new to him as to Lowther. It made a great impression upon him. He said it never had occurred to the King to argue the question in that way; that it had been discussed as a mere matter of civil propriety and expediency, but that this was a new and clear view, and quite decisive. 'If she was fit to be introduced as Queen to God she was fit to introduce to men. Yes, yes; the King is to see the Ministers today on it, and he shall in half an hour be in possession of this unanswerable argument.' On my return I repeated this line of reasoning to Lord Melville, and, wonderful to say, it appeared that the religious and moral effect of the prayer had been overlooked by the Cabinet also. They had considered it only as to its legal consequences. Three or four of the Cabinet are for praying for her as Queen, but they will be outvoted. This question is of great importance, and I do not see the end of it.

Feb. 12th – A [Privy] Council held today, and it is finally settled not to pray for the Queen by name. An order to this effect will appear in to-night's Gazette. The Archbishop was for praying for the Queen. . . .

Feb. 13th – A new and most serious difficulty has arisen. The King wants the Ministers to pledge themselves to a divorce, which they will not do. They offer to assist to keep the Queen out of the country by the best mode, namely, giving her no money if she will not stay abroad; but this will not satisfy the King. He is furious, and says they have deceived him; that they led him on to hope that they would concur in the measure, and that now they leave him in the lurch. It looks like a very serious breach. . . . The Cabinet offer all but a divorce; the King will have a divorce or nothing. His agitation is extreme and alarming; it not only retards his recovery, but threatens a relapse. He eats hardly anything – a bit of dry toast and a little claret and water. This affair becomes very serious on a more important account than the plans of the Ministers, but the King has certainly intimated intentions of looking for new and more useful servants.

Lord Colchester, a former Speaker of the House of Commons, was touring the Continent at the time of George IV's accession. Two of his friends at home, both Members of Parliament, sent him news.

Henry Bankes to Lord Colchester, 15 February

Dear Colchester, – Your kind letter of Jan. 29th (the day of our poor King's death) reached me last week. . . .

His present Majesty, who, by-the-bye, was in the most immediate danger of following, instead of succeeding, his father on the second and third day of his reign, is most firmly bent on a divorce from his odious and infamous consort. This, we must agree, is natural enough for him to wish, but as those who must carry his project into effect very naturally cast about and calculate their means, his Ministers report to him unanimously that it is *not feasible*, and neither can, nor ought to be, attempted. He perseveres. He insists most obstinately. The Ministers *positively refuse*. He threatens to dismiss them all, to which they reply that they are ready and willing to retire from his service. Written papers and argumentations of considerable length pass between them upon the subject of marriages and divorces. . . . This is our actual state of political uncertainty. . . .

Henry Legge to Lord Colchester, 16 February

My dear Lord Colchester . . . Three days after the good old King's death his successor was so alarmingly ill that serious apprehensions began to be entertained that the longest reign in our annals would be followed by the shortest known in history. His appearance at the Council on Saturday last was that of a person very much reduced by illness, very pale, very weak and tottering. . . .

The death of the Duke of Kent, of the King, and the danger of His present Majesty, and *a* divorce, have put minor subjects into the background. That some process is intended I have good reason to believe. What it is to be, or what shape it is to assume, I do not know. There seems to be a general expectation that the lady will return to this country. . . .

The evidence of criminality is, I am told, conclusive; if so, it is not to be expected that she will be permitted quietly to assume her new dignity and exert its privileges. . . . It is an unpleasant subject in whatever light it is viewed, and can hardly fail to make a disturbance. . . .

Caroline had now taken matters into her own hands and determined to go to England to claim her rights. She announced her decision in a letter to the Prime Minister from Rome on 16 March (the spelling and phraseology of the letter are her own).

Rome, the 16th of March, 1820

The Queen of this Relams wishes to be informed through the medium of Lord Liverpool, First Minister to the King of this Relams, for which reason or motife the Queen name has been left out of the general Prayer-books in England, and especially to prevent all her subjects to pay her such respect which is due to the Queen. It is equally a great omittance towards the King that his consort Queen should be obliged to soummit to such great neglect, or rather araisin from a perfect ignorance of the Archbishops of the real existence of the Queen Caroline of England.

The Queen is also very anxious that Lord Liverpool should communicate this letter to the Archbishop of Canterbury.

Lord Liverpool will be not able to believe, I am sure of it, how much the Queen was surprised of this first act of cruel Tyranne towards her, as she had been informed through the newspapers of the 22nd of February, that in the cours of the Debbet in the House of Common on that evening, Lord Castlereagh, one of the best friends of Lord Liverpool, assured the Attorney-General to the Queen Caroline, Mr Brougham, that the King's Servants would not omitte any attentions or use any harrsness towards the Queen, and after that speech of Lord Castlereagh to find her name left out of the Common Prayer-book, as if she was no longer for this world.

George IV as Prince Regent (I.R. Cruikshank)

The Queen trusts that before she arrives in London to receive satisfactory answer from Lord Liverpool.

CAROLINE QUEEN

Brougham, who had received the formal appointment of Attorney-General to the Queen in late April, resumed his efforts to prevent her from coming to England and to obtain for her a suitable title and income which would enable her to live abroad in comfort and be received at foreign courts. He details the negotiations in his memoirs:

Upon the King's death she had become Queen, and the difficulty became considerable of her position at foreign courts, which would have been easy while only Princess of Wales; and then, upon becoming Queen, she might have retained the title under which she had been known before. . . . She was at Geneva, and her best friends strongly recommended her to remain there until some arrangment could be made. But she received letters from less discreet parties in England, urging her to set out; and she conceived that if she came near England she could more easily negotiate. I was quite convinced that if she once set out she never would stop short. The Milan proceedings were the general topic of conversation, and the feeling which had been so strong in her favour before she left England, had been revived in consequence of those proceedings. Therefore it was quite certain that those who had written to her whilst she was at Geneva would influence her as she approached England, by speaking in the name of the multitude, and would advise her to throw herself on them for protection against the attempts of the Milan Commission and those who had set it to work. So it happened. I had taken the precaution of sending over my brother James to confer with her, and to ascertain who had been examined at Milan, and as far as possible to find out what kind of evidence they had given. It appeared that there was nothing of which she had any reason to be apprehensive, except that almost all the witnesses were Italians, and some of them turned-off servants, and others of disreputable class. But I remained of opinion, in which she entirely concurred, that, however impossible it might be to prove any misconduct, it was very much better to have an arrangement which should supersede all necessity of an inquiry, and leave her conduct entirely unimpeached.

She came to St Omer, where I went to meet her, accompanied by Hutchinson and my brother William. I was the bearer of a proposition that she should have all the rights of Queen-Consort, especially as regarded money and patronage, on consenting to live abroad. Lord Hutchinson was the bearer of an intimation that on her coming to England all negotiation must cease. I found her surrounded by Italians, and resolved to come to England. I advised her against this step, as it must put an end to all negotiation; for example, upon the right to use a royal title, or even to be presented at foreign courts as Queen. My impression was that she had been alarmed at the result of the Milan inquiry, of which most exaggerated rumours were purposely spread, and that those who urged her coming over had succeeded in persuading her that her safety would be best consulted by the popular feeling which her arrival was certain to excite. A long discussion with her had no effect in diverting her from her purpose, which I believed to have been fixed before she set out on her journey; and she left St Omer very suddenly, after refusing to let Lord Hutchinson be presented to her. . . .

Hutchinson set out the government's terms in a letter to Brougham:

'The *secret insult*! or bribery and corruption rejected!!!' I.R. Cruikshank (11 June 1820). Lord Hutchinson holds out a purse of £50,000 while the Queen, attended by Alderman Wood, indignantly rejects his terms

June 4, 1820 – 4 o'clock

Sir,

In obedience to the commands of the Queen, I have to inform you that I am not in possession of any proposition or propositions, detailed in a specific form of words, which I could lay before her Majesty; but I can detail to you, for her information, the substance of many conversations held with Lord Liverpool. His Majesty's ministers propose that £50,000 per annum should be settled on the Queen for life, subject to such conditions as the King may impose. I have also reason to know that the conditions likely to be imposed by his Majesty are, that the Queen is not to assume the style and title of Queen of England, or any title attached to the royal family of England. A condition is also to be attached to this grant, that she is not to reside in any part of the United Kingdom, or even to visit England. The consequence of such a visit will be an immediate message to Parliament, and the entire end to all compromise and negotiation. I believe that there is no other condition – I am sure none of any importance. I think it right to send to you an extract of a letter from Lord Liverpool to me. His words are: – 'It is material that her Majesty should know, confidentially, that if she shall be so ill advised as to come over to this country, there must then be an end to all negotiation and compromise. The decision, I may say, is taken to proceed against her as soon as she sets her foot on the British shores.' I cannot conclude this letter without my humble, though serious and sincere supplication, that her Majesty will take these propositions into her most calm consideration, and not act with any hurry or precipitation on so important a subject. . . .

Henry, 1st Baron Brougham and Vaux
(J. Lonsdale)

The Queen directed Brougham to answer:

Mr Brougham is commanded by the Queen to acknowledge the receipt of Lord Hutchinson's letter, and to inform his Lordship that it is quite impossible for her Majesty to listen to such a proposition.
5 o'clock, June 4, 1820.

She immediately left for Calais, followed by an urgent plea from Brougham:

St Omer, June 4, 1820 – 6 o'clock

Madam,
I entreat your Majesty once more to reflect calmly and patiently upon the step about to be taken, and to permit me to repeat my deliberate opinion. I do not advise your Majesty to entertain the proposition that has been made. But if another proposition were made instead of it, I should earnestly urge your Majesty to accept it – namely, that the annuity should be granted without any renunciation of rank or title or rights, and with a pledge on the part of the Government that your Majesty should be acknowledged and received abroad by all the diplomatic agents of the country according to your rank and station, but that your Majesty should not go to England. The reason why I should give this advice is, that I can see no real good to your Majesty in such an expedition, if your Majesty can obtain without going all that it is possible to wish. I give this advice, most sincerely convinced that it is calculated to

save your Majesty an infinite deal of pain and anxiety, and also because I am sure it is for the interest of the country.

Suffer me, Madam, to add that there are some persons whose advice is of a different cast, and who will be found very feeble allies in the hour of difficulty.

I know not that I have a right to proceed further, but a strong sense of duty impels me.

If your Majesty shall determine to go to England before any new offer can be made, I earnestly implore your Majesty to proceed in the most private and even secret manner possible. It may be very well for a candidate at an election to be drawn into towns by the populace – and they will mean nothing but good in showing this attention to your Majesty – but a Queen of England may well dispense with such marks of popular favour; and my duty to your Majesty binds me to say very plainly that I shall consider every such exhibition as both hurtful to your Majesty's real dignity, and full of danger in its probable consequences.

I know your Majesty's goodness and good sense too well not to be convinced that you will pardon me for thus once more urging what I had before in conversation stated. – And I have the honour to be your Majesty's devoted and faithful servant,

H. Brougham

Brougham also despatched an urgent letter to Lord Liverpool:

(Most secret.)
St Omer, Sunday night, June 4, 1820

My Lord, – My letter of last night may have prepared your Lordship for hearing that, five minutes after the Queen had rejected Lord Hutchinson's proposition, which she did the moment it was made – this evening at five o'clock – she set out for Calais, having previously prepared everything for her journey, and sent all her Italian attendants off to Italy. I had not advised her to accept that proposal, but I strongly urged her to offer terms – viz., to stay abroad, provided she were acknowledged and respected as Queen. I did this in the spirit which has always regulated my conduct in this affair – that of preventing whatever tended only to annoy, and to force on discussions unnecessary in themselves and hurtful to the country. In the same spirit I have most earnestly urged her Majesty to go (if she finally resolves to go) as secretly as possible; and I wrote to her at Calais to-night to repeat my remonstrances, and to entreat that at least she would give Lord Hutchinson time to send a courier to London for fresh instructions. Your Lordship will see from the enclosed what view I have taken of this matter.

I sincerely regret the failure of this negotiation, on every account. But even if the Queen had listened to me alone, and had paid far more attention to my advice than she has done, I feel that my sense of public duty could not have carried me further than I went, considering the duty which I owed to my client. To that length these two duties coincided perfectly; and though I cannot allow myself for a moment to suppose that the Queen runs any risk by the step she is taking, yet I am certain that she exposes herself to trouble which might have been avoided. – I have the honour to be your Lordship's obedient servant,

H. Brougham

P.S. – I afterwards wrote a still stronger remonstrance to Calais, which *may* produce some effect, though I hardly dare to hope it. Mr Alderman Wood and Lady Anne Hamilton went with the Queen; and neither of them are acquainted with *any one part of her case*. It seems difficult, therefore, to suppose that they should offer advice, and still more so to imagine that it can be taken.

The prospect of the Queen's return to England excited the attention of the Radicals, who saw a new opportunity to embarrass the King and the government. On 25 February *The Republican*, as its title implied a Radical newspaper, set out her wrongs and urged the people, and women in particular, to express support for the Queen's cause.

THE QUEEN

As Republicans, we should not deign to meddle with this question, if the rights of royalty were the only matter in dispute, but as men struggling to be free, we feel it an imperative duty to support this injured woman – this victim, first to unbridled lust, and now to despotism. We shall therefore take up this subject without looking at the parties as members of royalty, but as distinguished members of the society we live in. To do justice to this woman, it will be necessary that we go back to the period of her first arrival in this country. We believe that it was pretty well understood at the time of the proposal of this marriage, that, on the part of the then Prince of Wales, it was no more than a politic step to get his debts paid, which his unbounded extravagance and licentiousness had then brought to a considerable amount. So general was this belief, that the country abounded with ballads on the subject: a verse of one of them we well recollect, it was as follows:

> She is Caroline of Brunswick,
> And has a handsome hand, Sir,
> If you will pay off all my debts,
> I'll take her to command, Sir.

This ballad represented the late King as advising the Prince of Wales to marry, and to take this Princess, his first cousin, to wife, and this verse quoted is the answer put into the mouth of the Prince. Various reports were afloat at the time about the rude reception the lady first met with, one said that the cohabitation lasted for one night only, others that it extended to two, three, and four. However, be the precise time what it may, we know that it was very short, and that the late Princess Charlotte of Wales was the fruit of this short union. We also know, that the kind husband kept her in a separate part of Carlton House for some time, and made her situation such, that at last it became intolerable. A separation took place, as a reconciliation appeared impossible. The late Queen, it is well known, sided with her darling son, and the King endeavoured to do justice to this injured Princess. . . . It is well known, that prior to the marriage of the then Prince and Princess of Wales, Carlton-house was a complete brothel, and that on the arrival and marriage of the Princess of Wales the only females that surrounded her, with the exception of the few she bought with her, were the former courtesans of the Prince. It was a matter of course that these should study to keep the affection of the Prince from the Princess as their own fate depended on it. They but too well succeeded and this innocent, injured, and unfortunate Princess, had her future happiness sacrificed at the altar of profligacy. . . . The conduct of Henry the Eighth towards Ann of Cleves was manly when compared with the

Queen Caroline, 1804 (Sir Thomas Lawrence)

treatment of the present Queen. . . . It is not our purpose here, to notice those proceedings which have been termed 'delicate investigation', it is sufficient that we say, that the Queen triumphed over all the malice that villainy could urge, assisted by perjured spies. She has been twice arraigned and twice acquitted; and that by those persons who would have found their interest in according with the views of her persecutors. Another attempt has lately been made to impeach her character during her residence abroad, and venal as the law officers of the crown are, they durst not, at their master's most earnest desire, bring her to a fair and candid trial. All the prostituted part of the press, – that which Lord Castlereagh terms '*respectable*', is arraigned against her, and every artifice resorted to bring her into contempt. All this will avail nothing; the more the Queen is persecuted and reviled, by the court Sycophants, the more will she reign in the affections of the British people. It is of very little consequence, whether she is admitted to share the pageant of a coronation; she will still be the Queen of England, and as long as she remains excluded from Carlton Palace, she may venture to ride or walk about the streets of London, amidst the cheers, the congratulations, and the caresses of its inhabitants. She will not then need a troop of guards with drawn swords to protect her, nor a carriage that is bullet proof. It is equally unimportant whether her name be mentioned in the liturgy of the church; what is now called the established church, forms but a small portion of the inhabitants of this country. . . . Her husband has decoyed her into a marriage to answer his own private views, without the slightest affection towards her, he just condescends to consummate the marriage, and then drives her from his house, studies to insult her, by every means that can be devised, and utterly forsakes her by a public avowal that he will never meet her in public. What tie can a woman feel towards such a husband as this? . . . Who can blame the woman, who placed in such a situation as this, should yield her affections to some other person, when she perceives that the man who has seduced her into this situation, is daily revelling in adulterous harlotry. . . . We are aware that every virtuous female in the country already feels indignant at the treatment the Queen has uniformly received, and we trust that they will not fail to lift up their all-powerful tongues in her behalf. We particularly recommend, that on the arrival of the Queen in this country, that all who are well disposed towards her, should congratulate her by their joint addresses. . . . She has nothing to look to for protection, but the mass of the people. . . .

Henry Crabb Robinson, a barrister and former foreign correspondent for *The Times*, recorded in his diary a visit to the theatre at which the growing popular support for Caroline became apparent:

[26 April 1820]: I . . . [went] to see 'The King and the Miller of Mansfield'. But I heard scarcely any part, for the health of the King being drunk, a fellow cried out from the shilling gallery – 'The Queen!' The allusion was caught up, and not a word was heard afterwards. The cries for the health of the Queen were uttered from all quarters, and as this demand could not be complied with, not a syllable more of the farce was audible.

As later events were to show, the theatres in London provided a stage for popular demonstrations in favour of the Queen throughout her subsequent 'trial'.

The respectable classes, however, were more concerned with the implications of the Queen's character and the likely consequences of her cause being adopted by radicals and troublemakers. Lord Colchester, writing from Genoa, expressed these fears in a letter to Henry Bankes:

Genoa, April 29th, 1820

Dear Bankes,

Elections being over, and the account of votes in the House of Commons balanced, the result is such as I had anticipated, and I do not think that, upon any trial of strength in the new Parliament, the issue will be different from the former, in which the Opposition made so poor a show in competition with the existing Administration. You will rapidly, and probably better than if more slowly, settle Civil List, Budget, Parliamentary Reform, and Her Majesty's Establishment, before the middle of July; and I only hope that, upon the latter subject His Majesty's Ministers will take a larger view of the question than merely so far as concerns *His* Majesty and *Her* Majesty. The true question is not what *they* shall do, or what *they* shall personally agree upon as convenient to their respective ease and emolument, but how far it is fitting for the British Empire to acknowledge for its Queen and invest with all the dignity and influence of the Throne, a vagabond Princess, whose conduct has degraded the nation and lowered the standard of public morals. Surely this is a question of much higher importance than the likes and dislikes of any individuals, and it is to be judged of by other principles; and it must be decided *at the outset*, once for all. Should the present change in her situation be passed by and her relative position be slurred over by some temporary compromise, you will have her in a few months setting up her household in London, a rallying point for all the discontented politicians; and it will then be too late to talk of past occurrences after the proper day of inquiry has been suffered to slip by. Be assured that this is the plan by which she will be advised to evade all present questions of impropriety in her continental travels.

If, imprudently, she sets you all at defiance, then indeed she may bring down upon

'How to get un-married – ay, there's the rub!' L. Marks (July 1820). The Queen, supported by Justice, with Brougham on the left, resists the attempt of the King, assisted by Castlereagh, Lady Hertford, and Sidmouth, to break free of the marriage bond

herself what it seems the wish of Government to avoid; and she may do that for them which they seem wanting in spirit to do for themselves and their country. And so I quit this disgraceful subject.

Colchester's correspondents were equally alarmed:

H. Legge to Lord Colchester

Navy Office, May 8th

My dear Lord Colchester,
. . . I cannot yet believe that Her Majesty will venture to set her foot on this island. She may threaten, and she may bully, but I trust she will be better advised. If she comes, there can be no doubt that every palace will be shut against her, and that her treatment will be such as she *ought* to expect. She would, however, make a great disturbance, and would have all the Radicals and all the Reformers at her feet. . . .

Edward Bootle Wilbraham to Lord Colchester

London, June 20th, 1820

My dear Lord, – . . . The first subject, perhaps almost the only one about which the English world talks and thinks, is the Queen, who, a fortnight ago, took the bold and decisive measure of coming to this country in the prosecution of her royal rights. As she is not liable to be tried for high treason, the Baron de Bergamo being a foreigner, and owing no allegiance to us, and the act being committed in a foreign country, I am inclined to think that the step she took, however impudent, was not an unwise one for her own interest, and that Alderman Wood, reprobated as he has been by all parties, has really given her no bad advice on the present occasion. . . .

What will be the result of all this it is quite impossible to say, except that we shall have to sit very late in the summer; that Her Majesty will serve as a rallying point for the disaffected and Radicals, and that she will probably end in carrying what she wants, for already she gains ground in the affections of the middle and lower classes, who know nothing of her proceedings since she went abroad; all the newspapers having concurred in keeping silence on that subject during her absence from England. . . . By the common people she is looked upon as an injured and unprotected female. How long Parliament will sit, will depend on this topic of discussion, as we should otherwise be probably prorogued towards the end of July, whereas now we are quite uncertain. The Coronation also, though fixed for the first of August, will probably be deferred: indeed it is said that the preparations will not be ready for that time, which is not unlikely. The King employs himself a good deal, as I believe, in the arrangement of the dresses for this occasion, which is a subject which he enjoys thinking of: his health, I believe, is good, but he does not stir out much. . . .

F. Burton to Lord Colchester

Upper Brook Street, June 24th

My dear Lord, – . . . A full exposure is now inevitable. The Secret Committee of the Lords began their sitting this day at twelve; and it is expected they will decide upon proceeding by Bill, which of course must give rise to a tedious procrastination on account of witnesses. In the meantime Her Majesty will leave no stone unturned to gain popularity. This night she goes to Drury Lane: to-morrow, it is supposed, to Covent Garden; and doubtless the Opera, &c., will not lose the like honours. She has visited Mrs Damer, Lady Elizabeth Whitbread, and Lady Perceval; but the latter on foot, whilst her carriage was waiting on the heath at some distance. Lady Tavistock is the only lady of much consideration who is known to have called on her; but Dr Parr dined with her on Saturday. I hope she did know that he had given a grand dinner on a Sunday during the Warwick Assizes, to Hone, who was attending there for the purpose of assisting his friend then upon trial for publishing one of his own publications. . . .

Yours sincerely,
F. Burton

Notes

1.   William, Viscount Lowther, later 2nd Earl of Lonsdale, was a member of the Treasury Board.
2.   Sir Benjamin Bloomfield, the King's private secretary.

CHAPTER THREE

The Queen and the People

The Queen landed at Dover on 5 June and arrived in London the following day. The painter Joseph Farington wrote that it was 'a universal subject of conversation'; indeed it was much more, for as he recorded two days later crowds of people turned out in London shouting slogans in her favour and attacking houses which did not 'illuminate' – by putting lighted candles in their windows – in her honour. The Duke of Wellington was one of those stopped in the street by a gang of workmen brandishing pickaxes who demanded that he should declare support for the Queen. He obliged with the memorable reply: 'Well, gentlemen, since you will have it so, God save the Queen – and may all your wives be like her.'

Caroline went first to live in South Audley Street at the house of her chief supporter Matthew Wood, an Alderman of London, ex-Lord Mayor, and MP for the City, who was largely responsible for linking her cause to that of the London radical movement and who tried to exploit her to rouse popular indignation against the government. As Madame, later Princess, Lieven, the wife of the Russian ambassador, wrote to her friend Metternich in Vienna, 'the gauntlet has been thrown down'. The House of Commons discussed the situation and members urged the ministers to reach an accommodation with the Queen's representatives. Canning, formerly one of her lovers, was in a particularly embarrassing position; after a speech in which he expressed his continued regard for her it was expected that he would have to resign if his colleagues decided to prosecute her. He did not do so, but he shortly afterwards left for an extended tour of Italy which kept him out of the way until after the proceedings against her were over. Fears of popular violence were fuelled by the rioting of the mobs, the attacks of the popular Press, and the adoption and presentation of many addresses and petitions in the Queen's favour. There were also rumours of the disaffection of the Army, stimulated by a brief mutiny in one of the Guards battalions which, however, proved to have been caused by dissatisfaction over pay and living conditions. The offending troops were quickly marched off to Portsmouth but nervousness about the reliability of all the troops in London remained, and was increased by reports of their cheering the Queen and demonstrating support for her. By the end of June negotiations between the Ministry and the Queen's representatives had broken down. The Queen, now also advised by William Cobbett and encouraged by the Corporation of London, refused to accept exclusion from the Anglican liturgy or to go abroad with the promise of a parliamentary income. There seemed no alternative to a confrontation, the result of which no one could forsee.

The Times *announces the Queen's arrival*

THE QUEEN

There have been disembarkations on the British coast, bringing war and producing revolutions in the State, ere now. The chief of those were the landing of WILLIAM the Conqueror at Hastings; the landing of Henry VII at Milford Haven, and the landing of the Prince of ORANGE at Torbay. What were the feelings of the people at these momentous eras we know but feebly; events may be recorded, but the secret throbs of the heart cannot be counted: yet, if we might venture a guess on so obscure a subject, we should be inclined to say, that neither at the landing of WILLIAM the Conqueror, nor at that of the Earl of RICHMOND, nor of WILLIAM III, were the people's bosoms of this metropolis so much agitated as they were last night, when it was known her Majesty the Queen of ENGLAND had once again – bravely, – we will say – once again set her foot on British ground. The most important Parliamentary questions were adjourned – the KING'S Ministers fled to the council chamber – the streets were crowded: every one was inquiring, 'When did she land? Where will she sleep? Where will she reside? How will she enter London? Had she a good passage?

Had she a bad passage? How is the wind?' It was said of WILLIAM III, we recollect, that the winds enlisted themselves in his train. . . .

WILLIAM the Conqueror came attended by a force which at once subdued the army that was opposed to him – HENRY VII and WILLIAM III brought with them, or confidently relied upon finding, a train of armed followers. But this woman comes arrayed only in native courage, and (may we not add?) conscious innocence; and presents her bosom, aye, offers her neck, to those who threatened to sever her head from it, if ever she dared to come within their reach. . . .

News report from Dover, Monday, 2 o'clock p.m.

HER MAJESTY'S ARRIVAL IN ENGLAND

. . . At one o'clock her Majesty set her foot on British ground; the royal salute began to fire, and an universal shout of congratulation welcomed her arrival. For a few moments her countenance and manner bespoke considerable agitation: she was visibly affected by the cordial symptoms of regard which welcomed her home: but she soon recovered herself, and with a firm step, a composed manner, and a smiling but steady countenance, walked slowly along the crowded ranks of the principal inhabitants. Well-dressed females, young and old, saluted her as she passed with exclamations of 'God bless her: she has a noble spirit: she must be innocent'. The Queen returned the salutations with the warmest marks of affectionate pleasure, and

'A scene in the new farce of the Lady and the Devil,' Marshall (June 1820). The King and his advisers are thrown into consternation by the news of the Queen's arrival

repeatedly thanked the ladies for their expressions of cordial attachment. She appeared in good health, her blue eyes shining with peculiar lustre, but her cheeks had the appearance of long intimacy with care and anxiety. She is not so much *embonpoint* as formerly, and her manner and figure altogether seemed perfectly befitting her exalted station. She was dressed with great elegance. As she moved along, the crowd gathered so fast, and pressed so closely around her, that she was compelled to take refuge in the York Hotel. Mr Wright, of the Ship Hotel, seeing that it would be impossible for her Majesty to reach his house on foot, immediately despatched a handsome open carriage to the York. Her Majesty, Lady Hamilton, and Alderman Wood, ascended the carriage: the populace removed the horses, and drew it themselves. A band of music preceded her Majesty, and two large flags, bearing the inscription of 'God save Queen Caroline' were carried by some of the principal tradesmen. A guard of honour was placed at the door of the hotel, but the people did not seem to relish their appearance, and the Queen observing to Alderman Wood that their presence appeared rather to produce an unpleasant and angry feeling, the worthy Alderman suggested the propriety of their going away. After playing 'God save the King' the soldiers retired, and the populace seemed highly delighted. Her Majesty observed, that although she appreciated as it deserved the attentions of the Commandant, yet that she wanted no guard of soldiers: her firm reliance was on the just principles and cordial attachment of her people. Her Majesty then went to the principal window of the hotel, and bowed several times with great grace and sweetness of manner to the happy assemblage. She then retired, and, first taking a slight refreshment, lay down to rest after the harassing fatigues of body and mind which she had undergone. . . .

The Times *on the Queen's arrival in London, 7 June*

The general expectation that her Majesty would enter the capital on the evening of yesterday proved to be well founded. Neither the degree of uncertainty which accompanied it, nor the unfavourable state of the weather, could extinguish the ardour which prompted hundreds to assemble at an early hour, in order to hail and congratulate her return. From the moment that she decided as to the course she would adopt, and resolved to throw herself on the people of England, all her proceedings have been so open, so divested of the mystery usually attending a royal journey, that few were in danger of miscalculating the different stages of her progress. Her Majesty's arrival seemed to have been greeted not as an unlooked-for, but as a natural and almost necessary, event. On all those outskirts of the town which point or lead to the high Dover road, at the obelisk in St George's-Fields, at the Elephant and Castle, the Bricklayer's Arms, the multitude began rapidly to increase about 3 o'clock. The more loyal publicans hoisted a royal ensign on the staff of their sign-posts, and at Deptford the union jack was suspended in two or three places across the road. Symptoms of an impatient curiosity mingled with those of a deep and powerful interest became stronger in each succeeding hour. The throng of spectators became more dense the further an advance was made towards the point of anticipated meeting; Deptford and Greenwich poured out in indiscriminate concourse all ranks and conditions of their inhabitants; Blackheath resembled some great continental fair; and at Shooters-hill were drawn up in excellent order an array of barouches, chaises, and other vehicles filled with respectable and decent women. . . . Nothing certainly could exceed the warm enthusiasm or eager welcome with which her Majesty's presence was greeted as soon as she appeared amongst them. The descent of the cavalcade which preceded her down Shooters-hill, amidst the joyous waving of hats, and the reiterated shouts of thousands, had a fine effect. . . . On arriving at the Green Man, her Majesty's carriage drew up, and she alighted. A momentary depression, arising chiefly from fatigue, rendered a short repose desirable. The attraction now grew more intense, and in order to prevent confusion, and allay the thirst of curiosity, the Queen, at the advice of Alderman Wood, after partaking of some refreshment, condescended to appear at one of the windows of the inn. The crowd, at once satisfied and animated at this appearance, burst into a vehement and protracted shout of applause. Her Majesty bowed gracefully, and, notwithstanding her anxiety and fatigue, looked remarkably well. She was dressed in a black twilled sarcenet gown, a fur tippet and ruff, with a hat of black satin and feathers. . . . As the weather had now cleared up, and the rays of the sun increased the splendour of the scene, the carriage was thrown open, and everyone gratified with an immediate view of their Sovereign's consort. . . . The acclamations . . . continued without interruption until the entire cavalcade reached the metropolis, when they swelled into a yet louder strain. Her Majesty was evidently affected, though not overcome, by these testimonies of reverence and loyalty. It was obvious that she had anticipated no less, and that she had formed a right estimate of the national character. . . . The ladies, it may be supposed, felt a peculiar interest on this occasion, and testified the warmth of that feeling by every demonstration not unbecoming the delicacy of their sex. . . . It was now understood that her Majesty was to proceed to the house of Mr Alderman Wood, in South Audley-street, there to fix her abode for the present. Thither all parties, whether on horseback or on foot, now began to hasten, and soon swelled into a countless multitude those who, from better or earlier information, had already stationed themselves in that quarter. Considerable difficulty was experienced in leading up her Majesty's barouche to the door. The tide of popular feeling was at its flood, and the air rang with repeated cheerings. After the Queen had at length entered, there seemed to be no disposition to disperse: vehicles of every kind maintained their position, and the crowd stood compact and immoveable. In a few minutes Mr Alderman Wood appeared in the balcony of the first floor, and, we believe, intimated that her Majesty would in person testify the sense which she entertained of the respectful sentiments expressed towards her. The clamour then subsided, till, shortly after, the Queen herself appeared, and by a dignified obeisance acknowledged the tokens of affectionate loyalty by which her reception had been graced. The most splendid pageant, the most imposing theatrical exhibition, never imparted a more genuine delight than seemed to pervade all ranks of spectators at this instance of condescending kindness. Her Majesty, with a deportment perfectly graceful, walked from one end of the balcony to the other, and, having bowed to all around, withdrew. . . . The crowd instantly dispersed. . . .

The club-houses in St James's-street were illuminated, as were likewise the houses in Hill-street, Burlington-house, and some others in Piccadilly.

Brougham's account of the Queen's arrival

On her arrival in London she gave extreme offence to the King by allowing Alderman Wood to sit in the carriage with her, as she drove through the town to his house in South Audley Street, where she remained till a house in Portman Square was got ready for her. She afterwards occupied the house at Hammersmith, with a house in St

'Public Opinion!!' (June 1820) The Queen sits calmly on the scales of justice, outweighing the King despite
his accompanying load of green bags and the attempts of ministers and courtiers to pull down the scale.
John Bull and the soldiers applaud the Queen

James's Square when she had occasion to come to town. It is impossible to describe
the universal, and strong, even violent, feelings of the people, not only in London but
all over the country, upon the subject of the Queen. Of course, in London the
multitude were as unreflecting as they usually are when their feelings are excited. I
recollect one instance among many others. The crowd collected wherever they knew
her to be, and called her to appear at the windows of whatever house she was in. The
cheers and noise were excessive and exposed her to great annoyance and fatigue.
They called for cheers to individuals by name, and sometimes the cry was 'Three
cheers for Mr Austin, the Queen's son;' thereby assuming her to have been convicted
of the high treason of which the inquiry in 1806 had acquitted her.

On the 6th of June, Lord Liverpool in the Lords, and Lord Castlereagh in the
Commons, brought down a message from the King, accompanied by a green bag
sealed, which contained the evidence upon which the case against the Queen was
supposed to be founded.

In the Lords, a secret committee of fifteen peers was at once appointed to whom
the contents of the green bag were referred. In the Commons, ministers made an
attempt to induce the House to act with equal rapidity; but I was fully prepared for
this movement, and without much difficulty succeeded in defeating it. Without having
given the smallest hint of my intention to any one, save Denman, I effected this by at
once entering fully into the whole case. Canning, in answering me, while he
supported the ministers, acted most honourably, and bore such testimony to the
virtues and high bearing of the Princess whose honour, and I may almost say life, was

assailed by a husband whose whole life and conduct in the marriage state had been a barefaced violation of his vows – that ministers were forced to give way, and an adjournment was agreed to without a division. However, the counsels of men who were base enough to pander to the King's wishes, lest by opposing them the Tory ministry might be destroyed, prevailed; and it was determined to introduce a Bill of Pains and Penalties, to degrade the Queen-Consort, and to dissolve her marriage with the King. . . .

The painter Joseph Farington bears witness in his diary to the popular reception of the Queen.

June 8. – My Servant, Sarah, told me that she went yesterday even'g to South Audley Street which was full of People crying out in favour of the Queen, and obliging every person whether in Carriages – on Horseback or on foot to pull off their hats when they passed Alderman Wood's house in which the Queen was. She was hailed as being an injured woman, and the King was much abused. She was told that Alderman Wood had made a speech from his Balcony. – Such is the disposition of this vain, weak, mischievous man.

    This night abt. 12 oclock, a number of Rabble passed through the streets calling for a general illumination, knocking at doors and breaking windows, such is the Phrenzy raised by the arrival of the Queen and the fomentors of disturbance.

June 9. – . . . Illuminations again took place this evening from the general apprehension of the windows being otherwise broken by the Mob. – But Soldiers paraded Charlotte St and checked the mischievous strollers.

June 13. – A Lady in Charlotte St Fitzroy square – I was this day informed, died of fright in consequence of the brutal attacks of the Mob who were calling out for illuminations for the *the Queen*. She was playing Cards at 12 oclock when the rioting began & died at 5 oclock in the morning.

Princess Lieven, a close observer of the London social and political scene, sent an account of the Queen's arrival to her friend Prince Metternich in a series of letters.

June 5 [1820] – The only topic of conversation here is the arrival of the Queen; she is known to be at St Omer; but, even so, I doubt if she will come. Brougham has gone to meet her, to dissuade her from coming. On this question at least, if not on the side of the Ministers, he is entirely of their opinion; and it is on him that they count most to prevent a scandal. Wood will use all his influence to bring her to England. All we want in this country is a Radical Queen.

June 6. – That woman has had the unbelievable impudence to come to London; she will be here in an hour. . . . What a to-do, what dangers! One cannot ignore the huge section of the public which is for the Queen; in the eyes of the English people, she is a pure and innocent victim. Alderman Wood, who manages the Queen and also manages the London populace, is going to make a fine use of his influence. . . .

The 6th, evening. – The King went to Parliament. The mob neither cheered nor booed. There scarcely was any mob; everybody had gone to meet the Queen. She arrived late. She passed by the Houses of Parliament at the moment when the

Ministers were proposing to set up a secret committee to examine her conduct. The gauntlet has been thrown down. It is said that the King is very pleased about all this. He has laid a nice burden on the shoulders of his Ministers, and now he says, 'Let them get out of it'. The Queen is staying with Wood. . . . The mob streamed through the streets all night with torches, making passers-by shout, 'Long live the Queen!' You can imagine London at this moment: what a stir, what excitement, what noise!

I am very much afraid we may reach the crisis which I have long feared; I have told you of my anxiety on this score. The Ministers are in a most dangerous position. They have put up a glorious fight against a hostile Europe; they have triumphed over the greatest difficulties, foreign and domestic, that have ever confronted a government; and now they are going to be defeated by a woman. They are battling against public opinion and against their master himself; this double adversary will end by crushing them. The infamous publications of Wood, on the proposals made by Hutchinson at St Omer, have produced the most unfortunate impression against the Court and the Government. Read the *Times*, since the 5th inclusive; everything is there. If I am serious today, it is because all this distresses me. To amuse you I will add that the Queen, passing by Carlton House, stopped the procession and herself waved her fair hand, crying, 'Long live the King!'

Friday, the 9th. – . . . It is said that the Queen is detaching herself from Wood, in order to place herself entirely in the hands of her counsel. The Ministers are overwhelmed with business and worry; the Opposition anxious about the general harm which may result, but pleased at the particular benefit which they may secure; the mob noisy, amusing themselves by smashing windows – ours were broken last night; and the King calm and satisfied. It is a deplorable business, and I am sure that you will think the same. . . .

Sarah Lyttelton wrote to her brother, Captain the Hon. Frederick Spencer, to announce the Queen's arrival and reception.[1]

June 7, 1820. – . . . One great piece of public news I can tell you, which is that the Queen is arrived – came yesterday to London openly to declare war against her enemies and their malicious designs; and she has been received, as all the King's enemies should be, by the Government, who have filled two enormous green bags with evidence of her guilt, and have laid them before Parliament. The country is all for the Queen. But she is to be tried; whether by Parliament or by a court of justice nobody knows yet. The Opposition think the ministers have been silly about her and her concerns, and so do I. But what is to come of it all is another question. If I was the King, I think I should have died out of the way very quietly, with mere worry. . . .

Charles Greville continues the story in his memoirs:

June 7th. – The Queen arrived in London yesterday at seven o'clock. I rode as far as Greenwich to meet her. The road was thronged with an immense multitude the whole way from Westminster Bridge to Greenwich. Carriages, carts, and horsemen followed, preceded, and surrounded her coach the whole way. She was everywhere received with the greatest enthusiasm. Women waved pocket handkerchiefs, and men shouted whenever she passed. . . . It is impossible to conceive the sensation created by this event. Nobody either blames or approves of her sudden return, but all ask, 'What will be done next? How is it to end?' In the House of Commons there was little said;

George, Prince Regent, by Sir Thomas Lawrence, *c.* 1819

but the few words which fell from Creevy, Bennett, or Denman seem to threaten most stormy debates whenever the subject is discussed. The King in the meantime is in excellent spirits, and the Ministers affect the greatest unconcern and talk of the time it will take to pass the Bills to 'settle her business'. 'Her business', as they call it, will in all probability raise such a tempest as they will find it beyond their powers to appease; and for all his Majesty's unconcern the day of her arrival in England may be such an anniversary to him as he will have no cause to celebrate with much rejoicing.

June 9th. – Brougham's speech on Wednesday is said by his friends to have been one of the best that was ever made, and I think all agree that it was good and effective. The House of Commons is evidently anxious to get rid of the question if possible, for the moment Wilberforce expressed a wish to adjourn the county members rose one after another and so strongly concurred in that wish that Castlereagh was obliged to consent. The mob have been breaking windows in all parts of the town and pelting those who would not take off their hats as they passed Wood's door. Last night Lord Exmouth's house was assaulted and his windows broken, when he rushed out armed with sword and pistol and drove away the mob. Frederick Ponsonby saw him. Great sums of money have been won and lost on the Queen's return, for there was much betting at the clubs. The alderman showed a specimen of his taste as he came into London; when the Queen's coach passed Carlton House he stood up and gave three cheers.

It is odd enough Lady Hertford's windows have been broken to pieces and the frames driven in, while no assault has been made on Lady Conyngham's. Somebody asked Lady Hertford 'if she had been aware of the King's admiration for Lady Conyngham', and 'whether he had ever talked to her about Lady C.' She replied that 'intimately as she had known the King, and openly as he had always talked to her upon every subject, he had never ventured to speak to her upon that of his mistresses'.

June 16th. – The Speech which Canning made on the occasion of the King's message has been violently attacked by all parties, and is said to have given as great dissatisfaction to the Queen as to the King. It is not easy to discover what the Queen could have objected to in the speech, for it was highly favourable and flattering to her. It was generally supposed last Sunday that he would resign in the course of the week, and bets were laid that he would not be in office next Sunday. . . .

There was some indiscipline manifested in a battalion of the 3rd Guards the day before yesterday; they were dissatisfied at the severity of their duty and at some allowances that had been taken from them, and on coming off guard they refused to give up their ball cartridges. They were ordered off to Plymouth, and marched at four yesterday morning. Many people went from the ball at Devonshire House to see them march away. Plymouth was afterwards changed for Portsmouth in consequence of their good behaviour on the route. Worcester met many of them drunk at Brentford, crying out, 'God save Queen Caroline!' There was some disturbance last night in consequence of the mob assembling round the King's mews, where the rest of the battalion that had marched to Portsmouth still remained.

Lord Eldon, the Lord Chancellor, writes to his daughter, Mrs E. Banks.

[June 1820]

My Dearest Fan,

As nobody here talks about anybody but the Q., so nobody here can write about anything but the Q., save what they write in the expression of love and affection for those to whom they write. You will see by the impressions of the seal on this scrap, that Cabinets are quite in fashion; daily, nightly, hourly Cabinets are in fashion. The lower orders here are all Queen's folks; few of the middling or higher orders, except the profligate, or those who are endeavouring to acquire power through mischief. The bulk of those who are in Parliament are afraid of the effect of the disclosures and discussions which must take place, if there is not some pacific settlement: the Queen is obstinate and makes no propositions tending to that – at least as yet; the King is determined, and will hear of none – of nothing but thorough investigation, and of what he, and those who consider *themselves* more than him, think and talk of – thorough exposure of the Q., and divorce. To this extent Parliament will not go – but, amidst this mess of difficulties, something must arise in a few days, or it will happen, I think, in a few days, that the K. will try whether he cannot find an Administration which can bring Parliament more into his views than the present Ministers; I don't see how matters can go on a week longer with the present Administration remaining; I think no Administration, who have any regard for him, will go the length he wishes, *as* an Administration – and if they will, they cannot take Parliament along with them. That body is afraid of disclosures – *not on one side only* – which may affect the monarchy itself. There is certainly an inclination to disquiet among the lower orders, but it is so well watched that there is no great cause for uneasiness on that account. Alderman Wood, who has the Queen still in his house, has, in South Audley Street, before that house, a pretty numerous levée of the family of John and my Lady, as Townsend denominates them.

June 10th, 1820

The newspapers give long accounts of riots here, window breaking, &c, and it's true that the mob have insisted upon three nights' illuminations (which concluded on Thursday night) to give importance to the Queen's arrival.

Hardly anybody would comply with the commands of the sovereign mob, and therefore more windows have been broken than upon occasions of illumination usually takes place. The multitudes in the streets never came so far towards Hyde Park Corner as our house, and therefore we were not molested; and patrols of horse soldiers between the Duke of Wellington's and us kept us very comfortable and quiet. Last night there was not the least appearance of any disquiet in almost any part of the town – and I think it is all over. At all events, in our part of the town, all will be as safe as if we were at dear Encombe. Our nightly Cabinets don't agree with Mamma, and she, you know, will never go to bed when I am out; but, upon the whole, I think she has had less headache than usual in ordinary times.

It seems to me that both Houses of Parliament are determined to have an end of this business between K. and Q. *without* inquiry and disclosure. All seemed to be agreed that she shall not live in this country, but there is nothing but difference of opinion how she is to be treated abroad. The Ministers will be compelled to give way to Parliament – and they are in a pretty state; – if they give way, the K. will remove them – if they do not, they will be outvoted in Parliament and cannot remain. At least I don't see my way honourably out of this difficulty. I comfort myself to-day by a good dinner at Merchant Taylors' Hall, where I am going as soon as I finish this scrap, to assist as a Taylor in making the Marquis Camden a brother Taylor. . . .

William Cobbett, the Radical journalist and publisher of the *Political Register*, the most widely read Radical newspaper of the day, took up the Queen's case. He had supported her when she was Princess of Wales in the dispute with the Prince Regent over their daughter Princess Charlotte, and Alderman Wood had appealed to him for help the evening before Caroline's arrival at Dover. He wrote on 10 June to advise her to reject compromise and demand her full rights.

London, June 10, 1820

The humble individual, who hopes that the goodness of his motives will apologize for his addressing this paper to the Queen, most deeply regrets that her Majesty cannot be truly and fully informed of the sentiments of the people respecting her Majesty's case. He ventures to assure her Majesty that it is the universal hope that she will not suffer herself to be induced to accept of *any compromise*; but that she will insist on the full enjoyment of all her rights; that being the only thing which can completely put to silence the calumnious aspersions of her indefatigable and implacable enemies. He beseeches her Majesty to bear in mind, that though those enemies have been, thus far, baffled and discomfited, disappointment may tend to teach them dissimulation as well as to sharpen their malignity; and that what they cannot effect by force, they may endeavour to effect by craft; what they cannot obtain by menaces, they may endeavour to obtain by blandishments; what they have not been able to extort from her fears, they may endeavour to steal from her magnanimity. If her Majesty should have advice offered her, he implores her to consider what may be the possible ultimate objects of those who offer that advice, and to reflect that it may be possible for them not wholly to overlook, on so important an occasion, their own interests and the gratification of their own ambition. Her Majesty knows, perhaps, little of what is passing amongst the public. Already are the windows of the shops exhibiting her Majesty's Person, attired in Royal Robes, with a Crown on her head and a sceptre in her hand. And the person who humbly submits this paper to her Majesty assures her, that the united soul of this loyal and just nation is poured out in prayer, that she will not yield, either to threats or entreaties, any portion, or particle, of her rights as *Queen of this kingdom*. This prayer is founded on a sense of national honour; on a sense of what is due to the women of this kingdom; and, above all, on a most anxious desire that her Majesty should not do anything that might leave even her bitterest enemy the smallest ground for sustaining a supposition unfavourable to her Majesty's innocence. The writer begs leave humbly to add, that he hopes that her Majesty will reflect, that, though she *yield* only in the smallest degree, there is no form of words that can possibly be used in so doing that will prevent her enemies from afterwards ascribing her condescension to a motive, the very thought of which would give her Majesty pain to the end of her days.

Wm. Cobbett

Princess Lieven's letters to Metternich continue to express alarm at the popular violence:

[June the 11th]

We live here in continual tumult and anxiety. There is something happening every hour. This tension wears one out mentally and physically; I believe that the Queen will age us all.

Troops have been brought up round London, and, at night, cavalry pickets occupy the principal quarters of the town. We have some near us; so that I sleep in peace.

June 21

The other day the Duke of York was almost torn to pieces by the enthusiasm of the mob. About 6,000 people had collected near his house, and when he came out they pressed round him shouting: 'We like princes who show themselves; we don't like Grand Turks who shut themselves up in their seraglio – long live the Duke of York – our King to be.' They were very much frightened by this at Carlton House, and the object of these acclamations was more frightened still. The mob escorted him as far as the chapel where he was going.

Popular disturbances continued through June, and in the middle of the month rumours of a mutiny in a battalion of the Guards in London added to the concern of the upper classes.

General Sir Robert Wilson to Earl Grey, 16 June 1820[2]

The plot thickens –
The 3rd Regt. of G[uard]s stationed in the King's mews mutinied yesterday – Abt 3 days since a Private was heard to say to his Comrades – 'The Queen is going to the Tower.' The answer was – 'If she does the King will have blood for supper and a bloody Quantity too.' Yesterday the men demanded extra pay or drink money on account of their hard work and as they had it in Burdett's riots[3] – This was refused – They were then desired to give up their ball cartouches and mount the King's Guard – Every man declined – *Huzzas* were given for the Queen and this morning the Regt. received orders to march at daybreak to Portsmouth. It is said but for this part I cannot vouch, that the relieving battn hissed the officer when he gave the order to march and remonstrated with the men against their obedience to the order – It is also added that the Life Gds cheered the battn as it passed and there are reports the battn has stopped at Turnham Green and will proceeed no further but these reports come from very suspicious qu[arte]rs. . . .

Anxiety about the loyalty of the troops and the possibility of riots in favour of the Queen led the Duke of Wellington, the Commander-in-Chief of the Army, to write to the Prime Minister as follows:

MEMORANDUM TO THE EARL OF LIVERPOOL RESPECTING THE STATE OF THE GUARDS

June, 1820

I feel the greatest anxiety respecting the state of the military in London, and I think it best to adopt this mode of making known to you my opinion upon it, leaving it to you to draw the attention of our colleagues to it or not as you may think proper.

Very recently strong symptoms of discontent appeared in one of the battalions of the Guards, of which the most remarkable circumstance was that neither Government nor the Commander-in-Chief had any knowledge of the existence of discontent till some hours after it had appeared in acts of mutiny and disorder. This battalion was moved from London, and it has been reported, whether with foundation or without is not known, that the men on their march had joined in, and made use of, the cry of disaffection of the day.

The Secretary of State has informed the Cabinet that the Commander-in-Chief has felt great uneasiness respecting the Coldstream Guards; while the Commander-in-Chief, in a General Order, assures the army and the public that the symptoms of discontent have been confined only to one battalion of the 3rd Guards, and even to a few individuals in that battalion. In the mean time there are, as usual, reports without number in circulation respecting all the Guards, both cavalry and infantry, the greater number false, no doubt, but whether true or false no man can tell; and I am sure that none of us could say he was surprised if, at the next Drawing-room, he should hear as we did at the last, that there was a mutiny in more of these corps; and thus, in one of the most critical moments that ever occurred in this country, we and the public have reason to doubt in the fidelity of the troops, the only security we have, not only against revolution but for the property and life of every individual in the country who has anything to lose.

I certainly have had every reason to be satisfied with the army, and I should say generally that they are to be relied upon in all cases. But I thought that we ought not to rely solely upon the army when we were discussing the expediency of calling out the Militia in this year; and I am sure that if the principle on which we decided to call out the Militia was sound, it applies ten times more strongly to the adoption of some measure of the same description in London, where we have already been *surprised* by a mutiny in one corps, where we know not, and cannot know under existing circumstances, whether seeds of discontent are laid or not in other corps, and where the Government depend for their protection against insurrection and revolution, and individuals for their personal safety and property, upon the fidelity of 3,000 Guards, all of the class of the people, and even of the lowest of that class.

In my opinion the Government ought, without the loss of a moment's time, to adopt measures to form either a police in London or military corps, which should be of a different description from the regular military force, or both. The consequence would be that the mutiny of the regular force, if it should ever occur, would be of little or no importance. But it is probable that the feeling of emulation which would be excited by seeing these other corps formed, and particularly that of the nondependence of the Government upon these guards alone for their security, would prevent the breaking out of these mutinies, even if the danger of them should be greater than any of us think they are. . . .

MEMORANDUM OF PATROL DUTIES TO BE PERFORMED JUNE 9TH

TO THE COMMANDING OFFICER OF THE LIFE GUARDS

From King-street Barracks, a patrol of six men to set out at half-past nine, and to proceed by Gloucester-place, Portman-square, Manchester-square, Cavendish-square, Portland-place, Weymouth-street, Manchester-square, Portman-square, and King-street Barracks.

A patrol of six men to set out at half-past nine, and proceed by Weymouth-street, Cavendish-square, Holles-street, Oxford-street, Cumberland-street, Portman-square, and King-street Barracks.

Twelve men to proceed from King-street Barracks, at half-past nine, along Wigmore-street to Cavendish-square, to wait there till relieved, and the last relief to return with the last patrols to King-street Barracks.

Similar patrols to be sent out from King-street Barracks as soon as those above-mentioned will have returned, and the same to be repeated till half-past one in the morning.

Disturbance at Lord Sidmouth's London residence, June 1820[4]

The story is told by George Pellew:

One of the modes in which the mob expressed their joy at the Queen's return was by nocturnal attacks on the windows of obnoxious individuals. Lord Sidmouth's residence sustained three successive sieges, all of which it was the narrator's fate to witness. On the first night, Dr Baillie was visiting an invalid member of the family when the house was assailed; and the expressions of surprise with which he diversified his medical instructions as each intrusive missile formed acquaintance with the window shutters, afforded Lord Sidmouth materials for one of his most amusing anecdotes.

On the second evening, a very large family party happened to be assembled in the house, and the garrison being thus strong, it sallied forth, headed by Lord Exmouth, and attacked the assailants, who, disconcerted possibly by this unusual system of tactics, instantly dispersed. One prisoner was taken, a juvenile printer, who, by his insolence, which was consummate, obtained for himself the glory of a night's imprisonment, instead of a lecture. The third attack occurred on a Wednesday evening, whilst Lord Sidmouth was attending the cabinet dinner. It was feeble and of brief duration; and as no further annoyance was anticipated by the police officers, the narrator, who had been left in charge, retired to his lodgings in the same street. Shortly afterwards he heard the mob returning, and hastened back to his Lordship's door, against which the watchman had placed himself. Before, however, they could gain admittance, the Philistines were upon them, filling the whole footway, and hemming them up in the entrance. At this moment a carriage dashed rapidly down the street, drew up at the door, and Lord Sidmouth exclaimed from within it – 'Let me out; I must get out:' but another, and a commanding voice, replied – 'You shall not alight; drive on;' and instantly the carriage bounded forward, and disappeared, but not before the glass of the window nearest the speaker had been shivered to atoms by a stick or stone. In a moment afterwards, at a signal given, the mob dispersed, leaving the watchman and his companion the only occupants of the street. In a few minutes the same carriage returned, escorted by a small party of the Life-Guards. It was that of the Duke of Wellington, and contained his Grace, Lord Eldon, and Lord Sidmouth.

Notes

1. Sarah, elder daughter of the 2nd Earl Spencer, married W.H. Lyttelton, MP for Worcestershire until 1820, later 3rd Baron Lyttelton. In 1842 she became governess to Queen Victoria's children.
2. General Sir Robert Wilson was a veteran of the Napoleonic Wars, Whig MP for Southwark after 1818, and a friend of Lord Grey. He was dismissed from the Army in 1821 after being blamed for the disorder at the Queen's funeral procession.
3. Riots which took place at the arrest of Sir Francis Burdett, MP in 1810.
4. Henry Addington (1757–1844), 1st Viscount Sidmouth, was Prime Minister 1801–4, Home Secretary 1812–21. George Pellew was his nephew and wrote the first account of his life (1847).

CHAPTER FOUR

'The Die is Cast'

Parliamentary proceedings on the Queen's affair opened on the day after her arrival in London. The House of Lords agreed to appoint a secret committee to examine the evidence against her, but in the Commons there was a strong feeling that further negotiations should be attempted, in view of the strong public sentiment in her favour. Brougham and Thomas Denman, the Queen's legal advisers, had several meetings with the Duke of Wellington and Lord Castlereagh, representing the Cabinet, but, as Lady Charlotte Lindsay reported, they failed to reach any agreement. A last-minute attempt by the respected independent member William Wilberforce to persuade the Queen to accept the removal of her name from the Liturgy in return for a financial settlement was rejected by her. The government now determined to introduce a Bill of Pains and Penalties, containing a divorce clause, into the House of Lords. Lady Charlotte Lindsay chronicled the events:

Lady Charlotte Lindsay to Miss Berry [1]

Wroxton Abbey, June 18, 1820

My Dearest Friend, – The day after the Queen's arrival, Wednesday, June the 7th, a message was sent from the King to both Houses of Parliament, stating that the step that Her Majesty had taken in returning to England made it necessary that papers containing an account of Her Majesty's conduct during her residence abroad should be laid before them, and that a secret committee in each House should be appointed to examine into and to report upon their contents. A debate took place in the House of Commons, but they did not come to any decision upon the Message. The Ministers were very powerfully attacked by Tierney, Creevy, Bennet, and others of the opposition, upon the message sent to the Queen through Lord Hutchinson, and they made a very awkward defence. Canning spoke handsomely of the Queen, and declared his intention of taking no part in the proceedings against her; Brougham made a very able speech, setting forth in the strongest manner the evils that might be expected from pursuing these measures against the Queen; Wilberforce made a speech to the same purpose; and these speeches produced a great effect. The sense of the House appeared evidently to be against proceeding in any such enquiry. . . . On Friday, the 9th, Lord Castlereagh proposed in the Commons an adjournment upon the consideration of the King's message, on account of a message received by Lord Liverpool from the Queen, stating that Her Majesty was willing to listen to any propositions that did not compromise her honour. Mr Brougham said that Her Majesty had been induced to write this, in consequence of the great desire expressed by the members of both Houses of Parliament to give every possible facility to an arrangement. . . .

All parties seem so thoroughly aware of the incalculable mischief that may arise from pursuing this enquiry, that I have great hopes this matter may stop here, though both parties have gone too far to retract with honour. The King's party will always say that they had proof against the Queen, but were induced, for the repose of the country, to let it drop; and the Queen's will say that, notwithstanding all the spite and rancour evinced against her, they have never been able to bring forward any proof of criminality. They had better not have gone so far; but as I fear that the further they go, the deeper they will sink into the mire, they had better escape with their *dirty shoes* while they can. B[rougham] has written to me, and tells me that *even I* can have no idea of all the tricks and rogueries he has had to encounter; but he says that he got the sense of the House so completely with him in the first debate, and having kept it ever since, he thinks that he shall steer her safe. . . . The concourse of people that assemble round her house, and that follow her carriage when she goes out, continues to be as great as ever; but the visitors within doors are by no means so numerous. Some of her male friends – Sir H. Englefield, P. Knight, Mr St Leger, and Dr Holland – have called, and some few of the opposition – Sir R. Wilson, Sir F. Burdett, Mr Bennet, &c.; but none of the *great guns* – no Lords Grey, Lansdowne, nor Holland, which I rather wonder at. Lord and Lady Tavistock have left their names; the Queen having always been particularly kind to Lady Tavistock from the time she was a child, makes her probably feel this attention indispensable; but I have not heard of any other woman of fashion who has called except Mrs Damer, who I imagine thought this visit a respect due to the station of a Queen against whom nothing has as yet been proved. The only inconvenience that may result to her is, that no other woman of character (except Lady T.) having made this visit, it acquires greater consequence than should naturally belong to so simple an action, and she will be reckoned a decided partizan of the Queen's, when she probably only disapproves of the proceedings against her. . . .

Wroxton Abbey, June 26, 1820

Last Monday (19th of June) the Ministers in both Houses of Parliament announced that the negotiation between the Queen and the Government was at a stand, and they laid the documents of the proceedings before the two Houses. It appears by these documents, that after some preliminary correspondence between Her Majesty and Lord Liverpool, it had been agreed upon by both parties that the Queen's legal advisers, Messrs. Brougham and Denman, should confer with the Duke of Wellington and Lord Castlereagh for the purpose of settling the terms of the desired arrangement. It seems that they have had five meetings upon this business, but have hitherto failed in coming to any agreement. The Queen's advisers offer to give up the point of her residence in England, but insist upon the restoration of her name to the Liturgy, or to her having some equivalent for it, such as instruction to our ministers at foreign courts to receive her publicly as Queen of England, and to present her as such at the courts where they reside, if she should require to be so presented. I don't think in the present stage of the business that she can ask less. One can easily conceive that the foolish step of the Liturgy cannot now, without awkwardness, be retracted; but I should have thought the equivalent might have been adopted to settle this matter. Mr Brougham declared that no blame was imputable to the Queen with respect to the failure of this negotiation, nor did he impute any blame to the other party. Lord Castlereagh moved that this subject should be debated upon on Wednesday, the 21st of June; but Mr Wilberforce giving notice of a motion for the arrangement of the unhappy differences in the Royal Family, Lord Castlereagh consented to postpone his proposed motion. . . . On Thursday, the 22nd of June, Mr Wilberforce brought forward his motion, which was an address to the Queen, praying Her Majesty to accede to the wishes of Parliament, and to relinquish the point of having her name restored to the Liturgy; that the arrangement might not be impeded in order to avert a measure which, whatever might be its results, must prove '*derogatory from the dignity of the Crown, and injurious to the best interests of the country*'; that by such con-descension she should in nowise be deemed to compromise her honour, but to yield in compliance to the wishes of Parliament; and this address was seconded by Mr Wortley, and carried by 394 against 124, the Ministers voting for it, and thereby confessing that they had brought forward a measure that, *whatever may be its result, must prove derogatory from the dignity* of the Crown, and injurious to the best interests of the country. Lord A. Hamilton moved an amendment, 'That it is the opinion of Parliament that Her Majesty's name should be restored to the Liturgy.' This was seconded by Sir F. Burdett, but was negatived without a division. . . . The address was presented to the Queen on Saturday, the 24th, to which she returned an answer, very well expressed in words, but in substance I think most injudicious – for she declined complying with their request. The gentlemen that went up with the address were hissed and hooted by the populace. Wilberforce was called Dr Cantwell, and they would possibly have more seriously insulted him if Mr Brougham had not accompanied him back to his carriage. It is hardly possible to conceive anything more weak and inconsistent than the conduct of Ministers in voting for an address that cast such reflections upon their own measure; nor can one imagine anything more rash and unaccountable than the Queen refusing to avail herself of this loophole that would have let her out of the scrape, given her 50,000l. per annum, a frigate to take her where she wishes to go, and an acknowledgment from the Government here that she should be treated with the honours due to the Queen of England in foreign courts, which must have been granted had she acceded to the address. But this is what I feared. The weakness of her adversaries makes her rash; she thinks that everything that embarrasses them must be for her advantage, not recollecting that they may all fall to the ground together. Wood (who still maintains his influence over her) is supposed to have persuaded her to reject the advice of the address, either from a conviction that her innocence will be fully established by an investigation, or from a hope that by throwing the country into confusion he may defer his own ruin. Farewell . . .

[June 1820]

So now the die is cast, and this measure is adopted, though approved of by no one! – disgraceful it must prove to both parties, whatever may be its result. I only hope it may not prove very seriously dangerous to the country. . . . In one shape or other I have little doubt of this Bill passing in the House of Lords; but I think it by no means likely to pass in the Commons – and, if so, the sentiment in the country against the decision of the Peers will be violent indeed. Not only the common people, but the middle ranks, and also many of the upper class, who live retired in the country, are all warmly interested for the Queen; and the more harm the Italian witnesses depose against her – and it is likely that all the witnesses that can be brought against her will be persons of bad character and low stations, discarded servants, &c., who will probably prevaricate in their evidence; while she will bring respectable witnesses who know nothing against her, as respectable people are those before whom improprieties are not usually committed, and who don't seek to know more than comes unavoidably before their own eyes.

Whichever way it may terminate, the Queen will not be so well off as she would have been had she acceded to the address of the Commons. If the Bill passes, she loses title, income, pregogatives; and I am by no means sure that she would not be still more unhappy should she triumph and be obliged to remain in England, leading the same sort of life as her predecessor, Queen Charlotte, and surrounded by the same sort of Court. On the day that the Bill was brought in, the Queen's counsel desired to be heard in the House of Lords; they urged that as the proceedings had gone so far, and the Bill having been read the first time, that the second reading might follow as soon as possible.

. . . Friday, the 6th of July, Lord Castlereagh announced in the House of Commons that the coronation is put off. . . . The Queen may at least have the satisfaction of having discomposed his Majesty's favourite pastime. The 17th of August is fixed by the Lords for the second reading of the Bill.

Charles Greville, with his keen ear for the views and opinions of London society, deplored the way in which 'the Queen's business' monopolized conversation:

June 25th. – . . . The discussion of the Queen's business is now become an intolerable nuisance in society; no other subject is ever talked of. It is an incessant matter of argument and dispute what will be done and what ought to be done. All people express themselves tired of the subject, yet none talk or think of any other. It is a great evil when a single subject of interest takes possession of society; conversation loses all its lightness and variety, and every drawing-room is converted into an arena of political disputation. People even go to talk about it from habit long after the interest it excited has ceased.

Meanwhile the artists Joseph Farington and Sir Thomas Lawrence (the latter having been, according to rumour, one of the Queen's lovers in the past) expressed their fear for the effect of the campaign on behalf of the Queen on the volatile mood of the country. Farington wrote in his diary:

June 25. – Sir T Lawrence called & we had much conversation respecting the

'Coronation arrangements awkwardly interrupted, or Injured Innocence demanding her rights!' (2 June 1820). The King plans a lavish 'imperial' coronation but is interrupted by the arrival of Caroline, who demands to be crowned with him

negotiation with the Queen. He said the Ministers are pledged not to retract the conditions they have laid down, therefore if concessions are to be made to the Queen they must resign their situations; while, on the contrary, the opposition could yield what the Queen requires viz: *her name to be introduced into the Litany,* – and she to be *introduced to foreign Courts as Queen of England.*

He concurred with me in thinking these are fearful times and thought the object was *Revolution.* He is feared [*sic*] what strumpet audacity may be able to do supported by a headlong mob, and as Parliamentary opposition eager to remove the Ministers. – He still, however thought that an increasing Majority wd. appear to support Government in the house of Commons.

Much might be done by determined resolution in the King, but that is not his constitution. He shd. show himself at the Theatres and on horseback fearlessly. – Those abt. him shd. fully inform him of circumstances, but they are probably timid. The Vice Chancellor, Sir John Leach, is frequently at Carlton House and seems to have superseded the Lord Chancellors influence. – It is said that the Queen depends upon *recrimination,* and that she has two letters written by the King to her, the latter particularly leaving her at liberty to pursue any course of life she may choose. . . . – Lord Brownlow, said yesterday, at Sir H Hume's dinner that being in Italy he saw *Bergamo* riding before the Queen's Carriage and cracking his whip as her Courier, and 3 weeks *after* he saw him in her Carriage with a Gold Key as her Chamberlain. At Lord Castlereagh's last night (Her Ladyship's route) Sir T Lawrence put a question to his Lordship respecting the *Coronation.* – 'Coronation,' repeated Lord C, and laughed at the idea in these times.

Lady Cowper,[2] writing to her brother Frederick Lamb, also expressed fears for the stability of the country if the affair was allowed to go on:

June 26th and 27th, 1820

. . . We are all in a pretty mess and so, I think, is she, since she refused Wilberforce's terms. The two parties were both bullying and Ministers have been driven to open the bag, which nobody thought they had courage enough for. They should have done it at first, and not have cut such a foolish figure and increased the agitation of the public mind. B[rougham] and Denman are her ostensible advisers, but she has other private ones whom she minds much more. B[rougham] thought she would have taken Wilberforce's terms. Nobody knows who counsels her, or if she follows her own wild head. . . . Canning's seems the most curious situation. He is to keep his place, but to absent himself from the Cabinet on questions about the Queen – *voilà du nouveau.* His friends say he wanted to resign, but was begged to stay as it would perhaps dissolve the Ministry if he withdrew. He has had interviews with the King; people say His Majesty is pleased with his old friends standing so aloof on this question and being so quiet. The fact is nobody knows what to do, and no two people are of the same mind. . . . *Et voilà le malheur!* Nobody can tell what will come of it all. The common people, and I fear the soldiers, are all in her favour and I believe the latter more than is owned – this is natural enough; they look upon her as an oppressed individual, whereas she is oppressing. As for her virtue, I don't think they care much about it, for tho they call her innocent, the Mob before her door have repeatedly called out 'A cheer for Prince Austin, the Queen's son. . . .'

June 20th [1820]

. . . You are pretty right I think in what you say about the Queen and B[rougham] but I think she is half wild and follows her own head more than any body's. She has an unlimited power of money, but goes about in a miserable equipage to excite compassion. I think her popularity is a little falling, there is but a very small crowd about her door and a very miserable set follow her open carriage with the pair of Post Horses, when she goes out. Yesterday they took them off and dragged her up St James's Street – a miserable set. The soldiers are, I think, most to be feared; those who are behind the curtains say they are so much for her, and so dissatisfied at the K[ing] never appearing amongst them, that they think it is cowardice keeps him shut up. They have also an idea that they swore allegiance to G[eorge] 3d, and owe him nothing, and some of them cried to the D[uke] of G[loucester] on parade, 'You ought to be our King'. Now it may all go on smoothly, but should the population rise in her favour will they with their discontents march against them? *Voilà ce qui reste à voir*, and what I feel no security about. . . .

Cobbett now re-entered the fray to give the Queen more advice:

William Cobbett to the Queen

June 25, 1820

The writer of this paper begs leave most humbly to state to her Majesty the Queen:

That her Majesty's Answer to the Resolution of the House of Commons has given great satisfaction to the public, in as far as it contains a rejection of the advice of the House; that, however, great *anxiety* still prevails on the subject of her Majesty's possible intentions as to *going abroad*; that the public are all alive *upon this great point*; that it is of the utmost importance that *no doubt* should longer exist on the subject; that all such doubt would at once be removed by an expression of her Majesty, *on the first proper occasion*, that her Majesty has resolved *not to go abroad*.

The writer of this paper thinks it right that her Majesty should be informed that her strength and safety lie in the public opinion; that the Parliament will do nothing for her, except as it is influenced by the Public opinion; that the Ministers were *checked* only by that decided expression of public opinion which her Majesty's arrival called forth, and for which they were not prepared; that to yield anything in order to please the Parliament would only displease the public the more on that very account; that the four Members, who carried the Resolution to her Majesty, very narrowly escaped being personally handled by the people; that they made their escape all four in one carriage; that the people *leur crachoient à la figure* (spit in their faces) as they drove along the street, that these four worthy delegates of the House returned home actually covered with spittle; that it is clear, therefore, that to recede at the request of the Parliament would be to make a useless sacrifice.

It is very clearly seen by the public that her Majesty's enemies want but one thing, namely, *to get her out of the country*; because they well know that she would then be instantly deserted by the people. It is clear also that, unless her Majesty *go away, nobody can get money or honours by advising her to go!* For these reasons it will necessarily follow, that every art which hatred can suggest and which perfidy can put in motion will be employed *to induce her Majesty to depart*, or, at any rate, to *persuade the people that she is willing to depart.* The effect even of this last would be most injurious to her Majesty; and, therefore, effectual measures should, as speedily as possible, be taken to remove from the public mind all *doubt* on the subject.

The Ministers are in a state of difficulty not possible to describe. They cannot extricate themselves from that difficulty. They are at the mercy of the Queen, who has nothing to do but to remain in her present attitude for some days. Her Majesty ought to make *no overture* for negotiation; and if her Majesty find that the Parliament is *about to be prorogued,* she ought then to make, before they separate, a formal demand of her rights and privileges, of which a full detail ought to be given.

If this line be pursued with firmness, a short time will give her Majesty the full enjoyment of all her rights and privileges; and in the meanwhile her Majesty is safe in the Love and admiration of this generous people, who are *all* for her, in every part of the kingdom.

The Lord Mayor and Corporation of the City of London voted an address urging the Queen to stand firm. The address was drafted by Cobbett as follows:

The humble Address of the Lord Mayor, Aldermen, & Livery, of the City of London, in Common Hall assembled

May it please your Majesty,

We, his Majesty's loyal & dutiful subjects, the Lord Mayor, Aldermen, & Livery of the City of London, in Common Hall Assembled, beg leave humbly to approach your Majesty with heart-felt congratulations on your Majesty's safe return to this Kingdom, which feels itself most highly honoured in hailing your Majesty as its Queen.

Since the time when we last had the proud satisfaction of being permitted to appear in the presence of your Majesty, we have never lost sight of the causes which finally produced your temporary separation from us; and, therefore, we have heard with the less surprize, though not with diminished indignation, of the new and atrocious conspiracies, which have been carried on and are still carrying on, against your Majesty's peace, honour, and safety.

We have been attentive and deeply interested observers of the recent unexampled, the secret and dastardly proceedings with regard to the rights and privileges of your Majesty. We have viewed with feelings of sorrow and of shame, the means which have been resorted to in order to deprive your Majesty of those rights and privileges: sorrow, that there should be found, upon the face of the earth, persons capable of adopting such proceedings; and shame that those persons have been found in this Kingdom. But, we humbly and most earnestly implore your Majesty not to yield any portion or particle of your rights, and especially those essential rights, the Coronation and the Liturgy.

The result of former investigations; the proofs then produced of subornation and perjury employed against your Majesty, the frankness of your Majesty's character; its sincerity, openness and scorn of all disguise; your Majesty's instant rejection of the compromise tendered to your Majesty at St Omers; your Majesty's voluntarily and eagerly hastening to the scene of accusation, and challenging your adversaries to the proof: these, may it please your Majesty, are far beyond what was necessary to convince us of your Majesty's perfect innocence, and of the deep guilt of those who have so foully conspired against your Majesty.

'The royal green bag or another ministerial scarecrow' (19 June 1820). Castlereagh holds up the 'green bag' in the House of Commons before the King, depicted as the mace, and the Speaker. The Queen, on the right, declares her innocence

We clearly perceive that, it is the chief object of your Majesty's adversaries to drive your Majesty from amongst us; to deprive us of the inestimable blessing of your presence, and to deprive your Majesty of the cordial, the zealous, and the efficient support of the great body of his Majesty's loyal and dutiful subjects, whose sentiments we are sure we speak upon this interesting occasion. That your Majesty will ever be induced to withdraw yourself from this Kingdom, is what we cannot be induced to believe. Your Majesty may rest assured, that there is no sorrow, no affliction, no injury of any kind, that can befal your Majesty, in which every faithful subject of the King will not amply participate; and, that, there is no act of injustice that can be attempted against your Majesty, which the people of this Kingdom are not ready to prevent, or to avenge, at the hazard of their fortunes and their lives.

Early in July, Parliament decided, on the evidence of papers supplied to each House in green bags – soon to be a butt of satirical comment in the Press and caricatures – that the accusations against the Queen should be proceeded with in a Bill of Pains and Penalties – already christened 'the Queen's trial', as noted by Princess Lieven. A date was set – 17 August – for the introduction of the Bill in the House of Lords, where the detailed consideration of the evidence would take place. It was generally agreed in society that she must have been guilty of improper conduct, but, as Sarah, Lady Lyttelton noted, the King was considered no better than his wife and he was so unpopular that the outcome could not be confidently foreseen. There were also fresh rumours about the loyalty of the troops and fears that the Queen's attendance at the trial and the processions of her daily journeys to Westminister from her new residence, Brandenburg House in Hammersmith, would keep the popular agitation at fever pitch. *The Times*, a zealous partizan of the Queen, daily discussed the issues and reported the state of public feeling. Observers as diverse as Princess Lieven and Robert Peel noted the gravity of the situation and feared for the outcome.

Henry Bankes to Lord Colchester [in Italy]

Old Palace Yard, July 7th

Dear Colchester, . . . After trying all probable means of compromising with the Queen, in the last of which Wilberforce and myself were two of the principal performers, she has set us all at defiance; and the Bill, charging her with an adulterous intercourse with Bergamo, and dissolving her marriage, has been read a first time by the Lords, where a judicial proceeding is more fit to originate than in our House. The question now before them is at what time they shall proceed to the second reading, and begin to prove the case. The Queen's counsel urge it on, suspecting probably that some of the witnesses may be not yet arrived in England. There is an odd story whispered about with regard to this same Bergamo, that owing to a wound received when he served in the army, he is disqualified for an adulterous intercourse.

Considering the temper of the populace, and the spirit of discontent and disaffection which is very widely diffused, and, above all, some symptoms of the same feeling that have been observed in the military, I much wish that all this infamy and disgrace could have remained unnoticed, without being made the subject of public prosecution, of which I very much dread the progress and the ultimate event. The two Houses will most likely believe the testimony of some of the witnesses, and act accordingly. The popular clamour will discredit them all, and treat them as suborned and perjured; and this abandoned woman, instead of being degraded in public estimation, will be exalted into an innocent and much-injured victim. . . .

Letters from Princess Lieven to Prince Metternich

July 4

Do not be deceived by the appearance of calm here. The Queen is doing more mischief than ever; and there is one fact not yet generally known, which, however, I believe to be true – that the army is disaffected and is taking up the cause of the Queen. If she has the people on her side, and possibly the army too, what is left?

July 8

The day before yesterday I attended the debate at the House of Lords. I was allowed to go as a special favour; I behaved so modestly that I am hoping to deserve it another time. It was a remarkable sitting; the Queen's Counsel spoke. I had made enquiries from the Ministry and from the Opposition, to ensure that nothing would be said at the session which would make my presence improper – actually, it went off very gravely.

The debate was an impressive spectacle. Counsel were summoned to the bar with all the usual ritual; all the peers of the realm were present. As regards its object, it was perhaps the most remarkable that has taken place for centuries – a Queen indicted by the highest tribunal of the Kingdom. As regards detail – a lawyer (Brougham) sprung from the lowest ranks of society, inveighing against the Cabinet, against the secret Committee, against the whole House; and that House, that Committee, those Ministers allowing themselves to be ridiculed by a little attorney. The Opposition laughed; provided that its adversaries are humiliated, all is well. The Ministers were silent; firstly, because in the House none of them can speak except Liverpool, and he has not the energy; secondly, because their supporters are good at wearing ribbons, but not at upholding their patrons. . . .

The Coronation has been postponed by the Ministers. Postponed – that's the point to which they have degraded their office – gaining time, postponing difficulties; they never get beyond that. In addition, the postponement results, I believe, from a fact of which I have already informed you – that they are not sure of the army. The Duke of York, who tells me a great deal, has not told me this; but he boasts of sometimes spending three nights running at his office. He is not making plans of campaign. What is he doing?

The 10th

We go back to town this evening; and I shall go straight to one or two routs to find out what the peers have decided. There is great curiosity about the session this evening, since it is to decide the date of the Queen's trial. In the Ministers' place, I should want it at once; but that is no reason for their wanting it. The Radical families are already urging the populace to take up arms in defence of the Queen; and she herself, in her answer to the Westminster deputation, makes an appeal to the people. On such occasions, delay is the worst policy; they should strike quickly and decisively; that would daunt the mob. . . .

July 11

. . . The position in England is indeed extraordinary. I know a great deal more than the interested parties, for I am treated so much as an Englishwoman by both sides that nobody minds talking in front of me. The English, silent and cold about everything else, are particularly talkative and frank about their own affairs. They have not got the knack of ordinary conversation, and do not take the trouble to talk to you, if you want to talk of trivial things; but boldly propose the most intimate questions, and they are on their own ground. Above all, argue (you must not think of being wholly of their opinion) and they appreciate you much more than you could have hoped at the beginning of the conversation.

In this unmusical country, there are horrible barrel-organs which go about the streets – at the moment, there is one beneath my window which is playing so out of tune that I feel almost inclined to cry, and find it nearly impossible to write to you. . . .

H. Legge to Lord Colchester

Navy Office, July 10th

My dear Lord Colchester, – . . . We have indeed a Queen to dispose of, such as she is; and it will be well if her persevering impudence does not dispose of the tranquillity of this country, by raising disturbances to which I cannot foresee the termination so clearly as you foresaw the result of Signor Vil Berforce's address to her Majesty. It is marvellous that she would not listen to such an overwhelming majority of the House of Commons as carried that address; and it is most unfortunate for us all that her daring impudence, her folly, or her madness, would not permit her to withdraw herself quietly upon that occasion from English ground. She has completely jostled the coronation, which has been put off *sine die*. The common notion is that it will not take place till next year. After requesting delay for the purpose of bringing witnesses in defence from Italy, she now insists upon the proceedings commencing *instanter*, Lord Liverpool will therefore probably propose an early day for the examination of witnesses. This will be the employment of the Lords; the Commons will adjourn when their own business is finished.

I do not know what to say upon the subject of suspending all proceedings till the Queen arrived. The wish, I believe, to avoid all discussion on this most unpleasant subject was nearly universal. I am not surprised that Ministers partook of this wish, or that they hardly felt bold enough to begin till the step which she took made it necessary to throw off all reserve. I believe they have had no bed of roses to sleep on since the death of the late King, and that no Minister ever had so difficult a task to perform as theirs has been from that time to this. I cannot enter more at large into this subject in a letter which may be opened at some foreign post-office. God send us all a good deliverance from this most distressing occurrence. . . .

Ever most truly yours,

H. Legge

Mrs Arbuthnot's journal[3]

[July] 10th. – The House of Lords decided to commence the trial of the Queen on the 17th of August, & all the Peers were ordered to attend on pain of paying 500£ & being imprisoned in the Tower. Mr Arbuthnot told me that Brougham came to him in the H. of Commons and begged him to request Ld Liverpool to order the Queen's solicitor to account for the expenditure of her money in the same mode that the King's Law Officers do to the Auditor Genl. He made this request because he found that, since her arrival in London, without any ostensible cause for great expenditure, she had already spent 8,500£; and he suspected that she was plundered by Alderman Wood. He further stated that he & Denman never saw her but upon the subject of her trial, that they were not the least in her confidence, & that they had both determined, if Wood was allowed to interfere in the legal proceedings, to resign immediately. They state that, since the meeting in the City when Wood said he w^d not vote her a shilling if she went away, she has taken a great dislike to him but, as she builds all her hopes on the mob, she does not dare to quarrel with him.

Joseph Farington's diary

July 3. – In private conversation with Dance, the President, and Smirke, the gross impropriety of the Queen in soliciting the acclamations of the Mob by driving through the City, & her Carriage being dragged with ropes was reprobated as disgustingly offensive to propriety & delicacy. – On Friday last she sent to the Royal Academy that she would see the Exhibition *yesterday* (Sunday) at one oclock, but in the morning a note came to Fuseli from *Alderman Wood* informing him that she did not intend to come. – Thus did she make Wood her amanuensis.

July 6. – The Committee of the House of Lords yesterday presented their report that various evidence of the Adultery of the Queen with a Foreigner who had been in a menial capacity, also of her continued licentious conduct had been produced from the Green Bags & from other documents laid before them.

July 9. – Queen's business irritates & agitates the people, – the Mass disposed to cry against Government, – the Public mind very discontented. . . .

July 10. – Sir T Lawrence called & we had conversation abt. the Queen's business. He said, there appears to be no doubt of her guilt in the minds of the *Lords in Opposition*, though they differ from Ministers as to the course of proceeding. – He mentioned an atrocious scene between Her Majesty & Bergamo at an Hotel or Inn in the *Milanese*. She now, it is believed employs Cobbett to write for her, & her reply to the City address is reported to have been written by him.

July 12. – In Consequence of the Alderman's intercourse with the Queen, he had been pestered with applications for situations in her establishment. Wood's interference in her affairs was caused by his Son while travelling in Italy being introduced to her which led to communications with his Father. – Sir T Lawrence thought the Popular Cry for the Queen was lessening, at least among the higher classes. Lord Lansdowne does not think there was any impropriety in sending a *Commission* to Italy to enquire into her conduct. – He was supported in his opinion 'that if she be found guilty, Parliament will not allow her the income which was proposed to Her' – £50,000 pr. annm.

R. Price spoke of it as a fact, that a fortnight before her arrival Mr Brougham, her Attorney General, said, in company, that Ministers could not wish more that he did that she wd. remain abroad. – He is supposed by some not to like the business he has to do. – R. Price [says] she has a mass of letters written by the late King, – the Duke of Kent &c bearing upon the present King's conduct, but Lord Grey & others object to recrimination on acct. of any of his former improprieties. – Sir T Lawrence sd. the Queen's conduct & proceedings had been such that they thought her mad.

'The pageantry put off or the Raree Show adjourned,' W. Heath (13 July 1820). The Queen appears from a cloud to demand the postponement of the coronation in a time of popular distress. Canning, Castlereagh and Sidmouth attend the King

Lord Buckingham's correspondents expressed alarm and dismay at the turn of events.

W.H. Fremantle to the Marquis of Buckingham

Stanhope Street, July 19, 1820

. . . The language even of the Government is most croaking, and you may be assured the Queen's party is far from diminishing. The City is completely with her, not the Common Council, but the shopkeepers and merchants, – and I have great doubts if the troops are not infected. The press is paid for her abundantly, and there are some ale-houses open where the soldiers may go and drink and eat for nothing, provided they will drink 'Prosperity and health to the Queen'. The K— grows daily more unpopular, and is the only individual in the Kingdom insensible to it. . . .

Thomas Grenville to the Marquis of Buckingham

Cleveland Square, July 26, 1820

My Dear Lord B—,

The little that I hear is not worth sending you, either in quality or in quantity. The rumours about the military increase daily and frightfully. How much of these rumours is true, and how much is invented, and how much is exaggerated, I have no means to judge; but the prevalence of that topic of conversation, while it shews the generality of the apprehension, is itself but too much calculated to bring on the evil of which it treats.

Tierney yesterday told us he had heard Wood say the day before that the Q— had irrevocably determined to come down every day to the trial in her 'coach-and-six *in a high style;*' if so, she will very likely be attended by all the idle populace between Hammersmith and London, besides a host of radicals, who will not let go by such an auspicious opportunity. How the peace of the metropolis or the safety of the Parliament is to be secured under all these circumstances, might puzzle wiser heads than those whose business it will be to decide upon it. T— admits himself to be considerably alarmed, and describes the appearance of the Ministers in these latter days as betraying more anxiety and apprehension than vigour or decision. He said that the Attorney-General, in his speech yesterday in the House of Commons, was almost in tears, and used the expression that 'there was no doubt that a revolution was in contemplation'. Whether it is prudent to use such an expression in order to excite sufficient means of resistance, or dangerous from awakening such a topic may be a question; but of the extent of alarm which he must have felt to have led him to that expression, there can be no doubt. . . .

Reports continue of doubts about the Household Troops; probably some mere inventions, and others exaggerated; but the mischief of these reports is incalculable, because they promote distrust and suspicion on the one side, and agitation and restlessness on the other; and if one wished to create the evil, there could be no readier way than by the unremitted discussions which prevail everywhere upon this subject. . . .

C. W. Wynn to the Marquess of Buckingham

Barmouth, July 27, 1820

. . . The eagerness of popular feeling, even in this Tory tranquil part of the country – where there has not, since the extinction of Jacobitism, been an opinion ever expressed on general politics, but that all measures adopted by the King must be right – is inconceivable. I was stopped in this little village the first day of my arrival, by the master of a fishing-boat, to ask me whether I thought the House of Commons would take care that justice was done to the Queen. My wife, also, has met with two or three equally strong proofs of the interest taken in this question. Pray tell me what you hear of the disposition of the army. I have seen some allusions to fresh discontents among the Guards on the subject of some stoppage for breakfasts. The cause does not signify a pin, for if the spirit once exists, occasions for manifesting it will never be wanting.

Henry writes me word that he heard of scarcely anything at Milan, or in the neighbourhood of the Lake of Como, but the Queen's conduct, of which everybody seemed ready to give evidence. The witnesses had all been placed on an allowance of thirty francs per diem, which seems as good a device to invalidate their evidence as could have been adopted, and many are supposed to have come forward only *per chiappar il denaro*. The most material are said to be some bricklayers, who must have peeped, he concludes, through the windows.

Ever most affectionately yours,
C.W.W.

Sarah Lyttelton to Captain F. Spencer

Putney, July 24, 1820

. . . My Father and Mother have been spending a fortnight at Althorp. They return in two days, to wait at Wimbledon till the Queen's fate is decided in the House of Lords.

The debates on it began the 17th of August, and the ministerial people are very sanguine about proving her guilt conclusively. Everybody agrees in believing her to be guilty, except the very lowest classes; but really ministers and their master have so completely bungled the business that it forces everyone who has the least sense of justice to appear to take her part in many things. He [George IV] is so unpopular, his private character so despised, and everything he does so injudicious as well as unprincipled that one can hardly wish him well out of it, except for the fear of a revolution. There are some good caricatures about the business. One is a vast pair of scales; on one side is the Queen, alone, with nothing but a scrap of paper, inscribed 'public opinion'. And she is down, fast to the ground, while on the other side is the King, of an enormous size, and kicking the beam; all the ministers tugging at the scale he is in, to pull it down; but nothing will do, he will kick the beam. John Bull stands between, swearing 'I'll see fair play'.[4] That gives a perfect history of the state of the country. . . .

Princess Lieven suspected that the Queen's supporters were plotting revolution. She wrote to Metternich:

[July] the 27th

The troops are disaffected. They are being paid by the Queen's partisans; that much is certain. The Duke of York told me so himself. Last month, she distributed £9000 amongst the soldiers of the guard. All this is very bad, and we shall only get out of it by blood-letting. As it is not my business to be brave, I am feeling thoroughly frightened; and, if anything happens, I shall run away.

The Times pleads for restraint, and puts the case for the Queen.

Wed. Aug. 2 1820

Her Majesty the QUEEN will take possession of her new residence, Brandenburgh-house, in the course of the present week. If there are those who wish that she had, in her present humble habitation, been less exposed to the gazes of the multitude, or that she had more effectually withdrawn herself from the honest expression of their pity and respect, her MAJESTY is now on the point of fulfilling such wishes. To the retreat of Hammersmith she may still be pursued by the sneers and taunts and hourly libels, of her enemies; though, from what has passed in the House of Commons on that subject, the malice which assails her may be forced to assume a more decent and circumlocutory form. Yet; if the fastidiousness of that Court feeling which has placed barriers round the untried Queen of ENGLAND, impassable to females of any distinction except her own household – if that same harsh and intolerant etiquette which has condemned her to solitude, or to the greetings of the populace, requires from her the ostentation of that humility which belongs to guilt alone – let her MAJESTY satisfy the caprice of her foes, however foolish or unreasonable it may appear to her. . . . But now to graver things:– The 17th of August is fast approaching; and of such a solemn nature are the expectations associated with that fearful day, that there is scarce a company in which we mix, or an individual we casually converse with, altogether insensible to some anxious hope, that her MAJESTY's conduct will not, even after what has passed, become the subject of Paliamentary investigation. Were we disposed to indulge such wishes, it would not be for the sake of the QUEEN. Her honour is attacked, and her vindication calls for what she is not likely to obtain –

a full acknowledgement from her adversaries of their injustice in accusing her; or, what we trust she will yet obtain, a trial in its consequences equivalent to such a concession. In what various lights – and all, to this hour, how unfavourable – have the measures of this illustrious Lady's antagonists appeared! There are but two grounds on which it was conceivable that she could be prosecuted. One was *law*, provided that her conduct was illegal. But illegality can be defined by law alone – and on that ground the King's Ministers gave up the contest, declaring that her MAJESTY had violated no law, and that there was none by which she could be punished. Then the mode of attack was changed, and a degree of *immorality* which ought to be chastised became the next argument for prosecution. Now look at the nature of this new ground of *ex-post facto* punishment, and contemplate, those who have nerves to do so – the unavoidable fruits of which it must be productive:–

1st. The profligacy of a Queen of ENGLAND might lead to a corruption of the Royal blood, and place upon the throne her bastard issue. But this is not a case in point. The QUEEN is past the natural age of child-bearing; and if, while she lived apart from her husband, she had the fortune to bring forth a child, the circumstances of the birth would be an insuperable bar to its succession.

2d. A Queen-Consort may justly be deposed, if proof exist that she has lived licentiously, to the disgrace and injury of a virtuous husband. Now this might bear argument as a case in point, had not the King's Ministers abandoned it as untenable, recommending a procedure which disables Parliament from ascertaining the comparative morals of the parties, and substitutes the State (which is incapable of adultery) for the husband, whom the commission of adultery would have disqualified for the office of an accuser. On what score, therefore, of reason or justice is it, that the *State*, or Commonwealth, can become the complainant against a QUEEN no longer capable of tainting the succession to the crown of England?

3d. The preamble of the Bill informs us, we think, that the QUEEN'S licentiousness was a disgrace or scandal to herself and to the kingdom. This introduces a novel view of the ends of British legislation. Such was not the aim of the law of divorce in private life, nor of that which made it high treason for the QUEEN to forfeit her fidelity to her husband. It was from no such vague and loose description of the bad effects resulting from a QUEEN's immorality that our ancestors condemned her to lose her head. It is not from any scandal to herself, nor from detriment to public morals, that the Queen-Consort of ENGLAND can be prosecuted as a traitor under the law of England. It is because she may give *a spurious heir to the Crown*, and plunge the monarchy into civil commotion. If a Queen-Consort can be rightfully dethroned for adultery, which, except by the law of EDWARD, is not a criminal action – and if, in cases like the present, where that law is inoperative, she is to be deposed by an *ex-post facto* law, as a scandal to herself and as offering a bad example to her subjects – think for one moment where this principle would lead you. What should preserve a Queen-*Regnant* on her throne, if a Queen-Consort can be deposed for mere immorality? The scandal is as great, or greater, as the party is more elevated. . . . It is an enterprise changed with terrors, and which we would conjure the authors of it to relinquish, but that we are aware of its entailing on them a mortification perfectly insupportable. . . .

Aug. 3 1820

At the annual dinner of the Merchant-tailors' Company, which took place yesterday, the conviviality of the evening was disturbed by a contest which arose concerning the omission of the second toast selected for such occasions, which had usually been the Queen and Royal Family, it appearing to some of the company present that such an omission at this time was a marked disrespect to her Majesty. After the confusion had in some degree subsided, the chairman put it as a proposition from the chair, whether the health of the Queen should be drank or not, and, on a show of hands, decided that the question had been negatived. A great number of the Livery, however, were far from being satisfied with this decision, and insisted that the usual toast should be drank. Parties ran so high that harmony could not again be restored, and the company, in consequence, separated at a much earlier hour than customary.

Aug. 4 1820

THE QUEEN

For several days past it has been understood that her Majesty would take up her residence at Brandenburgh-house. From various causes her departure has been postponed, and yesterday was fixed positively for her Majesty to leave the metropolis.

At an early hour yesterday morning Portman-street was in consequence filled with carriages and persons anxious to see her Majesty before she quitted the capital. At about 5 o'clock, the hour at which it was supposed her Majesty would take her departure, the crowd opposite the house was excessive, and loud cries of 'God save the Queen, God bless her Majesty', were heard from every quarter. The Queen was graciously pleased, on two several occasions, to show herself at the balcony, and bowed condescendingly to the people. A short time after 2 o'clock it was understood that her Majesty had altered her determination, and in consequence of the indisposition of Lady A. Hamilton, had postponed her visit to Brandenburgh-house until Saturday next. The consequence was, that some part of the crowd was dispersed. We understand that the carriage was actually counter-ordered, and that a person was about to be sent down to Hammersmith, to postpone the preparation. At nearly three o'clock Mr Ald. Wood arrived on horseback and was greeted with loud huzzas. Soon after his arrival, a servant was despatched to order the carriage to be got in readiness, her Majesty having determined not to disappoint the expectations of the inhabitants of Hammersmith. At this moment the street was completely thronged with persons, some of them of the highest respectability, anxious to pay their respects to her Majesty. Many ladies of rank attended in their carriages, and gentlemen on horseback awaited the appearance of her Majesty. At length, at nearly 4 o'clock, her Majesty's carriage drew up to the door. It was an entirely new elegant open carriage, drawn by four beautiful bay horses: the near leader was mounted by a postilion. The livery was scarlet, trimmed with gold lace. On the panels of the carriage was painted a crown, and underneath the letters 'C.R.'. In about 10 minutes her Majesty made her appearance at the door of her house, and was immediately handed into the carriage. Her Majesty seemed to be in high spirits, and looked remarkably well. She was dressed in a dove-coloured pelisse, with a hat of the same colour, surmounted by a very handsome plume of white feathers. Lady Ann Hamilton next made her appearance, and was followed by Dr Lushington and Mr Alderman Wood. Loud cries of 'God save the Queen' accompanied by shouts of approbation, filled the air. The

'John Bull peppering the Italian rascals – or a kick from Harwich to Holland,' W. Elmes (July 1820). The Italian witnesses against the Queen landed at Dover on 7 July but were attacked by a mob and were shipped back from Harwich to Holland to await the opening of the 'trial'

carriage drove off at a fast trot into Oxford street, followed by a great concourse of persons. It proceeded through the Park, and out at Kensington-gate. In consequence of a misling rain which fell at this time, the carriage, which was previously open, was closed, and it continued shut during the remainder of the way to Hammersmith. The road was completely lined in many parts with people; ladies were seen from every window, waving white handkerchiefs, and crying 'God save the Queen'. At the barracks in Kensington we observed a great number of the military joined in the general shout; they took off their hats, and waved them in the air as her Majesty passed. When her Majesty arrived at Hammersmith the scene was extremely interesting. All were prepared to receive her Majesty, and the little charity children, dressed in their Sunday clothes, were stationed near the church, to welcome her Majesty's arrival. Before the carriage reached Hammersmith, a body of gentlemen on horseback, with white favours in their hats, came to meet her Majesty, and they were greeted with loud cheers. They accompanied the carriage until it reached Brandenburgh-house. The town of Hammersmith was completely filled, and on the arrival of the Queen the cheers were so vehement as to have a deafening effect: guns were discharged, and the bells of the church were rung. Her Majesty most condescendingly bowed to the people as she passed. The carriage proceeded immediately to Brandenburgh-house, and drove through the great gates at the grand entrance up the avenue of trees to the front of the mansion. . . . The carriage was followed by two or three others filled with ladies of rank, who were desirous of paying their respects to her Majesty. Her Majesty dined at Brandenburgh-house, and did not return yesterday evening. The town of Hammersmith was at night brilliantly illuminated, and fireworks were displayed.

W.H. Lyttelton wrote to his friend Charles Bagot to declare his anxiety, and Bagot's friend George Canning wrote on his way to Italy of his fear of revolution.

Hon. W.H. Lyttelton to Charles Bagot

Putney, August 8, 1820

My Dear Charles,

. . . Since you left us, matters have been getting worse and worse, and the disapprobation of all that has been done, and of all that is about to be done, in regard to the Queen, has spread and strengthened throughout the Country. Not only the mob (don't be deceived by what your Tory friends may tell you to the contrary) but people of all ranks, and the middle classes almost to a man, and I believe the troops too, side with the Queen – look upon the whole affair as a Court-job, and impute it to the wrong-headedness of one man, and the miserable servility of the instruments of his will. Constitutional men exclaim against the *mode* of proceeding. Ignorant men (the *great majority*) believe it to be groundless. Designing men work successfully upon these opinions and prejudices, and threaten, if not the monarchy, the public tranquillity – and men of sense are agreed that every thing is hazarded, and that nothing, in any event, can be *gained*, by the measures in question. Such is, I give you my word, the state of public opinion and the general position of things to the best of my judgment, without exaggeration. I won't venture on any predictions, but the alarm is general, lest the mob should overpower the *Civil* force and the troops refuse to act against the mob – and what can then be done, except to prorogue the Parliament, and how the business is ever to be brought to a termination consistent with the independence and authority of the Legislature and Government, it is not easy to divine. . . . Everybody without one exception, wishes the business were at an end. . . . As to facts, I have heard lately, the K. was sufficiently well received at the two reviews at Hounslow – nothing worse occurring than a cry from 2 Middlesex militia-men, as he was going off the ground – of 'God save the Queen and no Gout!' And, what is more important, that the Q. sallied forth in her new shewy Carriage on the first of the two days, and came as far as Hounslow or Brentford (I forget which), when she was stopped for some time by some obstacles in the street, as was at the same time the D. of Wellington; and the D. reports that there was no cheering at all, and it appears from other accounts that she missed that shot entirely. New difficulties have arisen, I hear, and unexpected ones, in regard to the Italian witnesses. Several of the chief refuse to come to England on any terms – not liking the pelting and hooting with which their immaculate countrymen were lately received – and Colnaghi and some other resident Italians quake, lest the mob should massacre them as spies. There is, it is true, very weighty English testimony (as I was assured not long ago by Sir G. of the Admiralty) – that of Naval officers of high character, whom he named to me, who will prove all but adultery, but the main fact can only be proved by the foreigners. Mr Canning is gone abroad – it is not certain whether with any Commission or not – but the story they tell about him, and which I am pretty sure I have traced to his own authority, is that he tendered (which is done every other day now) his resignation when the proceedings were resolved upon, and that the K. told him he would excuse his taking any part in them. So he magnanimously keeps out of the way till it is over. You will of course hear the truth of this no doubt from the best sources – so I need hardly have mentioned it. It is not admired; not only Lord Grey, but Lord Spencer and many men of character, say that in this as in many other instances, the principles that used to govern public men in such predicaments are lost sight of –

and Mr C. is again, for this step, and his celebrated speech on the Q., very roughly dealt with in conversation. Lord Anglesea is said to have sent a letter to the K. acquainting H.M. with the public feeling against what was going on – for which the K. cut him at the Levee. Lord A. thought it might be accidental, but he was re-cut, and more decisively, at the next Levee. Lord Stafford is quoted to me as having seen (thro' his queer medium) this second proof of Royal sense and temper.

. . . As to the duration of the trial, Lord Liverpool is of opinion that the case for the prosecution will take a month, but nobody can tell, and many think it will last longer. This must depend on their calling the Italians or not – for if several of those Outlandishers are to be examined thro' interpreters by 250 Peers – it may last till next century. . . .

Ever yours,
W.H.L.

George Canning to Charles Bagot

Antwerp, August 11, 1820

(Private)

My Dear Charles,

. . . Let me hear of you now and then. I landed here yesterday on my way to Italy to bring my wife and family safe out of the reach of revolutions. My journey will have the additional advantage of taking me out of the way of the first act at least of what I hope will not be a revolution (but what has at least some of the worst characteristics of such a process) at home.

God bless you, my dear Charles,
Ever affectionately yours,
G.C.

Robert Peel, too, was impressed by the potential danger of the situation.

Robert Peel to J. W. Croker

Mickleham, near Leatherhead, August 10th, 1820

I do think the Queen's affair very formidable. It is a famous ingredient in the cauldron which has been bubbling a long time, and upon which, as it always seemed to me, the Government never could discern the least simmering. They applied a blow-pipe, however, when they omitted the Queen's name in the Liturgy: when they established a precedent of dethronement for imputed personal misconduct. Surely this was not the time for robbing Royalty of the exterior marks of respect, and for preaching up the anti-divine right doctrines. If she be worse than Messalina, nothing but the united voice of King, Lords, and Commons should have degraded her. I certainly would have tried her the moment she set her foot in England, but I would have prayed for her as Queen till she had been tried. What is to be the end of it? What mean all the compliments to Colonel Bosanquet and 143 City light horse men? Did you read them? Is the army suspected? I *saw* the Queen the other day pass the barracks in Hyde Park, and at the moment of her passing there was an immense shout. I did not see whether the soldiers joined in it or not. The *Morning Chronicle* says they did.

Ever most affectionately, I am,
My dear Croker,
Robert Peel

Princess Lieven to Prince Metternich

The 12th [August 1820]

In a few days there will be a serious crisis in this country. The Queen's trial begins next week. Any day may bring trouble. The Opposition believes there will be a revolution; the Ministry perhaps fears it. The whole progress of the affair is so peculiar that it is difficult to judge of anything beforehand, and for the moment I find it prudent to wait and not commit myself to an opinion. There is one thing of which my experience of this country makes me certain: it is that trouble which is much heralded never comes off. All the same, the lessons of experience may be at fault in circumstances so extraordinary as these.

The Queen has changed her lodging once more. She will settle tomorrow in the house adjacent to Lord Castlereagh's, and will have to pass Carlton House every day to go to Parliament. Here is a pretty piece of spite. Castlereagh told me that it would not disturb him in the least, except that the mob might begin to pull down his house. Few men have Lord Castlereagh's intrepid coolness, and more than once nothing but his unruffled appearance has overawed the mob. One ought always to show courage, even if it is only through fright; it is the one infallible resource.

Tomorrow, at ten o'clock, all the sages of the three realms will be assembled; there will be a roll-call in the House of Lords. What a task they are undertaking, and who can tell how it will end!. There are fears of serious trouble. However, I do not feel very frightened; but I am determined not to give myself time to be; for, at the first threatening sign, I am off.

Lady Charlotte Lindsay continued to keep her friend Miss Berry abreast of events in London. She herself was recruited by the Queen's advisers to give evidence at the 'trial'.

Lady Charlotte Lindsay to Miss Berry

Sheffield Place, August 13, 1820

On Friday, the 14th of July, Lord Erskine moved, in the House of Lords, that the Queen should have a list given her of the names of the witnesses against her. The Lord Chancellor objected, giving as a reason that there is no precedent for the list of witnesses being given in cases of pains and penalties. The motion was lost, the majority against it being 78 to 28. On the 17th of July, Dr Lushington (the Queen's civilian) moved, in the House of Commons, that Her Majesty should have her plate restored to her, complaining that it had been refused upon her applying for it at the Lord Chamberlain's office. Lord Castlereagh in answer, stated that this plate belonged to the Crown, and was only appropriated to the Queen's use during her residence at Kensington Palace. Dr Lushington withdrew his motion.[5] A motion of Mr Favell's, in the Common Council, was carried, for petitioning both Houses of Parliament to stop the proceedings against the Queen. This petition was presented by Lord Erskine, in the House of Lords, on the 19th of July, and was, upon a motion of Lord Lauderdale's, rejected without a division. . . .

. . . The Queen has received and still continues to receive very numerous addresses; many of them have been presented by members of Parliament. Some of her answers at first were well written, but lately they have given strong indications of the absence of her legal advisers, who are gone into the country for the recruiting of their health – Mr Brougham being very ill, and Denman with the jaundice. The answers now, 'a variety of wretchedness', are, I suppose, intended to please all palates; there are seditious for the Radicals, pathetic for the sentimental, and canting for the Methodists – the productions probably of Alderman Wood, Lady P., and Lady A. H[amilton]. Doctor Parr has been living much with the Queen lately, and is supposed to have influenced her counsels; but these answers are, I think, too foolish to have been his composition. A letter has just appeared in the newspapers, addressed to the King, from the Queen; part of it is well written. It is very inflammatory and libellous against both Houses of Parliament – consequently, very injudicious in this stage of the business. The author is not known; some say it is Cobbett's, but I do not think that it is quite in his style; others give it to a Mr Fellows, a Unitarian preacher. . . . Her Majesty has lately taken Brandenburgh House for her villa, and Lady Francis's house, until the Government find her some other, which I suppose they will speedily do, as Lady Francis's house is next door to Lord Castlereagh's. A party of Italian witnesses that arrived in England some weeks since, were so ill-used by the populace at Dover that the Government had been obliged to send them to Holland, to be kept there in safety until they are wanted to give their evidence. It is disgraceful to the country that witnesses on either side should meet with such treatment, and it has produced great inconvenience; for in order to protect these witnesses, when they return here for the trial, from the resentment of the people, they are to be kept all together in a Government house in Cotton Garden, close to the House of Lords. So those who shall have been examined, and those who are about to be examined, will have every opportunity of conversing together; and it is scarcely possible that they will not talk upon the subject that must be uppermost in their thoughts. Farewell.

Notes

1. Lady Charlotte Lindsay was a friend and companion of Queen Caroline as Princess of Wales. She gave evidence on her behalf at the 'trial'. Miss Berry (1736–1852) was a well-known authoress.
2. Emily Mary, Countess Cowper, daughter of the 1st Viscount Melbourne (though probably, like her brother the future Prime Minister, the illegitimate child of the Earl of Egremont), married in 1805 Henry, later 3rd Viscount Palmerston, later Foreign Secretary and Prime Minister.
3. Harriet, wife of Charles Arbuthnot, Secretary to the Treasury, was a close friend of Castlereagh and of Wellington.
4. See page 33.
5. On the Queen's plate, see pages 100–2.

CHAPTER FIVE

'Accusation in Thunder'

The date set for the opening of proceedings in the Lords was 17 August. As the day approached, the tension in the capital mounted. Thomas Creevey looked forward eagerly to the amusement which he expected the 'trial' to provide, but others were more anxious about the reactions of the public and the 'mob' to the appearance of the Queen and of the prominent members of the government who were accused of persecuting her. The government poured troops into London, sending even to the far north for reinforcements, and hundreds of special constables were sworn in to line the Queen's route from Hammersmith to Westminster. Notables who rode or drove to witness the debate were hissed and hooted, and Princess Lieven had to run the gauntlet in her carriage. Lord Castlereagh, the most unpopular member of the government, was advised to leave his house and sleep at the Foreign Office to escape the attentions of the crowd, and on one occasion Wellington was almost pulled off his horse. It was remarkable how courageously they all faced the mob: Wellington and Lord Sidmouth, the Home Secretary, were particularly fearless though, as one observer remarked, the mob did not go to extremes but showed themselves ultimately 'as English mobs generally are, as manageable and good-humoured as at an election or a fair'. When Lord Anglesey turned towards them, as Mrs Wellesley Pole noted, 'They slunk away as they generally do when fronted'. Violence beyond the traditional exercise of the free Englishman's right to shout, to threaten and to break windows was in fact rare. Nor were the 'mobs' wholly composed of ruffians and members of the 'lower orders' out for plunder, assault or excitement. It was a remarkable fact that many of those who demonstrated for the Queen were members of the 'sober and industrious' middle classes of London's trading population. Princess Lieven reported that as well as 'the real mob', the streets were 'full of well-dressed men and respectable women, all waving their hats and their handkerchiefs'. William Fremantle also noted that, however strong the evidence against the Queen, the 'middling class, the shopkeepers' were 'determined to support her as an oppressed and injured woman'.

The Queen's affair brought to the surface many aspects of the political and social culture of early nineteenth-century England, not least the popular prejudice against foreigners, as represented by the Italian witnesses to the Queen's conduct abroad, where she was accused of adultery with Bergami, her major-domo. The first major witness, an Italian servant named Theodore Majocci, whose appearance seemed to startle the Queen so much that she rushed out of the chamber, exclaiming, according to various accounts, either 'Theodore' or '*traditore*', was quickly discredited and his evasive replies of '*non mi ricordo*' (I don't remember) to Brougham's questions provided a new catch-word for public amusement. Lady Granville also reported that the antics of the Italian interpreter were 'irresistibly comic' and kept their Lordships 'in a roar of laughter'. The Londoners regarded the Italians, who were housed in lodgings in Cotton Yard, almost as exhibits in a zoo or performers in pantomime, and the newspapers criticized the spending of money, which might otherwise relieve the distress of the English people, on the cost of bringing over and maintaining these foreigners. 'John Bull looks upon them as so many bugs and frogs,' Lady Granville commented.

The proceedings in the House of Lords opened with the usual formalities, followed by a debate on two motions, one by the Duke of Leinster in effect to throw out the bill without debate, and one by Lord Grey, the leader of the opposition, to proceed by the judicial process of impeachment, which would give the Queen an actual trial and therefore a proper opportunity to defend herself. Both were rejected, as were other motions designed to bring proceedings to a speedy end without considering evidence in detail. The 'trial' as it became known was in fact the review by the whole House of the details of the charges, the usual procedure in considering a parliamentary bill during the second reading. In effect it was a trial but with the whole House as judges and jury rather than before judges in a court of law. Both the government and the Queen were represented by learned counsel, the former by the law officers of the Crown, the latter by her legal advisers Henry Brougham and Thomas Denman. Her case was skilfully presented by the last two, Brougham excelling in cross-examination of the witnesses for the Crown (as in effect they were) and Denman in particular adding touches of humour which kept the Lords in a good mood. Individual lords could also take part in the examination of witnesses and speak on the evidence as in a debate, so that the proceedings were in some respects more informal than in a criminal court.

The details of the evidence and the speeches were reported at length in the newspapers and, of course, in *Hansard*, though parliamentary reports were not yet fully verbatim or official. The reports were provided by the journalists who worked for the major newspapers, and collected and edited at the end of the session on behalf of the House by Thomas Hansard, the printer. The newspaper reports were avidly digested by the public and indeed filled most of the columns of those, such as *The Times*, who championed the Queen throughout.

It soon became apparent that things were going badly for the 'prosecution' and by early September, when the evidence against the Queen had been completed, few expected that the case would succeed. Whatever the truth about her conduct and moral character might be, the case involved other political issues and touched the position of the monarchy itself, so that the bill was unlikely to pass the House of Lords in its original form and even more unlikely to survive the House of Commons, where the whole process would have to be repeated in face of even more weighty and persistent pressure from public opinion. The government's later decision, under pressure from the bishops in the Lords, to remove the divorce clause from the bill seemed to destroy its major *raison d'être* and the need to continue at all with the emasculated measure was questioned. The Radicals began to scent victory, as their organ *The Black Dwarf* suggested, while Tories like J.W. Croker were cast into even deeper apprehension for the future. If the bill should fail because of the pressure of public opinion, what would become of the British parliamentary constitution?

The authorities turned their attention once more to the state and readiness of the troops, in case they should be needed; and the case for the Queen's defence had not yet been opened when Parliament was adjourned on 9 September for three weeks. The occasion was celebrated by one of the most spectacular of all the demonstrations in the Queen's favour, when thousands of seamen from the Royal and merchant Navies sailed or marched to Brandenburg House to show their support for her cause. 'This procession decides the fate of the Queen,' Creevey confidently declared. Britons would never indeed be slaves so long as her beloved Navy stood for their liberties and between them and their enemies, abroad or at home. Observers were beginning to ask whether Liverpool's government could now survive its likely humiliation.

Extract from Lady Anne Hamilton's Secret History of the Court of England

Lady Anne Hamilton was the Queen's closest attendant during the time of her 'trial'. Her *Secret History* is a partial and often inaccurate account of the reigns of George III and IV, written to justify Caroline and to discredit her husband. Here she describes the preparations made for the opening of the proceedings in the House of Lords.

During the disgraceful proceedings against the queen, such was the public feeling in her favour, that the peers actually feared for their personal safety in going to and returning from the House. This threatened danger was, as might be expected, properly guarded against by the military, who poured into London and its environs in vast numbers. The agitated state of the public mind probably was never more decidedly expressed than on the 19th [*sic*] of August, the day on which the trial commenced. At a very early hour in the morning, workmen were employed in forming double rows of strong timber from St Margaret's Church to the King's Bench office on the one side, and from the upper extremity of Abingdon Street on the other, so as to enclose the whole area in front of the House of Lords. This was done to form a passage to the House, which was devoted exclusively to the carriages of the peers, to and from the principal entrance. Within this extensive area, a large body of constables was stationed, under the control of the high bailiff and high constable, who were in attendance before seven o'clock. A very strong body of foot-guards was also posted in the King's Bench office, the Record office, and in the other apartments, near or fronting the street. Westminster Hall was likewise appropriated to the accommodation of the military. All the leading passages from St Margaret's Church into Parliament Street were closed securely by strong partitions of timber. The police-hulk and the gunboats defended the river side of Westminster, and the civil and military arrangements presented an effectual barrier on the opposite side. At nine o'clock a troop of life-guards rode into the palace yard, and formed in line in front of the principal gate of Westminster Hall; they were shortly afterward followed by a detachment of the foot-guards, who were formed under the piazzas of the House of Lords, where they piled their arms. Patrols of life-guards were then thrown forward, in the direction of Abingdon Street, who occasionally formed near the king's entrance, and at intervals paraded.

At half-past nine the body of the Surrey horse-patrol rode over Westminster bridge and for a short time paraded Parliament Street, Whitehall, and Charing Cross; they afterward drew up near the barrier at St Margaret's Church. The peers began to arrive shortly afterward; the lord chancellor was in the House before eight o'clock. The other ministers were equally early in their attendance.

At a quarter before ten, a universal cheering from a countless multitude, in the direction of Charing Cross, announced to the anxious spectators that the queen was approaching. Her Majesty, attended by Lady Anne Hamilton, had come early from Brandenburgh House to the residence of Lady Francis, St James's Square, and from thence they departed for the House of Lords, in a new state carriage, drawn by six bay horses. As they passed Carlton Palace, the Admiralty, and other such places, the sentinels presented arms; but, at the Treasury, this mark of honour was omitted.

When the queen arrived at the House, the military stationed in the front immediately presented arms. Her Majesty was received at the door by Sir T. Tyrwhitt and Mr Brougham; and the queen, with her lady in waiting, proceeded to an apartment prepared for their reception. Shortly afterward, her Majesty, accompanied as before, entered the House by the passage leading from the robing-room, which is situated on the right of the throne.

During this initiatory part of the trial, and until nearly four o'clock, her Majesty was attended by Lord Archibald Hamilton and his sister Lady Anne, who stood close to the queen all the time.

Upon returning from the House in the same state in which her Majesty arrived, she was greeted by the most enthusiastic acclamations and shouts of applause from every class of society, who were apparently desirous to outvie each other in testimonies of homage to their ill-fated and insulted queen.

Each succeeeding day of the pretended trial her Majesty met with a similar reception; and, during the whole period, addresses were lavishly poured in upon her, signed by so many persons, and testifying such ardent regard and devotion, that every moment of time was necessarily occupied with their reception and acknowledgment. Thus, though the queen was insulted by the king and the majority of the peers, it must have afforded great consolation to her wounded feelings, while witnessing the enthusiasm and devotion manifested in her cause by all the really honourable of the community. . . .

Thomas Creevey, Whig politician and diarist, writes to his step-daughter Miss Ord on the preliminaries to the 'trial'.

Letters from Thomas Creevey to Miss Ord

Knowsley, 7th August, 1820

. . . I came here on Saturday. I like Lady Mary [Stanley] better every time I see her. You know what a d—d ramshackle of a library they have here, so I was complaining at breakfast this morning that they had no State Trials in the house; upon which Lady Mary said she was sure she could find some, and accordingly flew from her breakfast and came back in triumph at having found them for me. Upon the subject of the

Queen, my lord and my lady are both *substantially* right, i.e., in thinking there is not a pin to chuse between them, and that the latter has been always ill-used, and that nobody but the King could get redress in such a case against his wife. Little Derby goes further than the Countess, when she is not by; but *she* thinks it proper to deprecate all violence, and says, tho' Bennet and I are excellent men, and she likes us both extremely, still, that we are like Dives, and that Lazarus ought to come occasionally and cool our tongues. Is not this the image of her?

Liverpool, 12th August

. . . I cannot resist the curiosity of seeing a Queen tried. From the House of Lords or from Brooks's you shall have a daily account of what passes.

House of Lords, August 16th

. . . This is very convenient. There is not only the usual admission for the House of Commons upon the [steps of] the Throne, but pen, ink and paper for our accommodation in the long gallery. There is a fine chair for the Queen *within* the bar, to be near her counsel and the two galleries. This makes all the difference. Two hundred and fifty peers are to attend, 60 being excused from age, infirmities, being abroad or professing the Catholic faith.

Wilberforce told Bennet that the act of his life which he most reproached himself with was not having moved to restore the Queen to the Liturgy, and he was sure this was the only course. Grey says the Queen ought to be sent to the Tower for her letter to the King.

Here is Castlereagh, smiling as usual, though I think awkwardly. . . . Sir Thomas Tyrwhitt has just been here and tho' in his official dress as Black Rod, was most communicative. He says the Government is stark, staring mad; that they want to prevent his receiving the Queen to-morrow at the door as Queen, but that *he will*. . . .

The Times sets the scene (17 August)

The seat appropriated for the use of her Majesty during the inquiry, which commences this day, is that ordinarily occupied by the Bishop of Sodor and Man. It is in the body of the house, in the rear of the cross benches, and immediately adjoining the bar. In this situation her Majesty will have a perfect opportunity of hearing and seeing everything that occurs. . . .

Mr Lee, the High Constable of Westminster, proposed a plan for preserving the peace of that city by the exertion of the civil power only; but it will appear, from the resolution to which the House of Lords came on Tuesday evening, that they deemed the attendance of the military necessary. . . .

Yesterday a large body of artillery arrived in town from Woolwich, to form a part of the military arrangements during the Queen's trial. The Surrey horse-patrol are, it is said, to do daily duty in the Westminster-road, several of them yesterday took up their station in the livery stables opposite Astley's Amphitheatre.

Besides the cavalry and infantry which will be on duty to-day, a great number of special constables have been sworn in to attend in the line of the Queen's approach to the House of Lords to-day, for the purpose of preserving the public peace. The Thames police-boat keeps its station opposite Cotton-garden.

(Report from Lancaster)

On Thursday last (the 10th inst.) two troops of the 6th Dragoons arrived here from Carlisle, and yesterday . . . proceeded on their route for the South.

The northern roads are so crowded with troops on their march towards the metropolis, that it would seem as if the town was to be put in a state of blockade.

Thomas Creevey to Miss Ord

17th August

. . . Near the House of Lords there is a fence of railing put across the street from the Exchequer coffee-house to the enclosed garden ground joining to St Margaret's churchyard, through which members of both Houses were alone permitted to pass. A minute after I passed, I heard an uproar, with hissing and shouting. On turning round I saw it was Wellington on horseback. His horse made a little start, and he looked round with some surprise. He caught my eye as he passed, and nodded, but was evidently annoyed.

I got easily into the Lords and to a place within two yards of the chair placed for the Queen, on the right hand of the throne, close to its steps. They proceeded to call over the House and to receive excuses from absent peers. As the operation was going on, people came in who said the Queen was on her way and as far as Charing Cross. Two minutes after, the shouts of the populace announced her near approach, and some minutes after, two folding doors within a few feet of me were suddenly thrown open, and in entered her Majesty. To describe to you her appearance and manner is far beyond my powers. I had been taught to believe she was as much improved in looks as in dignity of manners; it is therefore with much pain I am obliged to observe that the nearest resemblance I can recollect to this much-injured Princess is a toy which you used to call Fanny Royds.[1] There is another toy of a rabbit or a cat, whose tail you squeeze under its body, and then out it jumps in half a minute off the ground into the air. The first of these toys you must suppose to represent the person of the Queen; the latter the manner by which she popped all at once into the House, made a *duck* at the throne, another to the Peers, and a concluding jump into the chair which was placed for her. Her dress was black figured gauze, with a good deal of trimming, lace, &c; her sleeves white, and perfectly episcopal; a handsome white veil, so thick as to make it very difficult to me, who was as near to her as any one, to see her face; such a back for variety and inequality of ground as you never beheld; with a few straggling ringlets on her neck, which I flatter myself from their appearance were not her Majesty's own property.

She squatted into her chair with such a grace that the gown is at this moment hanging over every part of it – both back and elbows. . . . When the Queen entered, the Lords (Bishops and all) rose, and then they fell to calling over the House again and receiving excuses. When the Duke of Sussex's name was called, the Chancellor read his letter, begging to be excused on the ground of consanguinity; upon which the Duke of York rose, and in a very marked and angry tone said:– '*I* have much stronger ground for asking leave of absence than the Duke of Sussex, and yet I should be ashamed not to be present to do my duty!' This indiscreet observation (to say no worse of it) was by no means well received or well thought of, and when the question was put 'that the Duke of Sussex be excused upon his letter', the House granted it with scarce a dissentient voice. Pretty well, this, for the Duke of York's observation!

Well – this finished, and the order read 'that the House do proceed with the Bill', the Duke of Leinster rose and said in a purely Irish tone that, without making any elaborate speech, and for the purpose of bringing this business to a conclusion, he should move that this order be now rescinded. Without a word from any one on this subject the House divided, we members of the Commons House remaining. There were 41 for Leinster and 206 (including 17 Bishops) against him; but, what was more remarkable, there were 20 at least of our Peers[2] who voted against the Duke of Leinster – as Grey, Lansdowne, Derby, Fitzwilliam, Spencer, Erskine, Grafton, de Clifford, Darlington, Yarborough, &c. Lord Kenyon and Lord Stanhope were the only persons who struck me in the Opposition as new. The Duke of Gloucester would not vote, notwithstanding cousin York's observations. Holland, the Duke of Bedford, old Fortescue, Thanet, &c., were of course in the minority. . . . This division being over, Carnarvon objected in a capital speech to any further proceeding, and was more cheered than is usual with the Lords; but no doubt it was from our 40 friends. Then came Grey and I think he made as weak a speech as ever I heard: so thought Brougham and Denman who were by me. He wanted the opinion of the Judges upon the statute of Edward III as to a Queen's treason,[3] and after speeches from Eldon, Liverpool and Lansdowne, Grey's motion is acceded to, and the Judges are now out preparing their opinion, and all is at a stand.

I forgot to say Lady Ann Hamilton waits behind the Queen, and that, for effect and delicacy's sake, she leans on brother Archy's arm, tho' she is full six feet high, and bears a striking resemblance to one of Lord Derby's great red deer. Keppel Craven and Sir William Gell likewise stand behind the Queen in full dress. . . . Lord John Russell is writing on my right hand, and Sir Hussey Vivian on my left. I have just read over my account of the Queen to the latter, and he deposes to its perfect truth. . . .

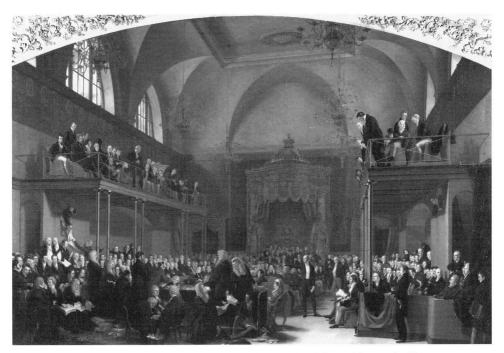

The House of Lords during the 'trial' (G. Hayter). Lord Grey addresses the House

Four o'clock

Well, the Judges returned, as one knew they would, saying there was no statute-law or law of the land touching the Queen's case. Then counsel were called in; upon which the Duke of Hamilton, in a most excellent manner, ask'd Mr Attorney General from whom he appeared, or by whose instructions. A more gravelling question could not well be put, as appeared by Mr Attorney's manner. He shifted and shuffled about, and Liverpool helped, and Lord Belhaven ended the conversation by declaring his utter ignorance of the prosecution – whether it was by the Crown, the Ministers, or the House of Lords. . . . There are great crowds of people about the House, and all the way up Parliament Street. The Guards, both horse and foot, are there too in great numbers, but I saw nothing except good humour on all sides. . . .

Princess Lieven and others describe the opening of the trial:

Letters from Princess Lieven to Prince Metternich

August 17th

. . . I am going to town this morning; it is the great day, and my road takes me by the Houses of Parliament. They want me to go a roundabout way, and I have said that I will. My husband goes ahead on horseback; and, as I shall be alone, I shall direct my coachman. I am not afraid of any harm that may come to me, and I am rather curious.

The 19th

I kept my word – I went by Parliament the other day. The crowd was terrific. I was stopped, and they wanted me to shout 'Long live the Queen', and my servants to take off their hats. I was in an open carriage. My heart beat quickly for a moment; but I put a bold face on it and I did not shout. I had forbidden my servants to take off their hats. The Russian cockade, which has three colours, gave me a certain constitutional look, which was a good thing in the circumstances. A smart touch of the whip set the horses bounding, and I got out of it. Esterhazy was standing cautiously at a window; he saw me pass and said that he was afraid for me. I reached home without accident and my husband scolded me; but I was able to prove to him by my experience that they were not killing people. All the same, five men were killed by the soldiers the day before yesterday in front of the Houses of Parliament. The newspapers say nothing of this; for the Jacobin papers do not want the occurrence, should it become known, to discourage the mob from going to the House, and the ministerial papers themselves are not anxious to boast about it. The Duke of York told me about it yesterday; he had got it from the military reports. The Duke is the idol of the mob; they are all for the Queen and for him. He frowns and does not bow, because they cheer him by the title of king. Wellington is terribly booed – and I believe he feels it. It is a shocking ordeal, coming out of the Houses of Parliament every day; the House rises at half-past four, and twenty or thirty thousand Radicals are waiting for you, greeting the peers with hisses or cheers, as it suits them. There are a great many soldiers and constables. This first stage of the trial may last three or four weeks, and every day the same spectacle. Your friend Wellington did something in very bad taste. He was the only person who kept his hat on, during the whole of the first hearing, in the Queen's presence. Lord Castlereagh has left his house; he was told that, however courageous it might be to brave the danger, his presence became criminal when it provoked a disturbance. So he has had his bed installed in the Foreign Office, in the room where he gives audience to ambassadors. To be reduced to that!

We shall go to town regularly twice a week during all this period. One must see and hear for oneself. As is reasonable, there are no social gatherings. but, as I am intimate with many households, I break through the impenetrable English barriers. The other day I amused myself by visiting first a Ministerial family, then an Opposition one, and then coming home. Lady Jersey is absolutely in a raging fever. How all this would amuse you; for, however regrettable the whole affair may be, and however tragically it may yet turn out, it still has its comic side!

Lord Holland's memoirs [4]

The proceedings on the bill were to be resumed, or as in common parlance it was described, the Queen's trial was to begin, on August 17, and on that day Parliament Street was lined by a crowd whose aspect was far more formidable that their numbers. Unlike English multitudes, their countenances seemed to indicate design, determination, and revenge. They hissed some and applauded other peers as they passed; but they performed both those tasks with such marked indifference that it was difficult not to suspect that they had some more serious undertaking in view. One man quitted his companions, and, placing himself at the head of the Duke of Wellington's horse (as he was riding down to the House), clenched his fist, and repeated the word *Ney*[5] three times with great emphasis and anger – an exclamation which surprised the bystanders exceedingly, and is said to have disconcerted the Duke himself not a little. Soon afterwards the railing which barricaded the street was broken down by mere pressure, and advantage was taken of this incident to augment both the military and the police. Owing to such precautions or to other accidents, the appearance of the people in the streets, though in numbers always considerable, gradually improved in character, and they became, as English mobs generally are, as manageable and good-humoured as at an election or a fair.

Lady Charlotte Lindsay's account of the opening of the trial

The House of Lords met on Thursday, the 17th of August, 1820.

After calling over the names, the Duke of Leinster moved that the order of the day for proceeding against the Queen by a Bill of Pains and Penalties be rescinded. The House divided: for the motion, 41; against it, 260. Lord Grey said that a Bill of Pains and Penalties could only be expedient where the law could not reach the offence alleged to be committed any other way. He moved that the opinion of the judges should be taken as to whether the offence of which Her Majesty is accused be high treason. The judges were consulted, and pronounced it *not* to be high treason. The Queen's Attorney-general, Mr Brougham, then made a most eloquent and powerful speech against the principle of the Bill. The Queen herself was in the House of Lords, attended by her lady of the bedchamber, Lady Anne Hamilton, and Keppel Craven, who officiated as chamberlain in the place of Gell. She was much cheered and applauded by the populace as she went down and returned from the House, but there was no riot.

Friday, August 18th. – The King's Attorney and Solicitor-generals, Gifford and Copley, and the Queen's Attorney and Solicitor-generals, Brougham and Denman, spoke in the House of Lords for and against the principle of the Bill. Brougham stated, and proved by various precedents, that any person may be subjected to impeachment for acts that are not offences by law, as well as for those that are offences by law. Lord Grey said that the arguments of Her Majesty's counsel had produced so strong an impression on his mind that he wished for time to give them due consideration before he could agree to the necessity of proceeding by this Bill.

Saturday, August 19th. – Lord Grey moved that they should proceed by impeachment. The House divided: 179 against the motion and 64 for it. Had the motion for impeachment been carried, I think the Queen would have been quite saved harmless. A majority of the peers would, I believe, vote for her degradation, provided the evidence against her would give any colour to their doing so, and many probably would vote for divorce; but I imagine few would be found to vote for *beheading* her, which must naturally be the consequence of impeachment, in case she is pronounced guilty. Lord King and Lord Calthorpe both moved against proceeding by a Bill of Pains and Penalites, but lost their motions. The Attorney-general then opened his charge. He made various mistakes in dates and little particulars respecting Her Majesty's attendants, but he brought forward some very strong circumstances. . . .

Lady Cowper to Frederick Lamb

London August 17th [1820]

The Peers are all gone to the House and had no difficulty in getting in. Details I will give you the last thing tomorrow. I think if there is to be any blow up that it is much more likely to be at the end than at the beginning, but I hope it will all go quieter than is expected. Active measures have certainly been taken in all ways for the preservation of peace. Troops have been marched to London from all quarters, regiments from Hertford marched on to Barnet, and Barnet to London. W[illia]m is ordered to be in readiness with his Yeomanry, and so of course are all the others. He has sent to Ld C[owper] to beg for four horses to be at his disposal in case he should want them. I dined with Huskisson at Whitehall yesterday. He says it is wonderful the terror people are in at a distance from the Metropolis. He says by the letters he gets one should fancy it was all over with us. . . .

The Queen and all her violent Radical Friends are furious with B[rougham] and say he betrayed her. The Ministers are also abusing him, for they say if he had not persuaded them that he could manage her, they would have sooner proposed measures of conciliation. In short, when a job has been thoroughly mismanaged, of course every body abuses every body. B[rougham] was jockeyed by her, and his vanity made him believe his influence with her to be very great, and she did with him what he intended to have done with her, which was to use her name for his own interest. I think B[rougham] feels that he wants friends very much, for he makes up to me greatly, but I am not his dupe as many others are. . . .

Friday 18th

All was very quiet yesterday, the Mob quite immense, but in good humour and little said by them. The newspapers will tell you what the L[or]ds do. . . . The Duke of York was much applauded going down, and the Duke of Wellington hissed, which much surprised him. The Duke of York's speech may very likely today *depopularize* him. Brougham's speech was in part good, but the beginning very tiresome and it sent the Queen to sleep. His attack on the Duke of York was very bad; stupid and in bad taste and no argument and very ill received, as he is highly popular with every body just now. Upon all these things being stated at Ly Jersey's I ventured a remark which was not well received either 'that the moral of the story only went to show how very little it signified whether people were hissed or applauded, for it was quite chance and ignorance, and likely every day to change'. Whigs cast an evil eye upon me. . . . They pretend to like truth, but it's only some truths they like. It is difficult to see through that future opaque cloud the Queen talks of, but I really believe the Bill will never pass the H[ouse] of Commons, if it does the House of Lords. There is no denying it, the feeling of the people is almost everywhere in favour of the Queen, not merely the rabble, but the respectable middle ranks. All their prejudices are in her favour. They hate the King, disapprove of his moral conduct and think all foreigners are liars and villains.

How Govern[ment]t have got the witnesses to come over, I don't know, but I suppose by power of money, and when this comes out it will still further invalidate their testimony. Besides, I cannot think they will be got to speak, for they are frightened out of their wits. They are confined in Cotton Garden [*sic*] and heard all the hurra and noise yesterday, which terrified them out of their senses. They thought the Mob was breaking in and coming to murder them. A messenger, who was very hot, comes into them wiping his throat, which they took for an explanatory gesture in lieu of the Italian language, to inform them they were going to have their throats cut. Think what a state of terror they must be in, and how they will shiver and shake and prevaricate in the House. If the thing goes on we shall have shocking work in the Winter with all this Mob on the long dark nights. Now they are good-humoured, but one cannot trust to its lasting, and all the time one thinks what a pity it is to see the country embroiled for a thing that signifies so little, merely to gratify the King's angry feeling and to enable Ministers to keep their places, which, however, I believe they will manage to do in any event. Really, when one thinks of it, the whole thing is too absurd and all brought on by the Litany omission, which, in fact, nobody cares about, and she has got herself hampered, and fighting to remain in this country, which is, in fact, the thing she would dislike most. Her manner was very good on entering the House, but she lay lolling in her arm chair in a ridiculous way and her head did not appear above the bar. She had a white veil over her face, which was the colour of brickdust. . . . Ld Archibald says on his conscience he believes the Queen guilty, but that he should still vote for her acquittal, because he thinks the K[ing] has no right to a divorce or to embroil us in a Civil War for a thing which signifies so little, and this I daresay, is the feeling of many other members of the House. . . .

Letters from Lady Granville to Lady G. Morpeth[6]

London: August 17, 1820

I have excellent accounts from Wherstead; so far good. I walk about the room a good deal, draw very long breaths and sometimes say out loud, 'It don't signify'. After I had written yesterday Mr Greathead called, a wise old man and a Whig. He doubted the Guards, blamed Ministers, dreaded consequences, hipped me to death. Charlotte Greville, Harriet, and a little dog followed and rather altered the scene. She was intent upon having me at her drum this evening, but I would not be taken in. It is with the utmost difficulty that they have persuaded Lord Castlereagh to leave his house and sleep at his office. There is to be a cordon of military, preventing the mob penetrating beyond Charing Cross on one side and Abingdon Street on the other. If the Guards are steady, nothing can be safer. There has been a sad *petitesse*. They have forbidden her going in at the royal entrance to the House of Lords. Urged by me, Lords Granville and Morley and Hart mean to get up when she enters. *Honi soit qui mal y pense*. I breakfasted this morning at a quarter before eight with Granville and Mr Wilmot and saw them off, armed with hard biscuits, and have this moment seen William Hissey, who went with the carriage and says that nothing can be more peaceable than the mob. Darlings they are. I am considerably happier.

One of the jokes is that the witnesses are to give their evidence *en récitative* and the Duke of Hamilton to interpret. . . .

I have just had the following note from good-natured, tumultuous Lady Bessborough, all the happier for the barricade and the cock: 'They are all safe in. I saw Lord G. get out, the place quite clear, not a soul near. Some mob broke in with the Queen but not much, and the soldiers have cleared them from the door steadily and gently, so I hope all will be quiet. I have not slept a wink, for, though our habitation is perfection, they chose to put up the barricade all night, and worse, *un coq matineux* has been crowing since three o'clock.'

I am so glad I have to write, as all these early hours must necessarily be passed in solitude. I cannot help looking out of window and spying out for ill-looking men. God bless you, dearest.

London: August 18, 1820

If I had not fancied a large hot buttered roll at breakfast I should be happy. My fears are subsided and my health is good. London is as quiet as a mouse and the mob cut their jokes even upon the Queen. Yesterday her carriage was for a moment followed by a stage-coach and a dray-cart, and some one called out, 'Mighty respectable carriages bring up the rear'. The Queen said to Sir Tommy [Tyrwhitt] as he led her into the House, 'I am sure you would have much greater pleasure in leading me to my coronation'. Archibald sat by his sister Anne and insisted upon her repeating to him all that was going on, which put this amiable virgin into somewhat an awkward predicament.

There have been gay doings at the cottage[7] at Windsor. His Majesty, Lady Conyngham, Princesse Esterhazy, and Lord Francis. This latter I hear makes a great fool of himself and is always showing off his favour with the King, displaying watches, snuff-boxes, and rings which he receives from him. The King is in outrageous spirits, discussing as we do. Amongst other subjects, they one day talked of the advantages and disadvantages of royalty, whether it was on the whole desirable. Another day they went upon the water. The King was in ecstasies until one of the subalterns, *soit* blunder, *soit* malice, said, 'One might almost fancy oneself upon the Lake of Como'.

London: August 19, 1820

The accounts of political proceedings are that the mob were as quiet as possible yesterday. The Queen as before quite tranquil and unmoved, retiring to sleep during a great part of the day, upon which Lord Holland has made a very good epigram. I did not hear it, but the point is that the nature of her crime is changed. Instead of sleeping with Bergami, she sleeps with the Lords. Lord Morpeth must forgive me, for impropriety is the order of the day. . . .

Thomas Creevey to Miss Ord

House of Lords, 19th August

. . . The Queen is not here to-day; and she does not mean to come, I believe, till Tuesday. I am rather sorry for this, because there was so very great, and so well-dressed, a population in the street to see her to-day. Where the devil they all come from, I can't possibly imagine, but I think the country about London must furnish a great part. It is prodigiously encreased since the first day. . . . Now Mr Attorney General has at last begun by opening his case against the Queen, and I have heard just one hour of him, and then left it. *Now* her danger begins, and I am quite unable to conjecture the *degree* of damage she will sustain from the publication of this opening. I say *degree*, because of course it is quite impossible that a very great effect should not be produced upon the better orders of people by the production of this cursed, disgusting narrative, however overstated it may eventually prove to be, and however short (if all strictly true) it may fall of the actual crime charged by the Bill.

Lady Charlotte Lindsay's account continued

Monday, 21st. – The Attorney-general concluded his charge this day; and Theodore Majoochi [*sic*], formerly a servant of the Queen's, and I believe a cousin of Bergami's, was brought forward as a witness. Upon his entrance, the Queen fixed her eyes upon him, started up, clenched her fists, and screamed out – 'What! Teodore!' and then rushed out of the House, to the astonishment of all present and of her own attendants, who followed after as fast as they could, keeping *their* madness in the background. I cannot make out the meaning of this exhibition, for it must have been done to produce stage effect, as she knew before she went down to the House of Lords that Theodore Majoochi was to be examined as a witness against her; but, whatever was the intention, the effect was not favourable, as it gave the impression of her being much alarmed at his evidence, and I fear that on the wrong side of fifty a woman does not create much interest by being in a passion.

Tuesday, 22nd. – Majoochi was examined and cross-examined again to-day; people see and hear according to their politics and their wishes. The Government people declare that he was perfectly consistent in his evidence, but Gell and Craven assure me that he was evidently perjured. I think that he did not *choose* to remember me, for, as I was the only lady who accompanied the Queen in her carriage from Naples to Civita Vecchia, it was extraordinary that he should forget my being there. He certainly made a greater impression upon me, for I was so much struck by his bad countenance that when talking about him with Craven and Gell, we used always to call him the *traitor*. . . .

Wednesday, 23rd. – Majoochi's cross-examination was finished. His answers became more and more evasive, till at last he said nothing but '*non mi ricordo*' about matters that he must necessarily have recollected. He is evidently a prejudiced if not a perjured witness.

'Preparing the witnesses – a view in Cotton Garden,' I.R. Cruikshank (August 1820). The Italian witnesses
are bathed by Castlereagh, Sidmouth and Liverpool in 'the waters of oblivion'. The Attorney-General
(Gifford) is in attendance

Lady Cowper to Frederick Lamb

Sunday August 20th [1820]

. . . the Queen, the Queen, and nothing but the Queen is heard of. Her impudence
surpasses every thing, and one requires great command of temper to keep within
bounds, for the folly of people and the absurdity they talk outdoes any thing you can
conceive. . . .

The Queen is tired out by her Advocates' long speeches and bored to death, so she
did not go yesterday. I believe she knew Saturday was a bad Mob day and did not
like to see herself ill-attended, so she has saved herself for Monday. She said to
Tommy Twyrrit t'other day, as he handed her in, 'Tell the King I am very well, and
that I shall live some years to plague him'. One thing surprises me that B[rougham]
told Ld C[owper] she had never had the curiosity to look into a newspaper since she
came to England. This must, one should think, be design, but he said it was a want
of interest on her part to know what was said. Wood, the foolish Alderman, has at
last found out that his proper place when he goes in her carriage, is to sit backwards,
so he has accounted for his arriving in London by her side on the score of his
stomach, so Henry Fox heard a woman say in Hammersmith the other day, 'Poor
dear Alderman, how sick he looks sitting backwards'. The Queen's colour is white,
the Symbol of purity, so you see some white cockades in the street on some of the
rabble – tis laughable!! One hardly knows what to wish should be the result. I should
much like to see her clearly convicted for being so impudent. At the same time, if the
Lords would throw out the bill, it would save a great deal of trouble and perhaps
danger, and the carrying it thro' can do no good. I assure you the rabble look in a
very unpleasant manner at the Peers' Carriages. I sometimes wish my royal crown
was off the arms. It is such a foolish hobble to have got into, and if it goes on I do
think we shall have blood shed before it passes the Commons. A Bill of Pains and

Penalties is an awkward name, it sounds to the ignorant as if she was going to be fried or tortured in some way.

George Pellew on Lord Sidmouth's experiences in dealing with the 'mob'

The second reading of the Bill of Pains and Penalties, or in other words, the commencement of the examination of evidence, touching the Queen's conduct, before the House of Lords, had been fixed for the 17th of August; and as this unhappy inquiry seemed to have called into activity all the evil spirits and passions of the times, Lord Sidmouth's exertions to maintain the tranquillity of the metropolis were almost unexampled. His Lordship's utmost vigilance, however, could not wholly secure himself and other noble peers from insult on their way to parliament for the fulfilment of their duty. During the period of the inquiry, Lord Exmouth was his guest at Richmond Park, and numerous were the little adventures which befell their Lordships, as they daily proceeded together on foot from the Home Office to the House of Lords. No serious insult, however, was at any time experienced; neither did Lord Sidmouth, though constantly threatened in anonymous letters, and having frequently, as in the cases of Thistlewood and others, very desperate characters to deal with, ever encounter any actual assaults or danger, in his daily journeys, often at very late hours, to and from Richmond Park. On those occasions he usually drove himself in an old-fashioned open whiskey, and at all periods of excitement loaded pistols were placed on the seat for the use of himself and his companion; but, providentially, there never was any necessity to employ them. Probably his confidence and fearlessness generated respect; for he observed, that the same persons who at the commencement of the inquiry into the Queen's conduct saluted him with hisses as he passed by, before its conclusion fell into the habit of touching their hats to him.

Journal of Henry Edward Fox [8]

Monday, 21 August. Went to the House of Lords, where, after hearing the conclusion of the Attorney-General's charges against the Queen, ill-delivered and wretchedly put together, I beheld a scene that I shall remember for life. As soon as he had finished, after a little conversation across the table, the Queen entered the House. I was close to her and observed every motion. She seemed to walk with a more decided step than I had seen her. Before she came to her seat she curtsied to the peers, she sat down, she bowed to Denman, and afterwards to Brougham, from whom she received a cold and distant acknowledgment. I observed she almost trembled, and she frequently clenched her hand and opened it as a person under great emotion. The witness was produced at the Bar. The moment her eyes caught him she sprang up with the rapidity of lightning, advanced two or three steps, put her left arm a kimbo, and threw her veil *violently* back with her right. She looked at him steadily for about two or three seconds during a dead silence; she then exclaimed in a loud, angry tone, 'Theodore!' and rushed out of the House. The whole was the affair of less than a minute. The consternation, surprise, and even *alarm* it produced was wonderful. Nothing but madness can account for it. It seems extraordinary, but she contrived to make that puny, dumpty figure of her's appear dignified. That it was a prepared scene I am persuaded. She had been to the House on Sunday night to alter her chair, and Sir T. Tyrrhitt told me before she came that she was only coming for a few minutes. Besides the frequent messages to and fro that had passed between her and her counsel, and

the displeased manner in which Brougham returned her bow, make *me* certain, who
stood very near, that she had planned it, if not *rehearsed* it, and that it was not either
violent fear or anger at the moment that prompted her, but that she intended making
a coup-de-théatre. Poor maniac! The effect it has produced is far from being of use to
her. Everyone felt disgusted at her impudence and convinced of her guilt. The
evidence I afterwards heard is certainly not strong enough to convict her upon. The
only material point is the going together into the bath. How it will end, God knows!
They say she means to kill herself. I should not be surprized. A woman capable of
what she has done to-day can do anything violent or disgraceful. How the people will
receive this remains to be seen. Our great-grandchildren will see it in operas,
tragedies, or melodramas, though it would better suit a *farce*. However,
notwithstanding the ridicule of it, it did make one shudder.

Lady Granville to Lady G. Morpeth

London: August 22, 1820

The witness examined to-day is a man who travelled all over Greece and Italy with
her as courier, a very shrewd, intelligent man, perfectly undaunted, and giving his
strong evidence without embarrassment or hesitation. It remains to be seen what
discredit can be thrown upon him. I hear Sir William Gell says he was turned away
for robbery, and that he perjured himself to-day the third question he answered.
Granville says that when he was brought in the Queen stood up, threw her head back,
and put both her arms akimbo, and looked at him for some time with a countenance
which those who saw it said was quite terrific. He returned the gaze with the most
unmoved composure. She then exclaimed, 'Ah, Theodore,' and trundled out of the
House, some say surprised and thrown off her guard, others, astounded at his
ingratitude after the kindness she had shewn him. Alderman Wood told Mr Ellis he
supposed she was taken ill, for she could not be surprised, as she knew he was to
appear against her, and in fact it was in the papers some days ago.

Mr Ellis begs to be most kindly remembered to you. He is charmed with London,
opera buffas in the morning, and discussions *chez moi* in the evenings. He proposes
having the Royal Family tried by turns, one every August. . . .

The interpreter is the man that delights them all. His name is Spinetto; he is an
Italian teacher at one of the Universities, as quick as lightning, all gesticulation, and
so eager he often answers instead of the witness. Between them they act all the
evidence, and at times they say this is so irresistibly comic that the noble lords forget
all decorum and are in a roar of laughter.

Princess Lieven to Prince Metternich

[August] the 23rd

Have you heard of the dramatic moment – the Queen's 'Oh Theodore'? It made a
very bad impression. She explains it as a start of indignation, at the sight of a witness
on whose gratitude she thought that she could count. But nobody is deceived about
the cause of the start. She was thunderstruck at seeing him; and this at the very
beginning of the proceedings was not very encouraging for her supporters. Lord
Liverpool immediately sent a messenger to inform the King, treating 'Oh Theodore'
as a fact of the greatest importance. I fancy that the Queen's party is diminishing a

little among the people; perhaps the rain has cooled their ardour – it's an excellent sedative, and there has been enough, in all conscience, the last few days to have an effect. . . .

What horrors in the newspapers! I read the speech for the prosecution; I have not had the heart to read the evidence; it is too disgusting. Is the Queen really a woman? And how can the House of Lords, uniting as it does all that is most dignified and most exalted in the greatest nation in the world, lower itself by listening to such vile trash? Was there no other way of treating her as she deserves? Worst of all, how could statesmen have allowed things to come to such a pass? One of the Queen's lawyers put the trial in a nutshell when he called it a solemn farce.

Hon. Mrs Wellesley Pole[9] to Charles Bagot

August 24, 1820

. . . The Lords go through fagging work and within these few days, they have added an hour to their sittings. The newspapers accurately report the proceedings, horrible and disgusting as it all is. . . . She is losing her popularity, and is not attended as she used to be, but she braves all. Even her friends hardly pretend now to say she is innocent, but they harp upon neglect, ill usage, and persecution, and when it comes to recrimination on her part, God knows what may not happen!. . . the witnesses yesterday substantiated every fact. . . . Some of the Opposition are behaving shamefully and it is as much as possible a party question with them. . . . I am sorry for our national credit to say that the Duke of W. is daily abused, hissed, and treated with the most opprobrious language on his way to and from the House of Lords. Lord Anglesey is also hissed and abused, and his two wives rubbed under his nose. Yesterday, *il n'en pouvait plus,* so he turned his horse short round and addressed the mob. They shrank away as they generally do when fronted.

Extracts from the examination of Theodore Majocci by the Solicitor-General, 21–2 August

. . . Do you remember the situations of the bedrooms of the princess and Pergami at Augusta? I remember.

Can you describe them? There was a small yard or court into which led both the rooms of her royal highness and Pergami; from the room of one you would pass into the yard, and also the other.

After they were in bed, could any person get into that court? No . . .

At Augusta did you embark on board any vessel? We embarked on board a polacre.

Was that an Italian vessel? It was said that it was a Neapolitan polacre.

Where did you go in this vessel from Augusta? to Tunis in Barbary . . .

Do you recollect where Pergami slept on board the vessel, the polacre? He slept in the cabin where they dined.

Was the princess's cabin adjoining to that cabin where they dined? It was near.

Did any other person sleep in that room where they dined? I do not recollect. . . .

At Aum did all the servants of the princess's suite remain in the day-time under tents? They were under the tents.

Were they in the habit of travelling by day or by night? In the time of night.

And they went to sleep in the day-time? Yes, they slept during the day.

Under tents, in the manner you have described? Yes.

A PEEP INTO
Cotton Yard Aviary,
WITH THE PECULIAR METHOD OF FEEDING TO SUIT A
R--Y--L PALATE.
New Version.

Most Noble Lords, cried G——e the Great,
I have a cause of wond'rous weight
  That claims your sage decision ;
A secret soon I'll bring to light,
'Gainst Brougham, Wood, or Denman's spite,
  Who hold me in derision.

My R——l Spouse, as 'twill be seen,
Has made me ope the Bag of Green,
  To prove her Guilt is certain ;
And then I've Friends who will, no doubt,
Most clearly make the Charges out,
  And draw the Mystic Curtain.

Besides, I've Witnesses a groupe,
In Cotton Yard, quite snug in Coop,
  With C—tl—gh their Tutor ;
They'll swear black's white, not over nice,
'Twas by L—d L—rp—l's advice
  I got them so confute her.

By none they're equall'd 'tis agreed,
I got them from the choicest breed,
  But mark—'twas by Permission ;
(At great expense depend upon't
I got Majochi and Dumont)
  Through the Milan Commission.

Then I've from the Restellian stock
(Allowed the best in all the flock)
  One—whom we'll soon be trying ;
Tho' I must own—truth by the bye,
He's lately seem'd so very shy
  P'rhaps he'll be after flying.

I've still a worthy friend beside,
To grant my wish is all his pride,
  S—d—th's a faithful Lord, O ;
But should things change, 'tis ten to one,
Like all the rest he'd cut and run,
  And say Non mi Ricordo.

Scarce was the R—y—l will proclaim'd,
And G—ff—d's speech all minds enflam'd,
  When O !—a sad disaster ;
Truth will come out—for truth defies,
E'en Bags of Green made up of lies,
  And crack'd Heads need a Plaister.

Majochi, first upon the List,
Thought none his statement could resist,
  So clear it was no doubt on't ;
But scarce was ope'd the Famous Bag,
'Bout which Great G——e had made his Brag
  When lo!—the cat jumpt out on't.

Published by C. E. Pritchard, Islington Green.
PRICE ONE SHILLING.
ENTERED AT STATIONERS' HALL.
N. B. Just Published, Price Sixpence, The Cock of Cotton Walk, and the Maid of all Work.

'A peep into Cotton Yard aviary, with the peculiar method of feeding to suit a R-Y-L palate,'
?I.R. Cruikshank (October 1820). The foreign witnesses are fed coins from a large green bag by Sidmouth,
while Liverpool and Castlereagh look on. Majocci, behind the bars, is 'Cock of the Walk'

Do you remember the tent under which the princess slept? I do . . .

Under the princess's tent was there a bed? There was . . . There was a little small travelling bed that her royal highness had ordered to be placed there, and there was a Turkish sofa. . . .

Did you see the princess there and any person with her? There was Pergami.

In the inner tent where the bed and the sofa were? Yes, and sometimes the little child.

Were the bed and the sofa placed within the inner tent? They were within the interior tent. . . .

Were Pergami and the princess there during the time that was allotted for sleep? During the time of rest.

Were the inner tent and the outer tent both closed? The inner tent was shut up by them, and the outer tent he might either close or leave it open as he chose.

When you say that the inner tent was shut up by them, by whom do you mean? Bartolomeo Pergami, because the tent was closed from the inside.

Did they remain there during the whole time that was allotted for sleep? Yes, they did. . . .

Do you remember on her embarking at Jaffa, on the voyage home, any tent being raised on the deck? I do.

What beds were placed under that tent? A sofa.

Was there a bed besides a sofa? A travelling bed . . .

Did the princess sleep under that tent generally on the voyage from Jaffa home? She slept always under that tent during the whole voyage from Jaffa till the time she landed.

Did anybody sleep under the same tent? Bartolomeo Pergami.

That was on the deck? Yes, on the deck.

Did this take place every night? Every night.

Were they shut in; were the sides of the tent drawn in, so as to shut them entirely in? When they went to sleep the whole was enclosed, shut up. . . .

Do you remember whether the princess bathed on board this vessel? I remember it.

Where was the bath prepared? In the cabin of her royal highness.

Who assisted at her bath? The first time I carried the water into the bath, and then Pergami came down and put his hand into the bath to see the temperature of the water; then he went up stairs and handed her royal highness down, after which the door was shut, and Pergami and her royal highness remained alone in the cabin.

Do you remember whether this bathing took place more than once? I remember that it has been more than once.

Do you remember, at any time, when the princess and Pergami were below in the room for the purpose of taking a bath, being called to supply any additional water? I do remember, two pails, one of hot and the other of cold water.

Do you remember who took that water in? I went with the water as far as the door of the cabin, and then Pergami came half out of the door and took the water, and took it in.

Do you know whether, at the time when you took the water in this way, the princess was actually in the bath or not? I cannot know.

Where was the cabin that you slept in situated, with reference to the tent you have described on the deck; was it under it, or how? I slept in the dining-room, on a sofa.

Was that, or not, under the tent? It was immediately under the tent, below deck.

Did you ever, on any occasion at night, while the princess and Pergami were in the tent, hear any motion over you? I have heard a noise.

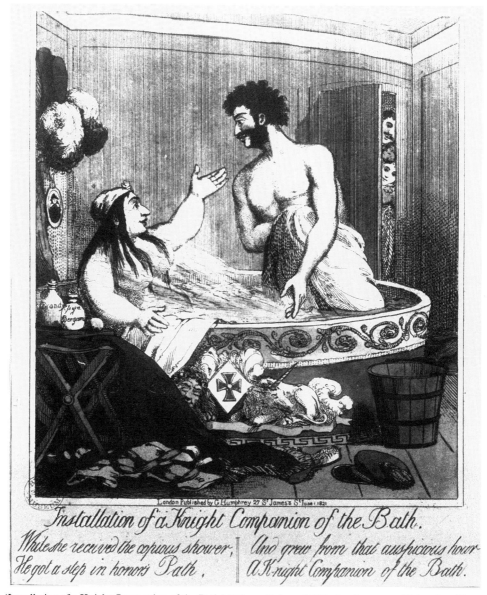

London Published by G Humphrey 27 St James's St June 1 1821

Installation of a Knight Companion of the Bath.

While she received the copious shower, | And grew from that auspicious hour
He got a step in honor's Path , | A Knight Companion of the Bath.

'Installation of a Knight Companion of the Bath,' T. Lane (1 June 1821). A reference to Majocci's evidence
about the occasion when the Queen and Bergami allegedly shared a bath

What did that noise resemble; what did it appear to you to be? The creaking of a
bench . . .

When you say that Pergami travelled in the same carriage with the princess, in the
journey to Bavaria, . . . was it your business to prepare the carriages, and the things
that were put into them? It was my duty. . . .

Do you remember at any time in examining the carriage finding any bottle in it? I
found one bottle.

Was that usually in the carriage on the journey, when the princess and Pergami travelled together? It was.

Will you explain the construction of the bottle, as far as it relates to the opening, or mouth of it, was it large or small? About three or four inches in diameter.

Do you know from what you found from time to time in that bottle, for what purpose it was used in the carriage? It was for Pergami making water. . . .

Extracts from Brougham's cross-examination, 22 August

Were there sheets and blankets upon the sofa under the tent, in which a person taking off their clothes could go to bed, as is usual in Europe? I placed the bed, and then I placed some feather pillows, and then I retired.

You did not put any sheets or blankets, or coverlid and sheets, did you? I do not remember.

Was it not exactly the same used for sleeping under the tent on board the Polacca afterwards, during the sea voyage? I do not remember. . . .

Will you swear you ever saw, either on the land journey in Palestine, or on board the ship during the voyage, one stitch of common bed clothes, sheets, blankets, or coverlid upon that bed? This I do not recollect. . . .

Did you ever happen to see Billy Austin, William Austin, rest under the tent in the same way upon the voyage, or on land? I do not recollect.

Did you ever see Hieronimus rest in the same way in the tent? I do not recollect.

Will you swear that they both of them have not so rested in the tent? I do not recollect.

In the room below the cabin on board the polacre, where did Hieronimus sleep in general ? I do not recollect.

Where did Mr Hownam sleep? I do not recollect.

Where did William Austin sleep? I do not remember.

Where did the countess Oldi sleep? I do not remember. . . .

When her royal highness was going by sea on her voyage from Sicily to Tunis, where did she sleep? This I cannot remember.

When she was going afterwards from Tunis to Constantinople on board the ship, where did she sleep? This I do not recollect.

When she was going from Constantinople to the Holy Land on board the ship, where did she sleep then? I do not remember.

Where did Pergami sleep on those three voyages of which you have just been speaking? This I do not know. . . .

Princess Lieven to Prince Metternich

[August] the 27th

You can see from the newspapers how the Queen's affair is progressing, if you have the time and the patience to read them. Nowadays I get my husband to read them to me; he reads aloud what he can – and what he does read gives me a fair idea of what he misses out. And that woman can sit there, listening to all these things being said and proved against her, and when she emerges after one of these scandalous hearings she is greeted with respect and enthusiasm, not by the mob – make no mistake about that – but by the solid middle classes who have won England her reputation for virtue and morality. You have to see for yourself what the Queen's escort is like to get an accurate notion of the cheering and the people who cheer. The streets are full of well-dressed men and respectable women, all waving their hats and their handkerchiefs. You see the real mob, too – the kind of blackguards whom the French newspapers translate quite seriously as 'black guards' – but they are certainly not in the majority. All this shows only too clearly how unpopular the King is and what people think of his behaviour, and how convinced they are that any woman who was protected and proclaimed guiltless by the venerable George III is bound to be the victim of calumny and vile persecution under George IV. You have to take this into account in trying to understand the inexplicable things that are taking place. . . .

The Italian witnesses are supplying not only the Press but even Society with all its jokes. Everyone is using the catchword '*Non mi ricordo*'.

[August] the 29th

. . . Things are going badly; the House of Lords deliberates and cannot agree, Brougham makes fun of both the House and the Ministers, the crowd swells and every day increases the Queen's popularity and the unwillingness of the public to believe in the evidence of the Italian witnesses. And every day adds to the difficulties of the Government. The Ministers spend half the day in the House of Lords and the other half at Cabinet meetings; and, in spite of that, I am sure that they are the last men in the world who can foresee how it will end. . . .

Lady Granville to Lady G. Morpeth

London: August 29, 1820

I have been doing my duty, reading the debate. I suppose it would not be easy to find an act of that sort so devoid of pleasure. The Lords seem to me to flounder deeper and deeper, and never was there a *marche* so *embrouillée*, so unsatisfactory, so interminable. You will see that Copley attacked Brougham, whom he affects to despise as not being what they call a close lawyer. Brougham flew into a passion, was flippant and insolent, and uttered the most unjustifiable falsehoods as to the conduct of government. This gave Lord Liverpool an opportunity of stating on his honour flat contradictions to the assertions of the learned counsel.

The mob direct all their violence against the Duke of Wellington. They tried yesterday to pull him off his horse. The police interfered and some of the mob were knocked down, some hurt in the struggle.

What an extraordinary man Brougham is! How do you think he was occupied the greatest part of Sunday morning? Playing at leap-frog with Duncannon's children at Roehampton. They say the Queen looks cross and pale, is blooded every morning before she comes to town and scarcely returns the bows made to her as she passes. . . .

W.H. Fremantle to the Marquis of Buckingham

Englefield Green, Aug. 30, 1820

My Dear Lord,
. . . I was in town for a few hours on Monday, and it appeared to me that in the streets the cry was increased instead of diminished for the Queen. I saw several lawyers, dispassionate men, and intelligent, who all confirmed this, and assured me

'Non mi ricordo. The captain of the gang . . .' W. Heath (8 October 1820). A vicious caricature of Majocci

that their belief was, that be the evidence ever so strong, and the facts proved, the public – and included in this, the middling class, the shopkeepers – were determined to support her as an oppressed and injured woman, and as hating and despising the character of the witnesses. It also has not a little benefited her cause, that it appears how much the King personally has prepared the evidence by his emissaries abroad, and more particularly by his Hanoverian engines. I assure you I am quite low-spirited about it. One cannot calculate on anything less than subversion of all Government and authority, if this is to go on; and how it is to end, no one can foresee. I think, however (what I did not do when you told me so in town), that the Commons will never entertain the Bill. But, again, when will it ever come to the Commons? The mischief will be all done previously; and the Press now is completely open to treason, sedition, blasphemy, and falsehood with impunity. This alone, if it continues, must debauch the public mind. I want some volunteer establishments to be formed, or something to be done without a moment's delay, by the well-disposed and loyal who have influence, to check the torrent and to guard against the explosion which must inevitably take place. I don't know whether you see the *Cobbetts, Independent Whig*, and many other papers now circulating most extensively, and which are dangerous much beyond anything I can describe. I have an opportunity of seeing them, and can speak therefore from knowledge; and the Government taking no steps (knowing, perhaps, they cannot depend on a jury) to prosecute. . . .

The King here confines himself to the Cottage, has *hourly* messengers – that is, dragoons, who are posted on the road by dozens – and we hear is in a state of the greatest irritation; but he is very seldom seen, and this is only what one picks up. – You have no conception how thoroughly the public mind, even in this neighbourhood, is inflamed by this melancholy subject, and how the Queen is still supported. . . .

The Times, *29 August*

The Italian witnesses in Cotton-yard were last Sunday engaged in dancing and singing, with the additional exhibition of music. The movements of some of them were so grotesque that it was fancied they had got their old companion Majomet once more among them, whose pranks furnished such grave matter for the Attorney-General's speech. Who supplied the music for these Italian observers of the sabbath?

Report from the True Briton

The expenses of the Queen's trial will be 200,000l, at the lowest, besides 50,000l for the Queen's expenses. This sum, which is thrown away upon Italians, would endow 50 hospitals, in England; or it would enable 20,000 of our suffering population to emigrate, and to relieve themselves and the mother country. It would provide 50,000 persons for a whole year: or, applied to the payment of debts, release from prison, at least 5,000 unfortunate men, who might thus be restored to the pursuits of industry in the bosom of their families.

Henry Crabb Robinson was touring the Continent in the company of William and Dorothy Wordsworth. He noted in his diary a visit to Lugano where they stayed at an hotel which had also been visited by Queen Caroline and her entourage during her European wanderings.

27 Aug. 1820, at Lugano

On the 27th we had a row to Luino, on the Lago Maggiore, a walk to Ponte Tresa, and then a row to Lugano, where we went to an excellent hotel, kept by a man of the name of Rossi, a respectable man. Our apartments consisted of one handsome and spacious room, in which were Mr and Mrs Wordsworth (this room fronted the beautiful lake); a small back room, occupied by Miss Wordsworth, with a window looking into a dirty yard, and having an internal communication with a two-bedded room, in which Monkhouse and I slept. I had a very free conversation with Rossi about the Queen, who had been some time in his house. It is worth relating here, and might have been worth making known in England, had the trial then going on had another issue. He told me, but not emphatically, that when the Queen came, she first slept in the large room, but not liking that, she removed to the back room. 'And Bergami' said Rossi, 'had the room in which you and the other gentleman sleep'. – 'And was there', I asked, 'the same communication then that there is now between the two rooms?' – 'Of course,' he replied. 'It was in the power, certainly, of the Queen and Bergami to open the door: whether it was opened or not no one can say.' He added: 'I know nothing; none of my servants know anything.' The most favourable circumstance related by Rossi was that Bergami's brother did not fear to strike off much from the bill. He added, too, that the Queen was surrounded by *cattiva gente*.

J. W. Croker to Robert Peel, 1 September 1820

My Dear Peel,
 . . . As to the Queen's affair, I can only tell you that all the disgusting details proved against her seem to make no change in the minds or numbers of her partisans. This is natural – they adopted her because she was in opposition to the King and the Government, and her personal conduct, if it only continues impudent and violent enough, is of no kind of importance to the mob. What the opinion of the sober middle classes may be, I do not know, but I have never met anyone of any kind who believes her to be innocent; and if the country believes her to be guilty, I cannot but think that they must approve of the proceedings substantially, and that there will be no difficulty in passing the Bill. . . .

 In fact, I now think the whole of the Queen's chance is narrowed to a point. She had two lieutenants of the English navy with her in the polacre, and through most of her journeys. Now if she does not produce them, as they are both on the spot, she is undone; and all that Majocci and Dumont, etc., have sworn will receive universal credit. I myself am persuaded that she will examine them; and I believe it for this reason, that Hownam, one of the lieutenants, is married in France, and was obliged to go thither lately to his wife's lying-in; now this was as good an opportunity and excuse as could be desired for his absence, but he is come back. I therefore conclude that they intend to produce him. Now can they be mad enough to produce him unless he will contradict the whole of what all the other witnesses have said? And if he does contradict them, I am afraid, as he is a man of hitherto good character, that he will be believed against the whole host of Italians. This consideration excites the only doubt I have on the case. . . .

 . . . If Hownam and Flynn will deny the facts stated, . . . the present ferment . . . would by the evidence of these two English officers be blown up into a conflagration that would reduce the whole proceeding to ashes, and might involve the Government, the Throne, and the constitution in the destruction. . . .

Lady Granville to Lady G. Morpeth

London: September 3, 1820

. . . I have been looking over Granville, who is writing to Mr Canning, and there I spy, progress slow, result uncertain, not sufficient evidence to carry the bill through the House of Commons. The Bishops will insist upon the divorce clause being left out. This would reconcile the saints in the other House, but the majority would be for her, not on the ground of her popularity, but of his unpopularity. The answer to 'Is she bad?' is, 'He is as bad' in the mouths of the country gentlemen. The Crown lawyers have conducted the business infamously, letting Brougham, etc., go on without interruption when they were irregular and insolent in their proceedings, stopping and interfering with them when there was no occasion for it.

These are the heads of his lordship's letter, and mine having no head at all, I have ventured to avail myself of them.

At Cleveland House, where I did not feel equal to go, there were only Lord Morley, the Archbishop and his son Henry, an evident Queenite. Lord Stafford, upon Lord Morley giving him some answer he did not approve of, said it was wonderful what arguments fools will make use of.

You must not expect such long affairs, dearest Sis., when the trial is over. I shall return to note-paper and a list of the game. . . .

London: September 4, 1820

Hart came to see me on my return from a Dowager drive. He was charmed with his Chiswick, says Lady Jersey was very amiable when she forgot, as she frequently did, her despair about the Queen. Granville has been riding in the Park with the said Countess and Mr Tierney. They met the Marylebone dames returning from their address, covered with feathers and white cockades, escorted by the mob. . . .

London: September 5, 1820

Yesterday's evidence was dull and neither one way or the other. The Lords say they never were so bored and consequently exhausted. It is true that Lady Harrowby is to be called. The object is to prove the King's having forbidden his Ministers to let their wives associate with her. Ministers are much charmed with the last two days, so much so that I heard the Duke of Wellington say to Madame de Lieven, complaining of his fatigue, '*Mais, vous savez, les grands succès fatiguent autant que les grands revers*'.

My visit to Brentford was bracing at ten o'clock in an open carriage. Miss Trimmer does not know where to shelter her morality, and her comments are for the most part groans. She told me, in answer to me as to my surprise at English people not being staggered by some of the facts that have come out, that their firm belief is that the King had sent a number of people for the purpose of assassinating her, and that Bergami was her only sure and tried protector, and that consequently if he had been half an hour absent from her, she would have been murdered. They are now keeping up the same impression by Alderman Wood and his sons actually walking up and down before Brandenburgh House armed with pistols and telling the people that without such precautions she would not be safe an hour. Miss Trimmer's brother had the curiosity to enquire of the scavenger of Paddington if his wife had been up with an address. Yes, he said, he was against it, but she would go, and that she kissed the

Queen's hand several times. Another woman on the top of a stage-coach, a better sort of housemaid, told him she had been, and that it was a very gay sight. She was not tired or faint, for plenty of gin and gingerbread was sold on the lawn. A man came out and read something, she could not say exactly what it was, all she knew was that it was exceedingly improper. So much for the present Court of Her Majesty.

London: September 6, 1820

You have been two days without writing, Lady Morpeth. I only mention the fact.

Sardi, the courier, has stated the strongest facts of all, but Trimmer and the young lords say it is of no use what is stated when people are resolved not to believe the staters. Lord Morley says nothing will induce him to vote for the bill if it comes to a division now, and I see both he and G. are anxious to have the thing knocked up in the Upper House. They think that without the divorce clause the proceeding is nonsense, with it quite unallowable. Ministers hold a different language. 'What is to be proved if this is not? What would you have more, no two witnesses contradicting each other? The Queen, the disgrace of her sex. How can anyone pretending to morality, decency,' etc. The fallacy of all this is that what we want is not belief, but proof-witnesses, but credible ones – ten Englishmen instead of a hundred Italians. John Bull looks upon them as so many bugs and frogs, and there is a Lieutenant Flynne coming on her side, who will be their demi-god. The real grievance is its having become, as everything does so much in England, a violent party question. Granville says there is a Ministerial mountain headed by Lord Ellenborough, as well as an Opposition one, and that both have been, and are, absurd beyond measure.

You will see we are coming to an end, though still unsatisfactory and tedious. . . .

Princess Lieven to Prince Metternich

September 2

Do you know, *mon Prince*, what the Queen does in Parliament? You will never guess. She plays – at backgammon. Since she announced at the start that she would be at the House of Lords every day in order to confound the witnesses by her presence, she does not like to go back on her word. So she goes; sometimes she goes in to the hearing, sometimes not; generally, she stays in the next room and plays with Alderman Wood.

It is believed that the Queen's counsel will ask for three months' delay to bring witnesses in her favour, and that the House of Lords will adjourn at the end of next week.

The 6th

. . . The Archbishop of York told me that neither he nor any of the ecclesiastical members of the House would vote for the Bill; that they could not do so without dishonouring their calling; and that, on this point, their party was absolutely firm. This will be a very strong argument for the Queen in the eyes of the public. The clergy say that the Act of Degradation might be passed, but not the divorce clause, and that no ecclesiastical court could grant a divorce in the present circumstances of the King and the Queen respectively. You may remember that Lord Liverpool let fall a few words in the House of Lords implying that the divorce clause might be abandoned. These were his words: 'This clause is the least important of the two.'

Brougham was talking about it yesterday evening in a way that struck me as very sensible. By these means the Queen, he said, would be deprived of her rank, and they would be saying to the King: You will keep your wife, but without her rank. The Bill would thus become actually a bill lowering the status of the King. It must pass in its entirety or not at all. Well, I tell you that I am certain it will not be passed. Anyway, the Queen is quite mad, and what surprises me is that they don't question the witnesses about that, or at least ask her doctor. If they pronounced her mad they would avoid all this scandal and be nearer the truth besides. Meanwhile I am expecting the crowning act of madness on her part – that she will throw up the game when she is on the point of winning. She wants to go to Ramsgate; the packet-boats are just under her window, and nobody would try to stop her flight, any more than they tried to stop that of James II. In the meantime, the Ministers are wretched; their position is terrible and grows worse every day. The only person who is cheerful and pleased with himself is the King of Parliament – Brougham.

The 8th

Well, my archbishop and my premonition were both right. The Bill has been cut in two – or that, at least, is what Lord Liverpool is proposing to the House. What a strange alliance! Lord Grey is taking the King's side against the Ministers. One false step, and all the rest have followed. Think for a moment of the state of England, the position of the King, the Government, the House of Lords, the Anglican clergy. Think on the other hand of what is brewing in the Commons – think of the Queen, the Radicals, above all of that lawyer, dominating, giving orders and being obeyed; and then find a solution. I don't think the Ministers will get out of it; every day they plunge in deeper. It was noticed that the King's counsel began his speech for the prosecution during a terrible storm, and went on with it yesterday during the eclipse. There is a couplet about it:

> Accusation in thunder,
> And proof in the dark.

The 11th

When the Ministers went to see the King at Windsor the other day to lay before him their proposal for abandoning the divorce clause, he listened to them and said: 'Do as you please,' and showed them the door. They were not even given anything to eat and came back famished. That's friendly and promises well.

The House of Lords has been adjourned till October 3. There was an argument between the Queen, who wanted the trial to go straight on, and Brougham, who asked for two months in order to be absolutely prepared. They compromised, and the Queen's counsel announced in the House of Lords, that, at the end of three weeks, he would appear with his defence and his witnesses.

Letters in The Times, 5 and 11 September

Sir, – I am an old-fashioned country gentleman, born and bred in the centre of England, where I have, thank God, lived happy during the long reign of our late most gracious Sovereign; and I will venture to say, that there never was a more loyal

'The kettle calling the pot ugly names' (23 September 1820)

subject, and therefore I do wish to express my astonishment that the noble Peers of this realm should degrade themselves, and have patience to sit day after day to hear and record such weak, wicked, false, and scandalous nonsense as is produced before them from the mouths of hired and perjured informers. I wish, in the most friendly manner, to tell their Lordships, that, if they are *not*, the whole country *are*, completely sick of so disgraceful a proceeding.

A Disciple of the Great Chatham
Devonshire-street, Portland-place, Sept. 3

TO THE EDITOR OF THE TIMES

SIR, – It is with much grief that I inform you of a circumstance which was communicated to me this day for a fact, relative to the Queen's going last week from Brandenburgh-house to Greenwich. A Mr B., coal-merchant, of Chelsea, had given his men a strict injunction not to cheer her Majesty as she passed; but, however, one of them thought he had an undoubted right so to do, and immediately saluted her; the man was in consequence discharged. So much for liberty of conscience!

Sep. 11
Z

Thomas Creevey to Miss Ord

House of Lords, Sept. 6

. . . Do you know this bill will never pass! My belief is it will be abandoned on the adjournment. The entire middle order of people are against it, and are daily becoming more critical of the King and the Lords for carrying on this prosecution. . . .

½ past 4

The evidence is closed – that is, all that is in England. Mr Attorney has been making his application for an adjournment of a few days to give time for the Lugano witnesses to arrive. Brougham's objection to this has been the feeblest effort he has yet made, and Mr Attorney is now replying. I suppose it will be granted, and this will fill up the measure of their lordships' iniquity.

P.S. – Erskine has made the *most beautiful* speech possible: Grey an excellent one: Eldon and Liverpool are *shook*, and I think the application will be refused.

House of Lords, 12 o'clock, 7th Sept

The first thing done to-day was Mr Attorney coming forward and stating that within the preceding half hour he had received letters from abroad, stating that the journey of the Lugano witnesses was unavoidably delayed, and that under such circumstances he should not persist in asking for time. So, after this *infernal lie*, he said his case was closed. . . . Mr Solicitor is now summing up.

Here's a breeze! The Solicitor having finished, Lauderdale moved that the Queen's counsel be asked if they were ready to go on, upon which Lord Lonsdale begged to state that, before such question was put, it would be a great satisfaction to him and others to learn that the divorce part of the Bill was to be given up; upon which Lord Liverpool said if it was the wish of the religious part of the House and of the community that this clause should be withdrawn, his Majesty had no personal wish in having it made part of the bill. . . . Well! Grey made a speech for the divorce part remaining! and Donoughmore is now asserting with great fury that Liverpool has given the King's consent without his leave.

. . . You know the Queen went down the river yesterday. I saw her pass the H. of Commons on the deck of her state barge; the river and the shores of it were then beginning to fill. Erskine, who was afterwards at Blackfriars Bridge, said he was sure there were 200,000 people collected to see her. . . . There was not a single vessel in the river that did not hoist their colours and man their yards for her, and it is with the greatest difficulty that the watermen on the Thames, who are all her partisans, are kept from destroying the hulk which lies off the H. of Commons to protect the witnesses in Cotton Garden. . . .

Brooks's, Sept. 9th

The House of Lords is adjourned to Tuesday three weeks, the 3rd of October. You can form no conception of the rage of the Lords at Brougham fixing this time: it interferes with everything – pheasant shooting, Newmarket, &c., &c. . . . Grey is just set out for Howick, the most furious of the set. . . . Brougham's chaise is now at the door to carry him home to Brougham Castle. He has performed miracles, and the reasons he has just been giving me for fixing the time he has done, shew his understanding (if one doubted it) to be of the very first order. The Queen is delighted at their going on so soon: she clapped her hands with delight when he communicated it to her last night. . . .

C.C. Western, MP, to Thomas Creevey

Buxton, 10th Sept.

. . . The abandonment of the divorce clause forms the ultimate climax of baseness, cowardice, folly, &c. It is a Bill of Pains and Penalties upon the King, to expose him to the most dire disgrace that ever was inflicted upon mortal man – to enact that, whereas his wife is the MOST ABANDONED of women, he is a fit associate for her! Oh, there never was the like!!!. . .

Thomas Creevey to Miss Ord

Brooks's, 13 Sept.

. . . Do you know they say the King is intent upon turning out Lord Hertford to make room for Conyngham as Lord Chamberlain, and Lord Cholmondeley to make way for Lord Roden. Was there ever such insanity at such a time? It is said the Ministers have exacted a promise from him not to make the first change, at least *pending the trial*. In writing the last sentence, I heard a noise of hurraing and shouting in the street; so I ran out to see. It was, I may say, the *Navy of England* marching to Brandenburgh House with an address to the Queen. I have seen nothing like this before – nothing approaching to it. There were thousands of seamen, all well dressed, all sober – the best-looking, the finest men you could imagine. Every man had a new white silk or satin cockade in his hat. They had a hundred colours, at least, or pieces of silk, with sentiments upon them, such as 'Protection to the Innocent', &c. M'Donald asked one of them how many there were, to which he answered very civilly – 'I don't know, exactly, sir, but we are many thousands, and should have been many more, but we would not let any man above forty come, because we have so far to walk.' Remember what I say – this procession decides the fate of the Queen. When the seamen take a part, the soldiers can't fail to be shaken.

W.H. Fremantle to the Marquis of Buckingham

Brighton, Sept. 27, 1820

My Dear Lord,
From all I hear, and from general conversation, I have no doubt if the Bill proceeds in the Commons we shall have a riot, and I doubt extremely whether the Divorce Bill can be carried. I dined yesterday with the Duke of York, who is here alone. His conversation was violent against the Queen, and fair and candid with regard to the state of the country. He spoke, however, with great confidence on the state and disposition of the army; in fact, after all that is said and done, it must eventually depend upon the troops, for sure I am they will be called upon. I took the opportunity of holding the language you suggested, and indeed it is what I really feel. He said it was not intended in the first instance to have troops to guard the avenues of the Commons, but they would be in the way; the whole arrangements would continue; and if the House found it necessary to call for them, there they would be. There has been, as you heard from the K—, a general quarrel between the K—, Duke of York, Lord Liverpool, and the Duke of Gloucester, none of them now speaking to the latter. He has acted like an obstinate —. What an abominable thing it is the King not going ashore, and not showing himself to any of his subjects! His conduct is an excitement

to popular hatred. What can it mean? Lord King is here, and appears to me to chuckle quite at the thoughts of what is likely to happen. I fancy a great number of Peers, when it comes to the close, will avoid the vote.

Perry, the editor, who is here, tells me the cry, instead of diminishing, increases in favour of the Queen; and he does not seem himself to favour her, or at least he does not speak in her praise.

Lord Bathurst is here, and from his language, and that of the Duke of B—, I should say the Government is confoundedly frightened; the latter certainly implied the necessity of strengthening it, and lamented once or twice the want of energy, and the whole line which had been adopted. He leaves this for town to-morrow.

> Ever, &c.,
> W.H.F.

The Times sums up, *11 September*

The accusation against the QUEEN being finished, the country has now a short period allowed to respire, and dwell at leisure upon the odious charges. . . .

Still, however, and we put it to the general sense of the country whether we err in the assertion – still, however, her MAJESTY does not suffer, from the delay, in public love and esteem. It is impossible but that addressing must have an end some time, and yet at this moment Addresses from what may be called all the good sense and sterling integrity of the country are pouring in every day with as much vivacity as they did immediately after the arrival of the undaunted heroine in England. . . . Who then can deny – who can have the impudence to deny – in the face of these facts, that she now stands as free and unsullied in the opinion of the people of England, as she did on the day of her first entrance among us to receive a husband's sacred vows that he would love, honour, and cherish her? Are we not right, then, in advocating such a cause?

But the public feelings are not confined to mere love of the QUEEN, or sympathy in her sufferings. The evidence against her is now before the country; and the natural and regular inquiry upon the production of evidence in all other cases is this – Does it tend to convict, or does it fail? But really, in the present instance, no one that we meet with, or hear of, ever thinks of asking himself such a question. The universal exclamation is 'What a set of villains!' and that indignation which it was hoped to point against the QUEEN is wholly and directly against her accusers. No one seems to conceive or imagine that her MAJESTY is affected by the late examinations, any more than that a cloud of dust could put out the moon. All speak of the witnesses – 'This rascal swore so and so,' says one, with astonishment: 'And only to think', says another, 'of that German chambermaid receiving more than ten years' wages, besides all expenses! Could they not get any better witnesses than these Italian devils? Why they are worse off now than they were at the last plot: they had then some decent people to perjure themselves for love or money.' These are expressions that you may hear in the streets. The QUEEN only comes in accidentally, with sighs of sorrow for her sufferings. Never – we can say it with confidence – never did a conspiracy more completely fail. But how deeply does it sink in the public mind, how painfully does it affect the best feelings of human nature, to have discovered that Majochi arrived at 'a great house in Pall-mall, with pillars before it, and sentinels, to concert measures against the Queen of ENGLAND, on the very day when the good old King, her protector, was buried!!' Oh, Shame! where is they blush?

The Black Dwarf, *20 September 1820, expresses the Radicals' view*

HEIGHO! SAID DERRY
A NEW SONG
TUNE – *A Frog he would a wooing go!*

A K—g he would a wooing go!
   Heigho! said Derry
Though fifty-eight, I'd have you to know,
With whiskers and wig, he was quite the beau!
    With whiskey, quite frisky,
    Each night got tipsy.
With Bags, the Doctor, and Derry, O.[10]

A kind, good wife, this K— had got,
   Heigho! said Derry.
He wish'd to get rid of her (the sot!)
Says Bags, we'll do't, for we know what's what:
    We'll bribe her – proscribe her,
    Accuse her – refuse her,
Aye that we will, *said* Derry.

Now these *honest* souls, by honour forsook,
   Heigho! cried Derry.
Fit company only for L— or for C—,
Swore they'd succeed in spite of the 'Book',
    With their blarney, carney,
    Fine speeches and gammon, O!
We'll talk her over, cried Derry.

Then they got a green bag, which prov'd all smoke,
   Heigho! said Derry.
Ev'n Majocchi himself couldn't keep up the joke,
For '*Non mi ricordo*' was all that he spoke!
    With his twisting, and shifting,
    His Daring, and swearing,
Heigho! *Non mi Ricordo*!

This put the poor trio soon to the rout;
   Heigho! Said Gifford.
Our tricks John Bull will discover no doubt:
Oh! dear! if he does, we must all turn out
    Of our places so pretty,
    Oh Lord! What a pity!
Quite shocking I declare O!

                             B.D.

Notes

1. A Dutch doll with a round bottom, weighted with lead, so that it always jumped erect in whatever position it was laid.
2. i.e. members of the opposition.
3. The statute which made it high treason for a queen to commit adultery. If the statute applied, Caroline might be liable to the death penalty.
4. Richard Vassall Fox, 3rd Baron Holland (1773–1840), Whig politician.
5. The French field-marshal executed on the orders of Louis XVIII after the defeat of Napoleon in 1815. Wellington had refused to intervene on his behalf.
6. Harriet, wife of the first Viscount, later Earl, Granville, diplomat. Lady Georgiana Morpeth was the wife of Viscount Morpeth, later 6th Earl of Carlisle.
7. The King's private residence in the grounds of Windsor Park.
8. Henry Edward Fox, son of the 3rd Baron Holland, later 4th Baron.
9. Wife of William Wellesley-Pole, Irish MP, later 3rd Earl of Mornington.
10. 'Derry' is Lord Castlereagh, son of the Marquess of Londonderry; 'Bags' was Lord Eldon's nickname, and 'the doctor' Sidmouth's.

CHAPTER SIX

The Queen and the Women of Britain

Much of Caroline's appeal to the people of England arose from the fact that she was a woman. Her cause was that of a wife abandoned and mistreated by a husband notorious throughout his life for his profligacy and selfishness. Indeed she had become a wife not because of mutual affection but merely as the result of a heartless affair of state. The kingdom needed an heir and Caroline had been selected to provide one: it was no secret that at the time of the marriage the Prince had been openly associating with a mistress, Lady Jersey, and if it was a secret from the general public that he was even married to another woman it was an open enough secret in circles close to the court. On every count – deception, betrayal, abandonment, rejection and hatred – Caroline was a wronged woman whose plight sounded a chord of alarm and concern in the breast of every wife in the Kingdom.

Her situation also emphasized the inequality of women and their lack of legal rights in a society dominated by men. No woman at that time could sue for divorce, even on evidence of her husband's open adultery or cruelty. No married woman had a right to her own property in marriage – even her marriage settlement, which wealthy fathers provided as a resource in case of her abandonment or widowhood, was controlled by (male) trustees. Men on the other hand could shut away their wives, deny them access to their children, or divorce them for unfaithfulness even if that unfaithfulness was the result of the husband's own desertion or immorality. The unfaithfulness of husbands was regarded as a fact of life; an unfaithful wife faced social ostracism, outside the aristocracy at any rate. Women were legally, socially and personally inferior to men, and they had no political rights – they were not themselves citizens of the state, had no right to vote, could not sit in Parliament and, though in certain circumstances they could acquire or inherit peerages they could appear in the House of Lords only on ceremonial occasions, and then not in their own right but as guests of husbands, fathers or brothers.

This had of course always been the case in England, as in other European countries, but by the early nineteenth century English women were beginning to demand more equal rights and treatment. There had been brief episodes of women's rights agitation in the past, most notably in the mid-seventeenth century when the breakdown of the social and political order after the execution of Charles I had spawned Radical movements among both sexes: there were Leveller women as well as men. These, however, were suppressed when the old order returned with Charles II and for most of the eighteenth century all but a few 'bluestocking' women of the upper and middle classes had to accept a position of dependence on men. The occasional novelist, female poet or intrepid traveller might appear, but these were exceptional women who were able to break the mould for themselves alone.

Things began to change in the 1790s, under the influence of Radical philosophy in the aftermath of the American and French Revolutions. Demands for equal rights for all men soon awoke similar sentiments in the minds of a few women, most notably Mary Wollstonecraft, whose *Vindication of the Rights of Women* (1792) and other writings followed on from Thomas Paine's *Rights of Man* and put the first coherent case for the political and social equality of the sexes. The feminist cause did not yet flourish, but it was never again to be entirely forgotten. In the period after 1807, when English Radicalism emerged again from the cloud of repression under Pitt and the fear of revolution was no longer so dominant, Radical feminism began to grow. It was most visible not in middle-class circles in London but among working-class Radicals in the north. In Oldham, Blackburn, and other northern industrial towns (where women supplied much of the underpaid labour-force in the new factory industries) societies of female reformers emerged – the Female Reformers of Blackburn and the 'Ancient Virgins' of Oldham among them. We know little about these groups apart from the satires directed against them, often by their male counterparts, but it seems likely that women of all classes were beginning to take a greater interest in the conditions of society which so overwhelmingly discriminated against them.

Just as the arrival of Queen Caroline in 1820 stimulated a new outburst of popular radicalism in general, so the nature of the 'Queen's affair' promoted especial activity by women. London Radicalism was still essentially male-orientated, but there appears to have been the beginning of a separate movement, or climate of opinion, for it lacked real grass-roots organization or structure, among women. Some were drawn into protest action by fellow-feeling for an oppressed member of their sex; others, like the wife and daughter of William Cobbett, rejoiced at the opportunity to identify the cause of women's rights with that of radical democratic reform in general. Women featured strongly among the numerous crowds who welcomed the Queen in June and demonstrated in her favour throughout the rest of the summer. In August the ladies and women (the distinction was still important) of the metropolis, in September those of Edinburgh, and several other female groups presented addresses and turned out in their support, while *The Times*, the organ of the middle-class Radicals, and *The Black Dwarf* among other representatives of lower-class opinion, published articles and other propaganda celebrating the support of female opinion. On 18 September *The Times* listed seventy-eight addresses that had been presented to the Queen so far, including nine from groups of ladies (and one from 'the young men of Hereford').

The Queen herself did not take up the feminist cause, but, as with her Radical supporters in general, maintained a passive attitude: she was interested only in her own case and not with its wider ramifications, and this may have been one reason why this sudden burst of feminist activity died away as rapidly as it had arisen at the end of 1820. The Queen Caroline affair, here as in general, proved to be a temporary phenomenon with little lasting effect, a memory of the past rather than a stimulus for the future, but while it lasted it brought women as well as men into the political arena.

The Black Dwarf, *12 July 1820*

PLACARDS RELATIVE TO THE PERSECUTION OF THE QUEEN

GLORIOUS DEEDS OF WOMEN!!!

Woe be to the age wherein WOMEN lose their influence, and their judgment is disregarded.

Reflect on glorious and virtuous Rome. It was there that the WOMEN honoured the exploits of renowned Generals.

All the Grand Events were brought about by WOMEN.

Through a WOMAN Rome obtained Liberty.

Through WOMEN the mass of the people acquired the rights of the Consulship.

A WOMAN put an end to the oppression of the *ten tyrants*.

By means of WOMEN, Rome, when on the brink of destruction, was screened from the resentment of an enraged and victorious outlaw.

France was delivered from her invaders and conquerors, in the fourteenth century, by a WOMAN.

It was a WOMAN that brought down the bloody tyrant, Marat.

A WOMAN nailed the tyrant, Sisera, to the ground.

A QUEEN caused the cruel Minister, Haman, to be hanged on a gallows fifty cubits high, of his own erecting.

And a QUEEN will now bring down the corrupt Conspirators against the Peace, Honour, and Life of the INNOCENT.

Letter in The Times, *3 August 1820*

TO THE EDITOR OF THE TIMES

SIR, – I have been a silent observer of the unmanly and unprecedented proceedings which have been carried on against one of my own sex, our gracious Queen Caroline, but I cannot help giving vent to my feelings in condemning the conduct of some great men in their last mean effort further to degrade her Majesty, by withholding the use of a service of plate which Ministers themselves acknowledge was appropriated by his late excellent Majesty expressly for her use. On reviewing the conduct of the accusers and the accused, how striking is the contrast! On the Queen's part all has been open, noble, candid, and anxious for public scrutiny: with the *great men*, all is dark, fearful, and ambiguous, showing evident fear to meet a magnanimous female, destitute of all power, influence, and patronage, arrayed in native innocence only. But I leave them, to the judgement of posterity. I leave them, while I propose to my fellow countrywomen the idea of presenting her Majesty Queen Caroline with a princely service of plate, as an expression of our attachment to her person, respect to her dignified rank, and of our high consideration of her exemplary conduct under the series of persecutions which she has been and still is enduring. Now suppose 100,000 females were to subscribe 5s. each, or 500,000 1s. each – and in either case I have no doubt a much greater number would be emulous of the honour – it would amount to 25,000l; a sum, I should suppose, quite sufficient for the purpose. As the idea originates with myself, and there may be difficulties in inducing the community at large to act in unison with an obscure individual, I will thank you to give publicity to it by inserting this in your independent paper, and I trust the subject will be immediately taken up by ladies of rank and influence in the metropolis. Let them but commence the business, and they may depend on the zealous and cordial support of almost every woman in the kingdom: only make a beginning, and I am persuaded the thing is accomplished. As a motto to be engraven on the principal piece of plate, I would propose the following:–

'Thus shall it be done unto the women whom the people delighteth to honour'.

I am, sir, yours, &c.,
JEMIMA

The Times, 12 August

The Address of the Married Ladies of the Metropolis and its vicinity will be received by her Majesty on Wednesday next at two o'clock, at the house of Lady Francis, St James's-square. A vast number of most respectable ladies have signed and are signing this address.

An Address of Condolence and Congratulation to her Majesty the Queen is in course of signature in Edinburgh, which has originated with, and is to be confined exclusively to, the Ladies. We understand it expresses a wish that her Majesty may take an early opportunity of visiting Scotland. . . .

SERENADERS. – A party of gentlemen, who are about to celebrate her Majesty's return to England by a concert, repaired the other evening to her residence, and in the most melodious manner serenaded her Majesty. The Queen was so much delighted with the singing that she requested a copy of the verses. . . .

We are sorry to learn that there has been some disturbance at Ipswich, in consequence of some of the men of the 10th regiment of dragoons, stationed in that place, having drank the health of the Queen. They were almost immediately secured and lodged in the guard-house, but were afterwards released by some of their comrades – *Chelmsford Chronicle.*

Anne Cobbett to Miss Boxall

Lambeth Road, Aug. 14, 1820

. . . Poor dear Papa is uncommonly well, to say the truth I believe our liege lady the Queen has contributed very largely to the keeping up of his spirits. I am sure I need not say I hope *you* are her friend for I am sure you must be so. Poor woman what

'Another green bag!! or plundering the Q—n's plate' (July 1820). Ministers rifle the Queen's plate from a large green bag while John Bull urges the people to rescue her property – a reference to the government's refusal to allow the Queen the use of the service of the plate given to her by George III in 1808 (see pp. 100–1)

persecution she has met with! But I think the tyrants are terribly puzzled just now, and they have made us suffer too much for me to pity them. Papa and I have been close prisoners here ever since May but yet we went to Blackheath to meet the Queen on the day of her arrival, and she one day drove by our door, so we have seen her, and quite enough to admire her greatly. She is in person just what one could fancy a *Queen* ought to be. It is not a little to the credit of our sex that all the reformers, radicals, jacobins &c. &c. have ever been able to perform in the work of years to shake the present system has almost failed, but been completed by a *woman*! at last. An *Old Woman* will not now be thought so foolish a thing. Papa says that for the future Husbands must be content to be henpecked, and he has given Mama notice that she may begin to exert her Sovereign authority forthwith. . . .

The Times, *17 August 1820*

Her Majesty came to Lady Francis's house in St James's-square at 12 o'clock yesterday and was received there, and indeed in the whole line of road from Brandenburgh-house, with the loudest demonstrations of popular attachment. . . . Her Majesty appeared deeply impressed with the warm enthusiasm of the people, and the repeated marks of affection shown to her by the most respectable persons as she passed along the streets. . . . Her Majesty was occupied throughout this important day . . . in cheerfully performing the same consolatory task in which she has been engaged at intervals during so many preceding days, namely, in receiving the cordial and unequivocal proofs of the confidence and attachment of a very large and respectable portion of his Majesty's subjects. The Addresses received by the Queen yesterday were from a very large number of married ladies of great respectability, from the inhabitants of Greenwich, and those of Aylesbury. The ladies, whose Address must have been peculiarly gratifying to the Queen, from the high and delicate sense of character which, happily for the moral reputation of the country, still characterises the ladies of England, assembled soon after 12 o'clock, in Leicester-square. The cavalcade, which consisted of twenty-eight private carriages, many of them drawn by four horses, and containing about 100 ladies, deputed from a very considerable number, several of them of rank, and all of them of the first respectability, proceeded on to her Majesty's residence in St James's-square, where they arrived, amidst the acclamations of the multitude of all classes assembled in the area of the square, about half-past one o'clock. The ladies were all in full dress; they were shown first into the suite of rooms on the ground floor, and afterwards conducted into her Majesty's presence in the drawing-room, which was nearly crowded to excess. The following address was then read to her Majesty by Mrs Thelwall, in a very impressive manner:–

'MADAM, – Whilst thousands and tens of thousands of our fellow-subjects are approaching your Majesty with assurances of homage and affection – whilst addresses even from the remoter parts of the kingdom are laid at your feet – permit us, your Majesty's neighbours, as wives, and the mistresses of families, in and near the metropolis, to approach you. We are unaccustomed to public acts, and uninfluenced by party feelings; yet we cannot be excluded from offering to your Majesty's notice our sympathy and devotion. Grateful to the constitution under which it is our happiness to live – saved also by our rank in the middle classes of society, from the dangers attendant on high rank or poverty, and protected by our husbands, we may hardly be supposed judges of all the value of your Majesty's conduct; but, Madam, we admire your magnanimity, and we adore that womanly feeling which has made your Majesty treat with contempt every offer, the tendency of which was to compromise your honour, and we thank you for it in the name of our sex.

Had your Majesty been treated with the respect due to your exalted rank, our hearts would have throbbed with ardent interest in your cause, and with love to your person; and, leaving to our husbands and sons all public expression of feeling, we should have confined ours to our domestic circles; but now, Madam, the indignation we feel for the cruel treatment of your Majesty bursts every barrier between us, and we hasten to express at your feet the warm, the almost overwhelming interest with which we are inspired: and be assured, Madam, our judgments are quite as much enlisted in your Majesty's service as our feelings: for, added to the dreadful charges against you, are not new crimes found out by your enemies? and new modes of judging them, unknown alike to common law and common sense? Under these circumstances, scarcely less than a miracle, we think, can procure your justification, refused as your Majesty has been every means of fairly meeting the accusations against you. We commit your Majesty's cause to the integrity of your own great mind; to the zeal, to the honour, and the ability of your legal advisers who will have for their reward a nation's gratitude; but above all, to our all-seeing and merciful God – to that God whom no one can prevent our addressing, and teaching our children to address, in fervent prayers for your protection.

And now, Madam, in simplicity of style, and sincerity of heart, we beg to subscribe ourselves

Your Majesty's dutiful, affectionate, and loyal subjects and servants. . . .

The Queen's answer

In this honest and affectionate address from my female neighbours, who are wives and mothers of families in and near the metropolis, I gratefully acknowledge the sympathy which they express for my many sorrows, and the indignation which they feel for my unnumbered wrongs. The approbation of my own sex must be ever dear to my heart; and it must be more particularly gratifying when it is the approbation of mothers of families in and near this enlightened metropolis.

When my honour is attacked, every loyal Englishwoman must feel it as an imputation on her own. The virtues of sovereigns are not circumscribed in their influence or insulated in their operations. They put in motion a wide circle of the imitative propensity in the subordinate conditions of life. Thus the virtues of the great become the property of the people; and the people are interested in preserving them from slanderous contamination. . . .

The Times, *17 August 1820*

. . . But a breach of *morality* in contradistinction to a breach of law . . . is the alleged foundation of this new Bill against her MAJESTY. If, then, the KING is to be allowed the benefit of moral considerations against the QUEEN; so, beyond all question, ought the QUEEN to be allowed them, when placed by the KING'S own will and pleasure in the light of a defendant towards her husband. All the technical forms in which Ministers can entrench themselves will avail them not one farthing against this broad principle of eternal justice. Fruitlessly will Lord LIVERPOOL strain his voice, and the Keeper of the King's Conscience appeal to his own, in behalf of this scandalous departure from first principles, and in defiance of the strong sense and blunt impartiality of the whole British nation. If it be attempted to execute, through the medium of artificial subtilties, a manifest outrage upon the clearest natural rights of one of the parties (and that the weaker party) in this great cause, which has roused from its resting-place every generous and every jealous susceptibility throughout the Empire, let Ministers beware of the consequence of their own rashness, for dearly will it be expiated. It is not enough to satisfy the doubts or to perplex the judgment of a lawyer on this occasion. The people, who can reason, but who know nothing of legal fiction, will say universally, that *justice is not done*, if the KING'S servants can prevail upon Parliament to protect the husband from that moral scrutiny, on the application of which to the wife's conduct is to depend her safety or destruction. If the wife be on her trial for immorality, what is it that, in the eye both of GOD and man, must be admitted to constitute the *degree* of immorality? What but the greater or less temptation encountered – the greater or less security against temptation which is enjoyed? Why is it, therefore, that by our laws, as regularly administered, divorce from his wife, against whom he sues for it, is granted to, or withheld from, an English husband, according as he has behaved towards that wife? Why but because, if he is a profligate husband, his bad example may have corrupted her – his infidelity wronged and provoked her; and because, if he has unjustly expelled her from his arms, she is liable to much temptation, and enjoys no protection; and thus his own criminal conduct leaves him without any title to redress. Oh! but, cry the Ministers, the State is the plaintiff – not his MAJESTY; it is the State which seeks to be relieved, his MAJESTY has nothing to say to it! Now this . . . is another of those impudent and monstrous

'Caroline,' S. Vowles (6 November 1820), commemorating the flood of addresses from London, Westminster, Southwark, Middlesex etc to support the Queen before the vote of the House of Lords

fictions which will convince no human being, and by which the people of England will be incurably disgusted. The State the plaintiff! You might as well persuade us that China or California was the plaintiff. The State, indeed, may, if she once gets over the vicious absurdity of legislating at all upon the *moral* character of the QUEEN'S life – the State, we admit, may call for the degradation from her royal 'pomp and circumstance' of a woman by whom the political station of Queen of ENGLAND is not respectably filled. But what connexion is there between degradation from high rank and a dissolution of the sacred bond of marriage? How, in the name of heaven, does it concern the 'State' whether a woman past the faculty of child-bearing, and an infirm man of nearly 60 years of age, continue man and wife, or cease to be so? It is the KING, then, and he only, who can be interested to accomplish the divorce; nor is it the worst feature in these unjust schemes against her MAJESTY, that the Bill for a divorce has been smuggled into the measure before Parliament, under another of those shameful fictions which would enable Ministers to fight their master's battles under the cloak of redressing the alleged wrongs of a people unconscious that such wrongs have ever been committed against them. . . .

The Times, *4 September*

Address from the Ladies of Edinburgh:

TO THE QUEEN'S MOST EXCELLENT MAJESTY

MADAM – Under the deepest expressions of sympathy for your unhappy situation, we beg leave to approach your Majesty with our best wishes for your speedy and honourable acquittal from those calumnies which have been so maliciously raised against your fame and honour.

We most sincerely lament the harsh and unprecedented usage which your Majesty has received in this country; but, while we deplore and deprecate that usage, we feel comforted in the buoyancy of your own magnanimous spirit, and in the general sympathy expressed for your sufferings by all ranks of people.

As your Majesty has justly observed, the principles and doctrines now advanced by your accusers do not apply to your case alone, but, if made part of the law of this land, may hereafter be applied as a precedent by every careless and dissipated husband to rid himself of his wife, however good and innocent she may be; and to render his family, however amiable, illegitimate; thereby destroying the sacred bond of matrimony, and rendering all domestic felicity very uncertain.

Such being the consequence of those principles and doctrines, your Majesty's case becomes a common cause with all the females in this kingdom, whose uttermost efforts ought therefore to be lawfully executed, to prevent innocence from suffering under the power and influence of servile and interested persons.

Trusting in that God who setteth bounds to the wrath of man, for your protection, and anticipating the triumph of Innocence in your honourable acquittal, we do earnestly and humbly solicit your Majesty, since you have declared your resolution to remain in Britain, to honour the ancient capital of Caledonia with your residence, where you will in a great measure be relieved form the intrigues of Court, and receive the warmest welcome and the most devoted services that a beloved Queen can expect from loyal and affectionate subjects.

The Queen's answer

I have long known, and, in several instances, have experienced, that the females of Scotland are inferior to none in the culture of their minds, in the purity of their principles, and in the steadiness of their attachments. This Address, therefore, from so many respectable characters of my own sex in the capital of Caledonia, has afforded me more than ordinary satisfaction.

In my progress through life it has been my first object to retain my own self-respect, without which integrity can have no strong hold upon the heart. My next desire has been to be esteemed by those who are themselves estimable; and whose approbation, while it is regulated by the judgement, is spontaneous and unbought. If I possess the good opinion of this better portion of the community, I am indifferent to the vile herd of venal traducers, or to that corrupt part of the nation who praise or blame not as themselves condemn or approve, but as higher authorities command. The praise or the blame of such persons, which is always to be purchased in the market of infamy, is a matter of little moment; for venality is equally contemptible, whether it deals in panegyric or invective.

The reasons which are employed to annul my marriage have a tendency to render every nuptial obligation fluctuating and insecure. The permanence of the institution would thus be made to depend more on inclination than on principle.

As far, therefore, as this Bill of Pains and Penalties may hereafter be employed as a precedent, it must be injurious to the moral interests of the community. I am glad that the discriminating and intelligent females of Scotland are beginning to view the question under this aspect; and to regard the experiment of a new mode of divorce, that is making in the House of Lords, as full of peril to the nation.

The more the good sense of all classes of the community and of both sexes is exercised on the present attempt to annul my marriage and to effect my degradation, the more they will be convinced that, if such an attempt should be successful, it must be hazardous in the extreme to the moral and political interests of the people, to the personal comfort of individuals, and to the general welfare of the community.

Letter in The Times, *20 September*

TO THE EDITOR OF THE TIMES

SIR – There is a mistake in your paper of yesterday. The number to the Address of the Married Ladies of London is there stated to have been 8,500. The fact is, Sir, that there were 17,652 respectable names to that Address, the ladies of the committee not suffering any person to be trusted with it but those who would guarantee that the names were such as they were designated – those of married women and the mistresses of families in the middle classes of society. Thus limited, there were seventeen thousand, six hundred and fifty-two names signed in *eight* days. As the committee thought (erroneously, as it has since appeared) that her Majesty ought not to be intruded upon, during her trial, even with expressions of sympathy, the committee are almost all out of town; but I thought it my duty, as their secretary, to request you will be pleased, Sir, to correct the statement of yesterday.

With ten thousand thanks for your noble defence of our persecuted Queen, I am, Sir, your obedient servant,

M.A.D.

'Which is the dirtiest?' W. Heath (5 September 1820). The King and the Queen throw mud at each other

J. Hatsell to Lord Colchester

Paultons, Saturday, Sept. 9th, 1820

My dear Lord, – . . . . For several months the people of England have thought, talked, and dreamt of no other subject than the Queen. The Lords, by permitting the evidence taken by the shorthand-writers to be published every morning, have not only supplied matter sufficient to occupy the leisure hours of the whole reading world, from breakfast to dinner, with subjects of conversation for the remainder of the day, but have exhibited to the world such a scene of profligacy and vice as were never detailed in any novel. . . . The whole is now adjourned to Oct. 3rd. And it is understood that the clause for divorce will be omitted. I hope *banishment* will be inserted in lieu of it! The women *in general* (owing, I believe, to that clause which inflicted a punishment that no other woman in the country could have suffered, who had cause for retaliation) have taken part with Her Majesty. Sir Thomas Acland told me that at Brighton, the ladies said, 'Well, if my husband had used me as hers has done, I should have thought myself entitled to act as she has done.' The mischief introduced into private families (where the father has not been cautious, like Lord Sidmouth and Lord Lilford, to prevent the newspapers from being read by his daughters) will be very great in corrupting the imaginations of the young ladies, and encouraging them to take part in every conversation, however indecent. . . .

In short, it appears as if all the world was run mad; and Her Majesty not the least in the throng. . . .

Yours very faithfully,
J. Hatsell

E.B. Wilbraham to Lord Colchester

Latham House, Sept. 12th, 1820

My dear Lord, – . . . . And now for news and politics. It would be wrong to think or talk of anything but the Queen , who is just now the object of public attention and irritation; – a feeling which Dr Parr, who writes for her the answers to the various addresses, seems determined not to suffer to subside without mischief. No lady whatever visits her, notwithstanding the lies of the Opposition newspapers; and she is reduced to radical society with here and there a fool with a *tête montée*. I forgot whether in my last letter I mentioned having heard that she *said at her own table*, when talking of the King, that 'by God she would blow him off his throne'.

Though your post only comes in once a week, yet, as I presume it brings you the English newspapers, I need not enter into details of the disgusting evidence, but merely tell you that Brougham has failed in his attempt to bully the House of Lords collectively and individually; and, not having succeeded in prevailing on them to suffer him to comment on the evidence for the prosecution before he opens his case for the Queen, he is said to reserve his energies for the House of Commons, where the Whigs and Radicals are to coalesce for the purpose of throwing out the Bill of Pains and Penalties, so that whenever it come to our inn, I expect very rough work and coarse debates, with a mob at our doors. This will be awkward, for Lord Castlereagh will be the only Minister to support the measure, (for I look on Bathurst, Vansittart, Robinson, and Pole as nothing,) and Canning will probably be absent, having committed himself awkwardly by talking of his *affection and respect* for the Queen, which must neutralise him on this question; probably much to the annoyance of his royal master; who, by the bye, is now living at his cottage in the Great Park at Windsor, with a male party only, having, it is said, been advised to dismiss the females by Lords Anglesey, Westmoreland, and Egremont (a good trio you will say). The mob seems determined to disbelieve the Queen's guilt, and the newpapers palliate what they cannot deny, which will do infinite mischief to the morals of young ladies at boarding-schools who are suffered to read them.

Radicalism has taken the shape of affection for the Queen, and has deserted its old form, for we are all as quiet as lambs in this part of England, and you would not imagine that this could have been a disturbed country twelve months ago. . . .

Yours very truly,
E.B.W.

CHAPTER SEVEN

The Queen's Defence

During the three-week recess after completion of the prosecution evidence the Radicals' campaign on the Queen's behalf reached its height. They increased their efforts to mobilize public support by attacking the credibility of the witnesses against her, and attempted to link the Queen's affair to the demand for reform of the political system. The unceasing flow of addresses and demonstrations, newspaper articles and satirical prints drove all other matters from the public's attention. J.C. Hobhouse, the moderate Radical MP for Westminster, took a leading part in the presentation of addresses to the Queen and described in his diary the great crowds and popular excitement that attended them. The unconvincing performance of the Crown's witnesses against the Queen lent credence to the allegations of her supporters that the evidence against her was fabricated or exaggerated, and that she was the victim, innocent or otherwise, of a 'flagrant conspiracy' for the benefit of a dissolute and unpopular monarch. Cobbett's address written for the inhabitants of Lymington, near his Hampshire residence, echoed those views as did the articles in his *Political Register*, now the leading Radical journal. Princess Lieven noted the signs of London's support for the Queen through addresses, deputations, and graffiti on the walls, and Cobbett's daughter Anne told her brother in America that 'nobody seems to expect anything but a revolution'.

When the Queen's defence was opened on 3 October, Brougham's speech was acclaimed as brilliant, but the evidence of the witnesses he and Denman called proved less impressive. Lady Charlotte Lindsay, the Queen's former companion, won much sympathy but the succession of servants and travelling companions which followed failed to generate much confidence in the Queen's innocence. The two British naval officers, Lieutenants Flynn and Hownam, who had served on the now famous polacca, were expected to be crucial witnesses if only because they were English, but they proved to be evasive about her sleeping arrangements on board, and damaged rather than upheld her case. Sir William Gell, a Derbyshire squire who had been in the Queen's suite before 1815, and her doctor Henry Holland, testified to her customary familiarity with servants without proving anything very specific. It was the general impression, as the Tory Harriet Arbuthnot wrote in her journal, that the Queen was probably guilty of immorality, but that she was no worse than her husband and that she ought not to suffer the penalties of the bill. Many of the peers were taking the attitude that while they would vote against her on the evidence, they would not support her degradation in the face of the public's attitude.

Denman's closing speech of ten hours for the defence failed to settle the issue. It was powerful and brilliant, but it was flawed by two miscalculations which offended many of his listeners. His famous comparison of the King to Nero and the Queen to his persecuted wife Octavia was thought too scurrilous an attack on a British monarch, however well-deserved, and it deeply offended George IV himself – Denman had to submit a grovelling apology and his future career was undoubtedly damaged. Secondly, Denman ended his speech with a reference to the biblical precept to 'go and sin no more' – which hardly helped his case that the Queen was innocent and which was ridiculed in the verse:

> Most Gracious Queen, we thee implore,
> To go away and sin no more;
> But, if that effort be too great,
> To go away at any rate.

Brougham's final speech retrieved some of the damage, but the Attorney-General's summing up for the prosecution was equally able and effective.

The verdict would in truth depend not so much on the legal view of the evidence as upon the political calculation of what was expedient in the circumstances of the country. As the peers rose in succession to give their views in the final debate, it became clear that the result would be close. Many believed the Queen guilty of misconduct, but it was a different matter to vote for the bill with all its likely consequences. In the Lords, the Peers customarily voted 'Content' or 'Not Content'. In this case, the latter did not necessarily mean 'not guilty'. As the verdict approached, nerves reached fever-pitch. It would be a momentous decision: if the Queen was acquitted the bill would fail, but would the celebrations of the Radical mobs get out of hand? If she was condemned by the Lords the bill must still go to the House of Commons and the country would face more weeks or months of agitation and tension – and Brougham was threatening, in that case, to disclose George IV's earlier marriage to Mrs Fitzherbert. The very existence of the monarchy might hang by that thread.

J.C. Hobhouse's diary, Monday 2 October

After a night without a wink of sleep, got up at seven – drest in court dress – breakfasted & set off in carriage for London – Arrived at Freemason's Tavern a little before ten – found there a number of respectable well drest females – tradesmen's wives & daughters waiting in a room for their carriages – which were drawn up in Lincoln's Inn Fields. After some time Peter Moore & Sir Gerard Noel came in court dress also – a great crowd before the door – the police sent the horse patroles to take care of us – I had four greys put to my father's carriage. The other carriages, in number 86, had all four horses, except Brooks & the committee with the address who went with six – very magnificent body, coachman &c. The procession set out, I leading it, alone – about eleven – paraded very slowly – down to Strand – then Pall Mall – St James St, Piccadilly – Shouts of Hobhouse for ever – & all sorts of demonstrations . . . all the way – those whom we met forced to doff their caps. A fine day – great crowds . . .

We did not reach Hammersmith & Brandenburg House till near two o'clock – Immense crowds there – and ballad singers amongst them – screaming about Theodore Majocci – and '*Non mi ricordo*'.

I first went up with the St James address – presented by Barber Beaumont – & a deputation filling 29 coaches & four – then came the Metropolitans – whilst they were unloading – I passed into the great drawing room and had some private conversation with the Queen – I cannot recollect it all or accurately – for it was long & desultory – but here are parts of it.

I asked her how her health was – she said 'why so so – pretty well considering – but your climate kills me'. (I should not be astonished if this were made an excuse for her leaving England again). . .

I ventured to ask her about Dr Holland – Oh yes he is all right – he came forward at once – I said I hoped that she would not let her counsel call many witnesses – oh no she said – I might have plenty – twenty-one came yesterday – but two or three good ones will be better than all . . . Hieronymus – her chief butler – came in – she asked him how late he had been out last night – he said 'I did not come home till three this morning your Majesty.' Ah, well, I wish you joy – said the Queen to him in a familiar manner – I at once saw what sort of manner she was likely to have had with her confidential Bergami – but is a Queen to be tried for words? . . .

She then said a word or two about her case & the People – What do you think – she asked me. I told her the People were unanimous almost – but I never counted on them – as they had been so often opposed to government and always failed – Well she added – and the *troops*? I answered – I do not believe the stories told of them – I have heard of only two regiments the 12th Lancers & the ninetieth who have expressed discontent – I do not believe anything beyond this. 'Nor I neither, she said – I believe the D of Wellington has been to the ninetieth.' This was delicate ground – I said no more – indeed I knew no more – and the Queen herself certainly seemed to think with me that it was very idle to reckon upon the soldiers. . . . She expressed great dislike of the Duke of Wellington – said Waterloo was a drawn battle – said he was her greatest enemy.

Expressed indignation at the confinement of Napoleon at St Helena.

I said that she had none of the nobility or higher gentry for her – but that they & all the Whig aristocracy would come to her if she triumphed – She said – I will not let them then – snapping her fingers. . . .

We waited some time & then went in to the saloon which was quite full of the metropolitans – Sir R. Wilson, Hume MP Sir Gerard Noel, Ald. Wood &c. supported the Queen who stood on a sofa with Lady A. Hamilton, – Gell, Craven and the Reverend Mr Fellowes were on her left. I read the address – kissed hands – & then the poor Queen went through the tedious ceremony of having her hand kissed by the hundreds present . . . . the women almost all said God bless your Majesty & burst into tears as they looked at her – I was obliged gently to push them on.

When this was over, I went into the inner room with the Queen & there presented an address from the St John's Union society five of whom kissed her hand – she received the address at the window in the sight of the rest, and of a great multitude who cheered violently. When I had done this – the queen said poor Mr Hobhouse – seeing me look very fagged – & then when I bowed out of the room, added 'God bless you'. I drove away amidst cheers – as hard as I could – to Hanover Square. . . .

Wednesday October 11

Rode up to Brandenburg House – immense crowds going there in procession – recognized & almost cheer'd off my horse. The Kensington address gone when I arrived – rode to Kensington spoke to my friends there & read the Queen's answer to their address aloud – Heard their opinions – one man said that he hoped to see Castlereagh punished capitally – I never heard this kind of language before – the feeling gone abroad is most intense. . . .

Address of the inhabitants of Lymington to the Queen

We, the Inhabitants of the Borough of Lymington and its vicinity, in the County of Southampton, humbly beseech our virtuous and magnanimous benevolent and gallant Queen to be graciously pleased to receive an assurance of our ardent attachment and a solemn promise of our support.

Great as are our own sufferings, deep as is the misery into which merciless taxation has plunged us; stung, as we are, to the soul by the deeds of the Traffickers in Seats and those of their twin-brothers in arrogance and cruelty who ought to set an example of Christian humility and charity; smarting under such numerous and intolerable wrongs, they all vanish from our minds when we reflect on the long series of wrongs, injuries, and insults heaped upon your Majesty. But, even these dwindle in our eyes, when we contemplate that mass of matchless wickedness, the now flagrant conspiracy, carrying on against your Majesty['s] honour and life. The mode of trial, the constitution of the court, the absence of all specific charge, the refusal of lists of witness [*sic*] and of places, the character of the witnesses, the rewards bestowed on them, the chusing of those witness by persons not necessary to name: at all these we have felt inexpressible indignation; how, then, are we to find terms to express our abhorrence of the sending away, in the face of a solemn pledge of the leading prosecutors, one of those witnesses, whom the prosecutors must have known to have been a perjured witness and also an agent in the hiring and suborning of other witnesses!

To say what we feel is impossible. It is deeds, and not words, that your Majesty has a right to expect from us; and, in the defence of your Majesty's sacred person, and lawful rights, we pledge ourselves to be behindhand with no part of his Majesty's and your Majesty's loyal, dutiful, and affectionate subjects.

Princess Lieven to Prince Metternich

London, October 3

Yesterday, the Queen received eleven more addresses, accompanied in each case by a deputation of several thousand people carrying banners with the most subversive inscriptions. With all one hears and reads, it is difficult to believe that there are still a King and a Government in this country. Just now, as I was passing by our stables, I read, written in large letters on the wall: 'The Queen for ever, the King in the river.' All the walls in town are scrawled over with nice things of this kind. I can't tell you what horrible faces one sees nowadays in the streets and the main roads, and how insolently they come up and bawl in one's ears, 'The Queen for ever'. As I was coming back to town yesterday, I was afraid that two of these awful creatures were going to jump into my carriage, to force me to bawl with them. . . .

'Arrival at Brandenburgh House of the watermen etc with an address to the Queen on 3 October 1820'
(M. Dubourg)

Anne Cobbett to her brother James in America

October 7, 1820

. . . You do not say anything about the works that have been going on here ever since the beginning of June last, that is to say, ever since the arrival of the Queen, so I suppose you have no means of seeing any English newspapers, which I lament very much, for the Press has been and is taking greater liberties than it ever did before; notwithstanding the new acts, passed last winter. You must read all the Queen's answers, which you will find in the registers, and that will give you an insight into her notions of things as they are, and what she thinks ought to be. Papa says you know, that whenever she sets about it in right good earnest, a woman is sure to beat her husband, in the end. In this instance it is so, at any rate, for the gentleman does not dare to show himself in London, or indeed, anywhere else, any more than he can fly over the Moon. He kept himself cooped up in Windsor Forest for nearly two months, and then, all of a sudden we heard of his going on board of ship at Brighton (at which place he was terribly hissed) and out to sea, where he was overtaken by the Equinox, and there being no such thing as getting into any port, no doubt he was very *sick*, and all we loyal subjects were in great alarm. However, Providence preserved him for greater things, and he returned to us in safety. Upon my word do you know Jumpy it is rather a melancholy thing to see a King playing at hide and seek in this way, not daring to stop in any town to change his post horses, but to have them brought out on some Common to meet him; really I could feel for him if it were not for the melancholy death of the Princess Charlotte. It is quite impossible to describe to you the state of this country at present. Nobody seems to *think* of anything but the Queen, nobody seems to *expect* any thing but a revolution. Three or four days in every week the whole population of London, as it were, turns out to see the different bodies of people that are going to wait upon the Queen. . . . Last week all the watermen of the whole river went in a body with an address to her, and they went by water. It was the most beautiful sight you can conceive. All the men dressed nice and clean with *white* cockades in their hats (about 5,000 of them!) with about 500 large flags and bands of music in their boats. All along the side of the river were people assembled to cheer them as they passed along. It really was sight enough to put fire and enthusiasm into even a Yankee. . . . You will laugh when I tell you, that Papa has become the most determined sight see-er. But he feels every cheer given to the Queen, as so much vengeance upon the Boroughmongers. One day last week the Old Major[1] carried up an address from some place or other, and the Queen invited him to stay and dine with her. So here is pretty confusion, a man convicted of sedition and expecting to go into prison, dining at the Queen's table! What strange times we live in Jumpy! That shows whether she be not a reformer. The Major *personally* was nothing to her, she never saw him before in her life, but she took that opportunity of shewing what she thought of the *cause*. . . .

In my last packet I sent you some of the *Peep at the Peers*, but I forgot to tell you who were the authors. Papa and I were just a month at it, and you would scarcely believe that it was the hardest job of work Gov[r] ever undertook, and every body says it has done more for the Queen than any other thing, because it has thrown such odium upon the Lords and her Judges, by showing how they are bound to the Government. . . .

Letters from Thomas Creevey to Miss Ord

House of Lords, October 3rd, 1 o'clock

. . . Brougham has been at it nearly two hours and a half, and may continue an hour or two more, for aught I know; but it is infinitely too hot to stay in the crowd, so I have just escaped. . . . I think I may say he was as good as I expected. . . .

4 o'clock

He has been at it again two hours, and will evidently be so till five – criticism in detail upon the evidence for the prosecution – damned dull and damned hot, so I have been walking about amongst my friends on Westminster Bridge.

House of Lords, Oct. 4, ½ past 1 [a.m.]

Brougham has just finished his opening. . . . I never heard him anything like the perfection he has displayed in all ways. . . . In short, if he can prove what he has stated in his speech, I for one believe she is innocent, and the whole case a conspiracy. . . . He concluded with a most magnificent address to the Lords – an exhortation to them to save themselves – the Church – the Crown – the Country, by their decision in favour of the Queen. This last appeal was made with great passion, but without a particle of rant. . . . I consider myself infinitely overpaid by these two hours and a half of Brougham, for all the time and money it has cost me to be here, and almost for my absence from all of you. . . .

Oct. 5th

. . . I had a very agreeable day at Powell's with the Duke of Norfolk, who called for me here, and we walked there together. We went to Brooks's at night, where, as you may suppose, the *monde* talked of nothing but Brougham and his fame, and the comers-in from White's said the same feeling was equally strong there. . . . [The speech] not only astonished but has shaken the aristocracy, though Lord Granville did tell me at parting this morning not to be too confident of that, for that the H. of Lords was by far the stupidest and most obstinate collection of men that could be selected from all England. This, I think, from a peer himself, and old virtuoso Stafford's brother, was damned fair. . . . General St Leger was called, and was only useful as a very ornamental witness. . . . Then came Lord Guilford, who is the most ramshackle fellow you ever saw. He is a kind of *non mi ricordo* likewise. He seems, however, to have been a pretty frequent guest at her Majesty's table . . . has dined more than once with Bergami at the Queen's table and that he never saw the slightest impropriety. . . . But the witness of all witnesses has just closed her examination in chief – Lady Charlotte Lindsay. In your life you never heard such testimony as hers in favour of the Queen – the talent, the perspicuity, the honesty of it. . . .

House of Lords, Oct. 6th

Wonders will never cease. Upon my soul! this Queen must be innocent after all. Lady Charlotte went on in her cross-examination, and could never be touched; tho' she was treated most infamously – so much so as to make her burst out a crying. . . .

House of Lords, 9th Oct., 10 o'clock

. . . The town is literally drunk with joy at this unparalleled triumph of the Queen. There is no doubt now in any man's mind, except Lauderdale's, that the whole thing has been a conspiracy for money. . . .

4 o'clock

Captn. Flynn of the polacre is just call'd. He is mad, and in trying to do too much has, for the present, done harm; but it will be all set right to-morrow.

House of Lords, 2 o'clock, October 10th

This cursed Flynn is still going on. He has perjured himself three or four times over, and his evidence and himself are both gone to the devil. He is evidently a crack-brained sailor. . . . he has fainted away once, and been obliged to be carried out.

Oct. 12th, one o'clock

By Jove, my dear, we are coming to critical times, such as no man can tell the consequences of. It is quite understood that the Lords – at the suit of the Ministers – are resolved to pass this Bill, upon the sole point of the Queen being admitted to have slept under the tent on board the polacre, while Bergami slept there likewise. . . . I predict, with the most perfect confidence, that commotion and bloodshed must follow this enormous act of injustice, should it finally be committed; but (tho' I stand alone in this opinion) I will not and do not believe the Bill will pass the Lords. . . .

Duke of Norfolk to Thomas Creevey

Fornham, 13 Octr., 1820

Dear Creevey,
Are you really become the champion of the H. of Lds., and suppose there is any atrocity they are not ready to vote for? For my own part, if they do pass this horrible Bill, I shall no longer consider it a disgrace or a hardship to be excluded [as a Roman Catholic] from a seat in their House; but, on the contrary, rejoice that I have not been implicated in so foul a crime. Is it possible that the slight evidence they have for the tent scene alone can establish their whole case? I am anxious beyond measure to hear the result. Ly. Petre desires to be kindly remembered, and we hope you will come down. If by any miracle the Bill should *not* pass, what a jolification we will have!
Yours sincerely,
NORFOLK

Lady Charlotte Lindsay's account of her examination by the House of Lords, 5–7 October

5 Oct. Then I was called, Mr Brougham having previously sent me a dose of lavender drops, and having desired the Court to permit me to sit down. I was first examined by Dr Lushington, who, being one of the Queen's counsel, of course gave me no difficulty; and this examination gave me time to get accustomed to my situation, and

to hearing the sound of my own voice. . . . The Solicitor-general Copley cross-questioned me, and in as harsh a manner as if he had been endeavouring to bring out the confession of a murderer at the Old Bailey. I was getting through it, however, better than I had expected, when four o'clock struck, which was the signal for an adjournment. I had to go home again, with the prospect of a further cross-examination the next morning.

Friday, 6th. – The business of this day began with my cross-examination, which was more distressing and severe still than that of yesterday. . . . I did not, however, flinch or falter. At last I was asked some questions respecting family misfortunes that had occurred in the year 1817 – the deaths of my brother Francis, and of my sister, Lady Glenbervie, which happened within a fortnight of each other. These questions, asked me in such a place, and when my spirits were so much harassed, quite overwhelmed me for a moment, and I burst into tears; but these tears, together with a glass of water that was brought me, relieved me immediately; and then, in answer to a question that was asked, 'Whether the state of my spirits, in consequence of these domestic misfortunes, was the sole cause of my resigning my situation of lady of the bedchamber?' I replied, 'No; certainly, my resignation was also influenced by the degrading reports that had reached me, although I had myself never seen any improprieties in Her Majesty's conduct while I was with her in Italy.' This answer seemed to give universal satisfaction. The counsel for the prosecution could not but own that it was an honest one, while the Queen's counsel were equally pleased, because it tended to strengthen their argument of a conspiracy to drive away from the Queen all her most respectable servants, by raising reports of her ill-conduct. I heard Denman whisper to Mr Brougham, 'that was well answered;' and Mr B. replied, 'Perfect! perfect!' After all this torment and fatigue, I was rewarded by a very gratifying compliment that was paid me by Lord Erskine, who, in speaking of my evidence, said, 'The fair and candid evidence of the noble witness at the bar'. These expressions produced a loud cheering, in which Lord Liverpool's voice joined; indeed, I must say that his conduct to me was remarkably gentlemanlike and good-natured during the whole of my examination. But my troubles were not yet quite come to an end, for it had appeared in my brother's examination that he had written me a letter advising my resignation, and offering to make good the income that I should lose by so doing. This letter, besides this offer, happened to contain some comical remarks, . . . which would by no means have been pleasant to hear publicly read in the House of Lords. When asked about it, I *really* could not recollect what I had done with it. The carelessness about a letter in which my interest was so much concerned appeared very extraordinary to many of their Lordships, who knew little of the brother and sister – the perfect honour of the one, and the implicit confidence of the other. I answered, that I believed I had destroyed it. . . . That if it was in existence, it would be at Lord Glenbervie's, in Argyll Street, where I left some few papers. . . . I was directed to make this search, and produce this letter, if I should find it, the next day. When I left the House of Lords I went to Argyll Street, where I did really search *honestly* among my papers; but I believe that no heir was ever more rejoiced at the discovery of the document that was to clear up all doubts of his right of inheritance than I was at not finding the object of my search. I was obliged to go again the next morning (Saturday, October 7th) to tell the Lords (what, perhaps, half of them did not believe) that I could not find this letter. . . .

C. Greville's memoirs, October 1820

Oct. 8th . . . The town is still in an uproar about the trial, and nobody has any doubt that it will finish by the Bill being thrown out and the Ministers turned out. Brougham's speech was the most magnificent display of argument and oratory that has been heard for years, and they say that the impression it made upon the House was immense; even his most violent opponents (including Lord Lonsdale) were struck with admiration and astonishment.

October 15th. – Since I came to town I have been to the trial every day. I have occupied a place close to Brougham, which, besides the advantage it affords of enabling me to hear extremely well everything that passes, gives me the pleasure of talking to him and the other counsel, and puts me behind the scenes so far that I cannot help hearing all their conversation, their remarks, and learning what witnesses they are going to examine, and many other things which are interesting and amusing. Since I have been in the world I never remember any question which so exclusively occupied everybody's attention, and so completely absorbed men's thoughts and engrossed conversation. In the same degree is the violence displayed. It is taken up as a party question entirely, and the consequence is that everybody is gone mad about it. Very few people admit of any medium between pronouncing the Queen quite innocent and judging her guilty and passing the Bill. Until the evidence of Lieut. Hownam it was generally thought that proofs of her guilt were wanting, but since his admission that Bergami slept under the tent with her all unprejudiced men seem to think the adultery sufficiently proved. The strenuous opposers of the Bill, however, by no means allow this, and make a mighty difference between sleeping dressed under a tent and being shut up at night in a room together, which the supporters of the Bill contend would have been quite or nearly the same thing. The Duke of Portland, who is perfectly impartial, and who has always been violently against the Bill, was so satisfied by Hownam's evidence that he told me that after that admission by him he thought all further proceedings useless, and that it was ridiculous to listen to any more evidence, as the fact was proved; that he should attend no longer to any evidence upon the subject. This view of the case will not, however, induce him to vote for the Bill, because he thinks that upon grounds of expediency it ought not to pass. The Ministers were elated in an extraordinary manner by this evidence of Hownam's. . . . They look upon the progress of this trial in the light of a campaign, and upon each day's proceedings as a sort of battle, and by the impression made by the evidence they consider that they have gained a victory or sustained a defeat. Their anxiety that this Bill should pass is quite inconceivable, for it cannot be their interest that it should be carried; and as for the King, they have no feeling whatever for him. The Duke of Portland told me that he conversed with the Duke of Wellington upon the subject, and urged as one of the reasons why this Bill should not pass the House of Lords the disgrace that it would entail upon the King by the recrimination that would ensue in the House of Commons. His answer was 'that the King was degraded as low as he could be already'. The vehemence with which they pursue this object produces a corresponding violence in their language and sentiments. Lady Harrowby, who is usually very indifferent upon political subjects, has taken this up with unusual eagerness. In an argument which I had with her the day before yesterday, she said that if the House of Lords was to suffer itself to be influenced by the opinions and wishes of the people, it would be the most mean and pusillanimous conduct, and that after all what did it signify what the people thought or what they expressed if the army was to be depended upon? I answered that I never had expected that the day would come when I should be told that we were to disregard the feelings and wishes of the people of this country, and to look to our army for support. . . . The last two days have been more amusing and interesting than the preceding ones. The debates in the House, a good deal of violence, and some personalities have given spirit to the proceedings, which were getting very dull. . . . It must be acknowledged that the zeal of many of the Peers is very embarrassing, displayed as it is not in the elucidation of the truth, but in furtherance of that cause of which they desire the success. There is no one more violent than Lord Lauderdale, and neither the Attorney-General nor the Solicitor-General can act with greater zeal than he does in support of the Bill. Lord Liverpool is a model of fairness, impartiality, and candour. The Chancellor is equally impartial, and as he decides personally all disputes on legal points which are referred to the House, his fairness has been conspicuous in having generally decided in favour of the Queen's counsel. Yesterday morning some discussion arose about a question which Brougham put to Powell. He asked him who was his principal, as he was an agent. The question was objected to, and he began to defend it in an uncommonly clever speech, but was stopped before he had spoken long. He introduced a very ingenious quotation which was suggested to him by Spencer Perceval, who was standing near him. Talking of the airy, unsubstantial being who was the principal, and one of the parties in this cause, he said he wished to meet

> This shape –
> If shape it could be called – that shape had none,
> Distinguishable in member, joint, or limb;
> Or substance might be called that shadow seemed,
> For each seemed either . . .
>   What seemed its head
> The likeness of a kingly crown had on.
>   *Paradise Lost*, ii. 666

Lady Cowper to Frederick Lamb

Tuesday, October 10th [1820]

. . . You will see by the papers the turn the evidence has taken, and there is every probability of the bill being given up. It was reported yesterday that some of the Ministers had been to the King to get him to comply. The fact is that tho the impression must remain very much the same upon all rational minds, yet there is not evidence to convict her, or at least so many parts of the evidence being disproved and the character of the witnesses taken in, and added to this the expediency of throwing out the Bill, and so many of their own Lords are of this opinion that, should the Ministers persist, I am told they would most probably be beat. The Polacca [story] is still uncontradicted. . . . Brougham says he will be obliged to allow by his witnesses that they both slept under the tent in the Polacca – and this I think for a month, which is awkward, but they were both dressed upon two beds, and this is not sufficient to pass the Bill upon them.

The Queen has a strange luck in her favour; the worse she behaves, the *more* it redounds to her credit. The only *good* I see in the turn affairs have taken, is that the

'The Queen returning from the House of Lords' (M. Dubourg). A contemporary print depicting the Queen's departure after a session of the House of Lords

Radicals are furious, and Cobbett makes a violent attack on Brougham for luke-warmness, and for having spared the King in his speech. The fact is that the Bill being thrown out is death to their hopes. . . . B[rougham] has certainly shown uncommon talent in the conduct of the whole business and what he is not in general famous for, great prudence and *temper*, except with a few exceptions. . . .

. . . (*entre nous*) I believe most of the Queen's witnesses are more or less perjured, but it is very different swearing to what you believe and what you know. The Queen is in high glee, but bored with it all, and they say when the whole thing is settled will *certainly* go abroad. . . . The Queen says she pities the King for having such *foolish* people about him; that if she had wished to get up a thing of this sort, she would have done it better. She says it is true she did commit adultery once, but it was with the Husband of Mrs Fitzherbert. She is a drôle woman. . . .

Wednesday [11 October 1820]

. . . After all this, how impossible it will be for any man to divorce his wife for the next 20 years, after such philippics as are daily uttered against spies and informers, and above all, servants' evidence, as if any body had ever objected to it before in any common case. We are really growing enlightened. . . . The most shameful thing that has appeared in the whole transaction is Col[onel] Lindsay having sold to Govern[men]t Ly Charlotte's letters written to him from Naples, and it was upon these that her cross-examination was founded. Did you ever hear of such a thing? She has satisfied nobody. The anti-Queens believe she told very great lies, and the Queen's friends think she did not do it boldly enough. They say if she had made up her mind to say a thing, she should not have hesitated. . . .

I believe the Almanac recommends, spring and fall, a little blood letting and a cooling diet. However, I now wish the bill to be thrown out. After all this evidence it is the only thing to do. The King might make his Party good by saying he was glad to find he had been deceived by false reports. The Bill being thrown out and the Queen well used, is death to the hopes of the Radicals, and may save us much unpleasant work. What does it signify letting her have a little Court and establishment? Her being received as Queen will disgust the Radicals of her, and no decent person will have any more to do with her than just leave their names. It is the idea of injustice that gets her so many partizans and raises a cry, for all know what to think of her, and I believe there are none who would trust her, perhaps excepting Denman, who is quite a fool on that subject. She has completely bamboozled him, and I believe made him in love with her. . . .

Friday Oct. 13th [1820]

The reports now are these:

Tho it is difficult to have a résumé, as the two sides see things in so different a light, the Queen's Court fancy the Bill will be thrown out, but somehow with a vote of censure attached. Ministers are in doubt what to do, they were very low before Flinn and Howman, but these have given them much to say and to lay stress upon, though I think there is not much to find fault with in the latter's evidence, tho he spoke evidently with a strong bias in her favour. Flinn is quite a mad Irishman, bother-headed and wild, with a neck cloth, which Lord Erskine says must be the sail of the Polacca, but as B[rougham] laid much stress upon small inaccuracies destroying the whole weight of the evidence of a person, this applies very much to these two witnesses, and he seems to feel it so and to be out of sorts. Many Peers who before said the Bill *must* be thrown out, are now in doubt. . . . Many Peers are against passing the Bill who would yet vote her guilty. . . . I hear the Duke of Y[or]k told the King on Saturday that the Bill must be thrown out. I am all on this side of the question now. I think so many witnesses having failed . . . and told evident and disgusting lies ought to vitiate the whole. I believe her *nearly* as guilty as ever I did, but it will not do to pass such a Bill in the teeth of such witnesses as Ly Charlotte and Gell and H. Craven and her respectable *maître d'hôtel*, and upon the evidence of such liars . . . it is neither just nor expedient, for I am sure it would put the whole country in a flame. . . . If the Bill goes to the House of Commons, we shall have dreadful scenes I do believe. This Bill never ought to have passed without the evidence being quite clear and decisive and untouched, so as to leave no doubt on one's mind. It will not do to force it on some points and quite failing on others. The Polacca is now what Govern[men]t mean to lay stress upon. I believe they have quite given up Naples, and the Polacca will not be strong enough, for it is just possible two people may lye in a tent on two beds in their cloathes, *en tout bien tout honneur*. One thinks it an *odd* proceeding, but it is not proof. . . . I think B[rougham] did well in his speech by not retaliating upon the King or putting in any offensive matter he could avoid, and really it is for every bodies interest now to keep up the Monarchy, for it is in a sad low state. I always fear that B[rougham] will lose his temper, and that if M[inister]s force the Bill, they will drive him to it.

Princess Lieven to Prince Metternich

October 12

How boring London will be when there is no more Queen to be tried! It is curious how either party is thrown into extremes of joy or depression according to the way the evidence goes against her or in her favour. For the last two days, her stock has been very low. An unfortunate English lieutenant, bent on serving her, by ill luck made an indiscreet remark which had no reference to her; and from this followed a string of contradictions which so played on the poor man's nerves that he fainted in the House. The impression against her was unmistakable; perhaps the fate of the trial rested with the lieutenant.

Lady Cowper to Frederick Lamb

Tuesday, Octr. 17th [1820]

. . . I am all for the Bill's being thrown out, I think many of the disgusting details having failed, and considering the exaggeration of ordinary low Italians, one may look upon her case as one of no particular horror, and it merely remains with her having taken a Courier for her Lover, which Lover, if he had been a gentleman, she had, in my opinion, a good right to have, without anybody objecting, (if he did not). She is a coarse low-minded woman, I have no doubt, but it is hard on her to have such disgusting details invented about her, and they really must have done so in many instances, for they say the Attorney General's opening speech was not a third part up to his brief, and there are many people ready to swear to stories of the green bag, ten times more extraordinary, which they did not bring forward from thinking them impossible. Two witnesses on oath were ready to prove they had seen her dance naked before an open window, and many other things of this sort. Ld Erskine says the only good of this Bill is to separate everybody. The Queen cannot see Bergami; the King cannot see Ly Conyngham. He is obliged to pass his time alone and bored at the Cottage, and she is going to Spa. . . . Canning cuts a miserable figure, loitering about at Paris, to see what turn affairs will take. . . .

Thursday night, October 26th, 1820

. . . Denman's Speech was very fine everybody agrees. I think he would have done better if he had spared the King more, all that abuse is of no use whatever, Ld Essex calls Carleton House, *Nero's Hotel.*[2] Leopold[3] has been today to call on the Queen; this looks as if the Bill would not pass. Ly J[ersey] is *toujours comme un cheval qui prend le mors aux dents,* when the Queen is mentioned. Ministers and their friends say the bill will certainly be carried through and that the King is so set on it that he would urge it on if he thought to have only *one* majority. They say Ld Ellenborough carried a sort of proposal to Ld Grey that Ministers would let the bill be thrown out if there could be a means hit upon of saving the Ministers, but he said he could hear of no arrangement of that sort, that he had come unprejudiced, listened to the evidence, and should act accordingly without any arrangement. I don't see what should drive them from their places even if they were to be beat, which is not likely. The King dare not, they would only say it was his act and not theirs. In Denman's speech there is a violent attack on the Duke of Clarence, who has been about in an indecent manner abusing the Queen which is not so bad as his abuse of Howman and Flinn, saying *I shall* take *care* they shall never rise in the Navy. The Duke of York is also violent. The Duke of Gloucester for her stoutly; this is not so much believed to be his generosity as he pretends for former friendship, as the Duchess's doing to prevent the Queen fulfilling her threat of Publishing Memoirs of herself and the rest of the Princesses. By the way such a threat as that shows what a degraded person the Queen is, yet people are so blinded now [that] if she were to do such a thing they would reckon it all fair. . . .

Mrs Arbuthnot's journal

18 October. – I have this last two days had conversations with several of the Peers, particularly Lord Ellenboro', & it seems *at present* the general idea that the Bill will not pass, but the larger proportion of those who w^d vote against the Bill itself are most anxious to have an opportunity of expressing their opinion of her guilt & their strongest censure upon her conduct; but they objected to passing the Bill because they felt that the treatment she had uniformly met with from the King was such as certainly to encourage any bad propensities she might originally have had, & because the whole nation with one voice exclaimed against it. Not the mob only or the Radicals, but the whole of the respectable yeomanry & gentry of the country who, tho' all convinced of her guilt, always say, 'But then the King is worse &, if she is bad, he made her so'. I think the vote of guilt & of censure would answer all the purposes of the Bill; it w^d justify the Ministers who advised her exclusion from the rights & priviledges of Queen of England and w^d keep her in that private station which is alone fit for her. No pains & penalties can place her one inch lower in the scale of society than that to which she is already sunk. Shunned & contemned by all who have any sense of decency or propriety; made the rallying point of all the disaffected & infamous throughout the country, & without one friend on earth, God knows her bitterest enemies need not wish her a more deplorable existence than that to which she seems doomed for the remainder of her life; an existence the miseries of which must be rendered still more insupportable by the consciousness she must have of what a different position she might & would have occupied now, if she had only conducted herself with common prudence & decorum. It is thought the proceedings in the Lords will last still another month.

28th. – The last five days have been taken up in the House of Lords with the summing up of the Queen's Counsel, & the reply of the Att^y & Sol: Genl. Mr Denman was violently abusive of the King, compared him to Nero & the persecution of the Queen to the persecution of Octavia. It was universally felt that, tho' very eloquent, it did not improve the Queen's case; & his quotation from the Scriptures, appealing to the House of Lords to address the Queen in the words used by our Saviour to the woman taken in Adultery, 'Go thou & sin no more,' was certainly strangely indiscreet. He was answered by the Att^y Genl in a most excellent speech, in which he clearly proved the Queen's guilt from the admissions of her own witnesses, & he particularly dwelt upon the inference to her disadvantage which must be drawn from her not having called any of those persons who, from habitual intercourse with her, were most capable of speaking to the purity of her private conduct.

The day before the Att: made his speech, I happened to read in Dr Holland's Tour in Greece an account that the people in those countries never undress, but rest for the night in the same dress that they wear by day. Very great stress had been laid by the

Queen's Counsel upon the circumstance of her not appearing to have ever undressed during the voyage when she slept with Bergami, & I sent this quotation to the Att: who read it in his speech & ridiculed the nonsense of Mr Denman asserting that no impropriety could take place because they were not undressed. I afterwards heard from a person who did not know I had sent the quotation (Lord Ellenboro') that it was the happiest part of the Attorney's speech, so that I was *très glorieuse* upon the occasion. . . .

The Times, 19 October

COVENT-GARDEN THEATRE

Shakspeare's play of *Cymbeline* drew a very full house, probably as much on account of the story, as from the beauty of the sentiments, or the harmony of the language. The subject of the drama is, as we suppose most of our readers know, the danger incurred by a faithful wife, in consequence of the persecutions of a jealous husband, whose mind has been worked upon to a pitch of phrensy by the artful tales of a scoundrel Italian: the catastrophe is the triumph of innocence. The not very remote analogy to present circumstances, both in the progress and conclusion of the drama, kept alive the attention and excited the sympathies of the audience. Some passages of peculiar applicability were seized upon with great avidity and enthusiasm. In the fourth scene of the second act, *Iachimo* tries to convince *Posthumus* of *Imogen's* infidelity, by producing one of her bracelets. The husband is staggered, but his friend *Pisanio* thus re-assures him:–

> Have patience, Sir;
> It may be probable she lost it, or
> Who knows if one of her women, being corrupted,
> Hath not stolen it from her?

The most vehement applause followed this suggestion, and lasted for two or three minutes. In the next act the following passage was received with tumultuous and repeated shouts:–

> Oh, master! What a strange infection
> Is fall'n into thy ear! What false Italian,
> As poisonous tongued as handed, hath prevailed
> On thy too ready hearing? Disloyal! No:
> She's punished for her truth.

But the climax of sympathetic exultation was reserved for the last act, when the lying Italian thus records his penitence and the lady's wrongs:–

> The heaviness of guilt within my bosom
> Takes off my manhood; I have belied a lady,
> The Princess of this country.

The company was highly respectable; and we did not observe above half a dozen

Jacobins, who disloyally hissed, when the general audience seized occasion to express their conviction of their Queen's innocence.

The play was not very well acted. Miss Foote would do very well if she were never to speak, for her looks and motions are always pretty and interesting. We have seldom seen Charles Kemble to more, or Macready to less, advantage.

Extracts from Thomas Denman's summing up for the Queen, 24–5 October 1820

Denman's speech occupied the major part of two days and lasted about ten hours.

. . . The worse he [the King] makes his wife, the more profligacy he imputes to her, the more he increases his own shame in having thus thrown her abandoned on the continent of Europe. We have heard of examples supposed to be similar to the present taken from English history; but, for my part, I find no example in English history. I can find no example in any history of a Christian king, who has thought himself at liberty to divorce his wife for any misconduct whatever, when his own misconduct in the first instance was that which threw her into temptation and vice. I find some little resemblance – I find a case in some degree parallel – if I go back to the history of imperial Rome; and, upon that subject, I will venture to call your lordships' attention to the only case in the history of mankind, that appears to me to bear any close resemblance to that which your lordships have taken upon yourselves to try. My lords, scarcely had Octavia become the wife of Nero, when almost on the very day of marriage, she became the subject of his unjust aversion. She was repudiated and dismissed on a false and frivolous pretext. A mistress was received into her place, and before she had been very long banished from the house of her husband, a conspiracy was set on foot against her honour, to impute to her a licentious amour with her slave; and it is stated by the great historian of corrupted Rome, that upon that occasion some of her servants were induced, not by bribes, but by tortures, to depose to facts injurious to her reputation; but that the greater part persisted in faithfully maintaining her innocence. My Lords, it seems, that though the public were convinced that she was innocent, the prosecutor persisted in maintaining her guilt. He banished her from Rome. Her return was like a triumph. The generous people of that country received her with those feelings that ought to have existed in the heart of her husband. But, a second conspiracy was afterwards attempted; and in the course of that conspiracy, it seems that she was convicted and condemned. She was banished to an island in the Mediterranean where she was soon (and this is the only act of mercy), by poison or the dagger, removed from her miserable existence. My Lords, the words of Tacitus are indeed striking. He says, '*Non alia exsul visentium oculos majore misericordia afficit. Meminerant adhuc quidam Agrippinae, a Tiberio; recentior Juliae memoria observabatur, a Claudio pulsae. Sed illis robur aetatis affluerat. Laeta aliqua viderant, et praesentem saevitiam melioris olim fortunae recordatione levabant.*' The death of her father and her brother deprived her of those natural protectors, who might, perhaps, have stood between her and misery and disgrace. But then, says Tacitus, there were still two disgraceful circumstances to afflict her while still under the roof of the palace. '*Huic primus nuptiarum dies loco funeris fuit, deductae in domum, in qua nihil nisi luctuosum haberet erepto per venenum patre, et statim fatre. Tum ancilla domina validior. Et Poppaea non nisi in perniciem uxoris nupta. Postremo crimen omni exitio gravius.*' [No exiled woman ever earned greater sympathy from those who saw her. Some still remembered the banishment of the elder Agrippina by Tiberius and, more recently, of Julia Livilla by Claudius. Yet they had been mature women with happy memories which could alleviate their present sufferings. But Octavia had virtually died on her wedding day. Her new home had brought her nothing but misery. Poison had removed her father, and very soon her brother. Maid had been preferred to mistress. Then she, Nero's wife, had been ruined by her successor. Last came the bitterest of all fates, this accusation.][4]

My lords; her royal highness, the princess of Wales, left this country when the first conspiracy only had been attempted and had been defeated – she left it, the known and unfortunate object of her husband's displeasure. Those who had most basked in her noon-tide rays, had then deserted her. She went abroad to the continent with reports and rumours indeed of a most afflicting kind. Those reports and rumours have at length (perhaps we ought to thank them for it) assumed something of a tangible shape. They may now be grappled with in the shape of substantial charges; and I trust we have demonstrated to your lordships, that they are utterly unfounded and untrue. . . . May I say one word more? I know there is a spirit gone abroad in the world – at least that is the suspicion of your lordships – upon the subject of her majesty the Queen; and I have heard it said, that there has been a low sort of rabble encouraged to acts of mischief; but I know that the same person who uttered that expression was obliged to admit, in the course of a few weeks, because the truth could not be concealed, that the whole of the generous population of England had taken her majesty's part. It is possible that these things may be true. It is certain that among all the sound and middling orders of society, these feelings do exist on behalf of her majesty. It is possible, for aught I know, that there may be some apostles of mischief in some corner, lurking to strike a blow at the constitution, and who may seek to avail themselves of an opportunity for open violence. My lords, if that be so, these generous feelings will be gratified by a verdict of acquittal that your lordships must pronounce; as those mischievous and disaffected men who must be supposed to exist would deprecate nothing so much as to see your lordships, in the face of the power of the Crown, venturing to pronounce a verdict of not guilty against a defendant so prosecuted. My lords, I trust your lordships will not allow the idea of having fear imputed to your minds, to direct you from the straight course of duty. I will venture to say it would be the worst of injustice towards the individual accused, and the worst of cowardice and baseness in any man who acted on such a principle. And therefore, I say, if your minds go along with the evidence – if you are satisfied that all that appeared important has been scattered like dew-drops from the lion's mane, and that we have even supplied some facts to the case of my learned friends which, resting on belief and apprehension, and upon circumstances which they never could bring against us – under such circumstances, your lordships will never think yourselves justified in considering whether your conduct will be imputed to dread of a mob, or Radical mobs, as they are called in the jargon of the day, which I detest – but will pursue that straight course which the principles of justice require. That course is, where the case has not been proved, to acquit the Queen of those charges foully brought up against her. Never was there such an inquiry! Never were there such means of accusation! . . .

. . . My Lords, we have done. This is an inquiry unparalleled in the history of the world – this illustrious lady has been searched out and known – her down-sitting and her up-rising has been searched out – there is no thought in her heart and no word in her lips, but has been brought to this ordeal – there has not an idle thought escaped, or idle look by which she has been betrayed into a moment's impropriety which has not been, by the unparalleled and disgraceful assiduity of her malignant enemies, brought against her. It is an inquisition of the most solemn kind. I know nothing in the whole race of human affairs – I know nothing in the whole view of eternity – which can resemble it, except that great day when the secrets of all hearts shall be disclosed –

He who the sword of Heaven would bear,
Should be as holy as severe:

And if your lordships have been furnished with weapons and powers which scarcely – I had almost said, Omniscience possesses, for coming at the secret, I think you will feel that some duty is imposed on you of endeavouring to imitate, at the same moment, the justice, the beneficence, and the wisdom of that Divine Authority who, when even guilt was detected and vice revealed, said, 'If no accuser can come forward to condemn thee, neither will I condemn thee: go and sin no more.'. . .

Thomas Creevey to Miss Ord

House of Lords, Oct. 24th, 2 o'clock

. . . Denman begun to sum up, and is now engaged in so doing. Their mighty case, you see therefore, is now finished, and a miracle no doubt it must appear to after times that all these charges of an adulterous intercourse which have been got up with

'Meditations among the tombs.' The King inspects the corpse of Henry VIII, who was more successful in getting rid of his unwanted wives, while Castlereagh points out the beheaded Charles I

so much secrecy – that begun six years ago and continued three years – that have had absolute power and money without end to support them, have been one by one demonstrably disproved by witnesses unimpeachable. . . . This admitted fact of the Queen sleeping on deck under the awning, and Bergami doing so likewise, under all the explanatory circumstances of the case, is the sole foundation of the Bill. . . . And now then – will the Lords pass the Bill? I say *No* – I say it is *impossible*: and yet something the villains of Ministers must do to save their own credit. . . . The Duke of Portland told Lord Foley he was one of 60 peers who usually supported the Government, and who would vote against the Bill. This Foley told me himself. I fear this is too high an estimate, but the Duke of Portland himself is a most fair and honorable person.

Brooks's, 5 o'clock

Denman's last two hours have been *brilliant*. His parallel case of Nero and his wife Octavia was perfect in all its parts. . . . I am just going to dinner at Sefton's, and then to go and see Cymbeline with him and Brougham.

York St., 26th Oct.

. . . I wonder when Lauderdale and idiots like himself will begin to think of the situation into which this infamous Bill has thrown this town. Every Wednesday, the scene which caused such alarm at Manchester is repeated under the very nose of Parliament and all the constituted authorities, and in a tenfold degree more alarming. A certain number of regiments of the efficient population of the town march on each of these days in a regular lock step, four or five abreast – banners flying – music playing. . . . I should like anyone to tell me what is to come next if this organized army loses its temper. . . .

30th October

I never saw such a beautiful sight in my life as the Brass Founders' procession to the Queen to-day.[5] I had no notion there had been so many beautiful brass ornaments in all the world. Their men in armour, both horse and foot, were capital; nor was their humour amiss. The procession closed with a very handsome crown borne in state as a present to the Queen, preceded by a flag with the words – 'The Queen's Guard are Men of *Metal*'. I am quite sure there must have been 100,000 people in Piccadilly, all in the most perfect order. . . .

Princess Lieven to Prince Metternich

25th [Oct]. . . As I was coming back from the country yesterday, I ran into the processions which were going to present addresses to the Queen. When they caught sight of my aristocratic equipage, they surrounded me and wanted me to shout, 'Long live the Queen!' I was reading the newspapers in the carriage, and I did not look up. The crowd got bored and left me alone. What an extraordinary sight! I was exactly opposite the King's palace. There were probably 30,000 people in the street, and the processions were made up of some thousands of men on foot and in carriages, the pedestrians marching gravely two by two, carrying inscribed banners: 'Virtue triumphs,' 'Down with the conspirators,' '*Non mi ricordo*;' and shouting 'Hurrah!' Next came the guild of workers in crystal. Two hundred masters and apprentices were each carrying in procession on the end of a fork some specimen of their handiwork – a crown, a sceptre, vases, urns, everything you can think of which might come from that type of shop, all of the very finest workmanship. In the distance, the effect produced was that of walking diamonds; the sun glittered on it; it was really beautiful. Next came the bakers displaying samples of their trade. Yesterday, the Queen received thirty addresses; meanwhile, she is on trial, and the King is in hiding. I forgot to mention the Quakers, accompanied by their wives and daughters – the most moral people in England. . . .

The Black Dwarf, *25 October 1820*

TO THE REFORMERS OF GREAT BRITAIN

THE QUEEN AT THE HEAD OF THE REFORMERS

It is impossible not to congratulate the countless myriads, who have every where gathered round the banner of reform, upon the present most satisfactory aspect of that all-important cause; and upon the consternation which has every where seized upon its enemies. The fatal massacre at Manchester appears to have been the crisis of the question. Since that awful period, *madness* has seemed to seize upon the Borough faction, and as Mr Cobbett justly observes, the frenzy has now encreased to such a height, that it is utterly impossible to calculate upon what its fury may next attempt. But of this, we may be certain – whatever partial mischief may result to individuals, from its ill-judging vengeance, it is sure at last to fall down, impotent and lifeless. . . .

There wanted but a bond of union, a means of understanding each other, among the enemies of corruption, to enable them to breathe the defiance in her ears, which had long terrified her heart. This has been supplied by the wanton, and atrocious attack upon the rights and reputation of the Queen. There were people weak enough to believe that the reformers were the personal enemies of royalty; and it was necessary that this opportunity should be given them of demonstrating that they could respect the royalty, which was respectable – and admire the dignity which was not indebted to any of the external pageantry of a court. You have been enabled satisfactorily to prove that it is the *Borough Faction*, which enslaves the throne, while it oppresses the people, to which you are in reality opposed. You have shewn that, while contending for public rights, you were equally ready to contend for the rights of the monarchy:- and while accused of an intention to destroy the throne, you have been chiefly instrumental in the preservation of your Queen, when *abandoned by the Church*, – fearfully avoided by the aristocracy – and threatened with destruction by the state!. . . .

Their nefarious attempts to stifle the voice of Reform, has had the appalling effect of placing the QUEEN at the head of the REFORMERS. Her Majesty has perceived, that while her safety depends upon the people, her INTERESTS are the same with the interests of the *people*! She has done yet more – she has *proclaimed* those truths – and denounced that *corrupt faction*, which has persecuted her, as it has persecuted the nation at large. A community of feeling, promoted by similarity of suffering, has united the Queen with the people, in the most indissoluble bonds – the bonds of reason and justice – the basis of all rights, and the foundation of all law. . . .

Hobhouse and the moderate Radicals were becoming tired of the long series of popular addresses to the Queen and fearful of either stirring up too much popular excitement for the benefit of their more extreme colleagues, or of wearying the public by over-repetition. As so often in the past and the future, the Radical cause was liable to fail through internal quarrels and disagreements even when victory seemed within reach.

J.C. Hobhouse's diary, Wednesday 25 October

. . . Went in procession heading fifty carriages of St George's addresses to Brandenburgh House – through immense crowds – a foot pace and took 3 hours to go.

30 deputations went up today. I presented four addresses. . . . She then took me aside. I told her that I had just been saying a word to Lady A. Hamilton relative to the propriety of her Majesty not receiving any more addresses in person – You think so, said she – so do I. We had better leave off whilst we are well – we must not keep squeezing the orange till all the juice is out – do pray speak to Mr Wood about this. I told the Queen that it would be necessary to keep her counsel on this subject, that there were a certain set of men who thought they never could have enough of a good thing – & who were very jealous of any prudent advice given to her majesty – I said this pointing to Cartwright. Oh – I understand you she said – yes – he would go on to the day of judgement.

I told the Queen that I thought popular feeling had been so manifested that if the addressing were to go on for ever it could not be more clear than it was now – and that after a certain time all exhibition became futile & ridiculous – she agreed with me. We talked of the bill – I told her I heard it would not pass the Lords – but that there would be a censure. She snapped her fingers & said – *that for their answer*. She then asked me what I thought the Commons would do – my answer was – 'any dirty thing they were desired by Castlereagh'. I quite agree with you, said she – some about me tell me otherwise, but I think as you do. . . . Soon after we went into the great room & I presented the St George's address – Hume & others presented addresses – when the kissing hands had been performed – the Queen withdrew. Mr Fellowes came up to me and said that he very much wished to speak to me as to the manner in which some use might be made of public feeling. I said that the great thing now, was to take care not to exhaust it. He agreed with me & said he had often told *Wood so*, but he was a vain man & liked the continuation of the shows. . . .

Shortly afterwards I went away. The carriage was a long time in getting away from the crowd – cries of gin, beer & apples – like a fair . . .

Sarah Lyttelton to Captain the Hon. F. Spencer

Althorp, October 30, 1820

My Dearest Fritz, –. . . As to your hopes from the coronation promotion, alas they are very groundless! No coronation, nor festivities, nor promotions are in fashion just now truly! If we do but keep tolerably safe from revolutions, massacres, or ruin, we ought to be thankful enough. . . .

Althorp don't come back here, but expects to be obliged to attend the House of Commons, which meets the 23rd November; if indeed the Bill to degrade the Queen is not thrown out by the House of Lords first, which people of all sides seem to be growing to wish. If after all they do condemn her, great riots are to be expected; the whole mob is for her. And immense processions are constantly going up from different sets of people, carrying her *addresses* – fifty open carriages in a string filled with women of the lowest class, both as to rank and character, all dressed out in tawdry silks, old plumes of feathers, white gloves and bare shoulders, went to kiss her hand almost every day while the weather was fine, attended by ten thousand people on foot, choking up Piccadilly and covering the road to Hammersmith. This was early in her trial. But now it is closed they say many people of the highest rank, the Duke of Bedford and Lord Fitzwilliam at their head, will go and leave their names, to shew they think her deserving of acquittal and protection. Her trial has been carried on by the most infamous means – spies, wretches of the meanest kind, bribed and perjured over and over, have been called by the persecutors – and her long life of barbarous ill-usage from her *natural protector* gives a strong bias in her favour. . . .

Princess Lieven to Prince Metternich

The 31st [October]

The peers are collecting their thoughts for the great discussion which begins on Thursday; and, among other methods of arriving at the requisite frame of mind, a large party of them have just gone gadding off to Newmarket. I cannot resist telling you an English pun, interesting because Brougham, the Queen's defender and champion, is the author: 'The Queen is pure innocence (in no sense)'. It bears striking witness to the moral opinion people have of her; legal opinion is another matter; and party opinion another again.

People are beginning to call on the Queen. Lady Jersey wants to go too. Meanwhile, Lady Fitzwilliam has cleared the way by going first. She is a great lady of the most impeccable reputation. . . .

Today, the English have a grand opportunity to gratify their passion for betting. The odds are that the Bill will not pass. It will be decided in a few days; the first debate, fixed for the day after tomorrow, will give one an idea of what is going to happen to the Bill. I am as anxious about it as any Englishwoman. They say that the Queen is in a pitiful state of nerves. Really, I am soft-hearted enough to feel sorry for the woman.

Notes

1. Major John Cartwright (1740–1824), the veteran reformer.
2. Nerot's Hotel was a fashionable London hostelry.
3. Prince Leopold, former husband of Princess Charlotte.
4. *Annals of Imperial Rome*, trans. Michael Grant, Penguin revised ed. 1973, bk xiv, p. 343.
5. See page 173.

CHAPTER EIGHT

The Queen Triumphant

The closing debate on the Bill of Pains and Penalties began with a summing-up by the Lord Chancellor, Lord Eldon, on 2 November. On the following day Lord Grey, the leader of the opposition peers, made one of his most notable speeches, described by Creevey as 'beautiful – magnificent – all honor and right feeling, with the most powerful argument into the bargain'. Grey had refused to make the trial a party question but had attended conscientiously throughout the proceedings and claimed that he was influenced only by the evidence. He told Princess Lieven that at the outset he would have voted against the Queen, but that despite his disgust at the disclosures of her conduct which had been presented he could not support the drastic measures proposed in the bill. His fine oratory and his distinguished reputation swayed many votes. The Prime Minister who followed Grey also took a fair and moderate line, advising the peers not to support the bill unless they were satisfied of the Queen's adultery.

At 3 p.m. on 6 November the House divided, 123 peers voting for the bill and ninety-five against. The minority included all the leading opposition peers but also many Tories and one archbishop, some of whom believed the Queen guilty but were opposed to the divorce clause. As Princess Lieven wrote, the ninety-five included 'all the greatest, richest, and most respectable members . . . an imposing and alarming body for the Ministry to have to face'. The size of the minority was indeed considered fatal to the bill. Creevey immediately pronounced it dead, and at Princess Lieven's that same evening Grey declared it 'tantamount to a defeat'. The ministers in a last effort to salvage the bill then proposed to leave out the divorce clause, in the hope that this would placate some of their usual supporters, but the opposition voted to keep it in in order to retain the maximum numbers against the bill as a whole. As Creevey noted, the majority included all the opposition, while all the ministers and almost all the bishops voted in the minority.

The end was clearly in sight, and when the majority for the bill fell to nine on the third reading two days later the Prime Minister rose to announce that the bill was withdrawn. The Londoners, as Princess Lieven reported, were 'mad with enthusiasm for the Queen', firearms were let off and the town was illuminated for five nights in succession, while the young Thomas Macaulay, an undergraduate at Cambridge, exclaimed that 'the Country is saved!' – an opinion he may have revised a few days later when the townspeople's celebrations triggered a great riot and confrontation with the university. The Cobbett family were exultant, and William's daughter Anne called it 'the greatest triumph . . . gained by the people of England that ever was gained in this world'. Her brother John declared that 'the Queen is a Radical' and that her cause had mobilized 'the whole of the people' against 'the King, Ministers, and all courtiers and all Parsons and Priests of every description'. From the opposite end of the political spectrum a correspondent of Lord Colchester bewailed that she had become 'the rallying point and the tool of all the enemies of every description of the King, the Ministry, and the Constitution'. Radical journals rhapsodized in verse over their triumph, and the citizens of Westminster, among many others, voted an address of congratulation to their heroine. *The Times* had particular reason to rejoice: its consistent support of the Queen resulted in the doubling of its circulation to 15,000 copies a day during the 'trial'.

However, calmer observers foretold that the mood would pass as quickly as it had sprung up. Lady Erne thought that 'many will discover their own folly and the imposition to which they have yielded', and when the Queen's attempt to exploit her victory by demanding a palace, an allowance, and the restoration of her name to the liturgy was rebuffed, it soon became apparent that if the government stood firm the crisis would die away. By the end of November, with Parliament prorogued for a breathing-space, things were beginning to return to normal.

Yet the crisis seemed likely to have some permanent significance. Richard Rush, the American ambassador, was impressed by the strength and resilience of the British political system, in face of the tremendous popular pressure of the day and the 'unconquerable resolution' of the people, and by the wisdom of the government in allowing the tempest to blow itself out. Creevey was more pessimistic: the people, he wrote, 'have learnt how to marshal and organize themselves, and they have learnt at the same time the success of their strength'. Most ominous of all, at the mast-head of the tallest ship in the river there hung 'the effigy of a Bishop, twenty or thirty feet in length, with his heels uppermost'. Who was the better prophet a short time would tell. In the meantime, the Radicals celebrated the Queen's triumph by organizing a thanksgiving service in St Paul's Cathedral on 29 November, preceded by a great procession from Brandenburgh House in Hammersmith described by *The Times* in terms almost of an imperial Roman triumph. The service, attended by large numbers of the middle classes of both sexes, appropriately included psalm 140: 'Deliver me, O Lord, from the evil man.'

The Bill of Pains and Penalties as voted on by the House of Lords, 9 November

Bill entitled, An Act to deprive Her Majesty, Caroline Amelia Elizabeth, of the Title, Prerogatives, Rights, Privileges, and Exemptions of Queen Consort of this Realm; and to dissolve the Marriage between His Majesty and the said Caroline Amelia Elizabeth.

Whereas, in the year 1814, her majesty Caroline Amelia Elizabeth, then princess of Wales, and now Queen Consort of this realm, being at Milan in Italy, engaged in her service, in a menial situation, one Bartolomeo Bergami, a foreigner of low station, who had before served in a similar capacity:

And whereas after the said Bartolomeo Bergami had so entered the service of her royal highness the said princess of Wales, a most unbecoming and degrading intimacy commenced between her said royal highness and the said Bartolomeo Bergami; and her said royal highness not only advanced the said Bartolomeo Bergami to a high situation in her royal highness's household, and received into her service many of his near relations, some of them in inferior and others in high and confidential situations about her royal highness's person, but bestowed upon him other great and extraordinary marks of favour and distinction, and conferred upon him a pretended order of knighthood, which her royal highness had taken upon herself to institute, without any just or lawful authority:

And, whereas also, her royal highness, whilst the said Bartolomeo Bergami was in her said service, further unmindful of her exalted rank and station, and of her duty to your Majesty, and wholly regardless of her own honour and character, conducted herself toward the said Bartolomeo Bergami, both in public and private, in various places and countries which her royal highness visited, with indecent and offensive familiarity and freedom, and carried on a licentious, disgraceful, and adulterous intercourse with the said Bartolomeo Bergami, which continued for a long period of time, during her royal highness's residence abroad; by which conduct of her said royal highness, great scandal and dishonour have been brought upon your majesty's family and this kingdom.

Therefore, to manifest our deep sense of such scandalous, disgraceful, and vicious conduct on the part of her said majesty, by which she has violated the duty which she owed to your majesty, and has rendered herself unworthy of the exalted rank and station of Queen Consort of this realm; and to evince our just regard for the dignity of the Crown, and the honour of this nation:

We your majesty's most dutiful and loyal subjects, the Lords spiritual and temporal, and Commons, in parliament assembled, do humbly entreat your majesty that it may be enacted; and be it enacted by the King's most excellent majesty, by and with the advice and consent of the Lords spiritual and temporal, and Commons, in this present parliament assembled, and by the authority of the same, that her said majesty, Caroline Amelia Elizabeth, from and after the passing of this act, shall be and is hereby deprived of the title of Queen, and of all the prerogatives, rights, privileges, and exemptions appertaining to her as Queen Consort of this realm; and that her said majesty shall, from and after the passing of this act, for ever be disabled and rendered incapable of using, exercising, and enjoying the same, or any of them; and moreover, that the marriage between his majesty and the said Caroline Amelia Elizabeth be, and the same is hereby from henceforth for ever wholly dissolved, annulled, and made void, to all intents, constructions, and purposes whatever.

Thomas Creevey to Miss Ord

House of Lords, 2 o'clock, 2nd November

Eldon begun this morning, and it was expected he would have made a great masterly judicial summing up; instead of which, he spoke for an hour and a quarter only, and a more feeble argument for his own vote I never heard in all my life. He begun by intimating very clearly that the preamble of the Bill was to be altered, and the divorce part given up: then, without reserve or shame, he abandoned Miocci and Demont, and, in truth, all the filth of his own green bag, and all the labours of the Milan commission. Howman's evidence and the admitted fact of Bergami's sleeping on the deck under the same awning as the Queen, was his sheet anchor. . . . He said he was perfectly convinced of her guilt, and he further said that no one who had not the same opinion ought to vote for the second reading. Erskine followed, and had spoken for about three quarters of an hour, when he fainted away, and was carried out of the House; since when, that villain Lauderdale has been speaking.

Yesterday and today have altered most materially the state of public opinion as to the fate of this diabolical Bill. The cursed rats are said to have returned most rapidly to their old quarters, and the ministerial majority is rising in the market to 40, 45 and 50. It is added, too, that the Bill is certainly to pass, and to be with us on the 23rd. I will not give my assent to any one of these reports till I have ocular proof of their being true; at the same time, with such rogues and madmen as one has to speculate upon, it is being almost mad oneself to expect anything being done that is right. . . .

House of Lords, 3rd Nov., ¼ past 3

I have not heard *all* Lord Grey's speech, being obliged to go into the City, which I am truly sorry for, as what I did hear was quite of the highest order – beautiful – magnificent – all honor and right feeling, with the most powerful argument into the bargain. There is nothing approaching this damned fellow in the kingdom, when he mounts his best horse. . . . Lord Liverpool is now answering Lord Grey, and is as bad as one would wish him to be.

Princess Lieven to Prince Metternich

November 3

I am closing this without having any news to add. I don't know what will happen at the debate today. Yesterday's was to have been distinguished by the presence of the Queen and her delivery of a speech she had composed herself. Her lawyers prevented her from coming. Her plan was, and still is, to give her own account of the relations between the King and herself, to reveal everything she knows about his behaviour, and not to confine herself to that alone but to give a little historical narrative of the behaviour of each member of the Royal Family, not forgetting the offspring of the unmarried princesses. She is quite capable of telling the whole story. . . .

. . . It is thought that the Ministers will get a majority today; but it is not so certain that they will obtain a majority for the adoption of the Bill. In fact, nobody has any news, and everyone's longing for it. Meanwhile, Lady Jersey is wearing the Queen's portrait round her neck!

The 6th

I am going to town to hear about this idiotic affair. Today the Bill has its second reading, or if it hasn't, that means it is rejected – one hardly knows which to pray for. It needs talent to have brought things to such a pass that you can only jump out of the frying-pan into the fire. I don't remember if I told you what Brougham said to me one day. He was asking me what people on the Continent thought of events in England. I replied: 'Don't tell me you don't know.' 'Quite true,' he said, 'they are laughing at me.' 'Exactly.'

Thomas Creevey to Miss Ord

Brooks's, 5 o'clock [6 November]

All is over – that is with the 2nd reading – 123 for the Bill and 95 against it – leaving a majority for the Bill of 28 only. This is fatal. Eleven Bishops voted for it, and the Archbishop of York alone against it. . . .

Brooks's, 4 o'clock, 8th Nov.

The House has been up these two hours, a division having taken place upon the question whether the divorce clause should be part of the Bill. In favor of this 129 voted, including all our people: against it there were 53, including *every one* of the Ministers, and all the Bishops but three. Was there ever such a spectacle! . . . In ordinary times a Government would instantly abandon a measure over which they had no control; there is an end, however, here to speculating upon men's conduct. . . .

Brooks's, Nov. 9

. . . Castlereagh got roughly handled at Covent Garden last night; so much so, as to be obliged to decamp from the house. Erskine was greatly applauded. . . .

Princess Lieven to Prince Metternich

The 7th [November]

You cannot imagine how triumphant the Opposition are over yesterday's division in the House of Lords – a minority of 95, among them all the greatest, richest and most respectable members. Many people attached for thirty years to Mr Pitt's Ministry and sworn enemies of the Whigs; others whose positions and fortunes are dependent on the goodwill of the Government; an archbishop – all these make up an imposing and alarming body for the Ministry to have to face. Lord Grey is delighted. I spent the evening with him; he gave me his word that he had intended to vote for the Bill and said that, if I had taken the trouble to watch him at the beginning to the trial, I should have seen what horror the very name of the Queen inspired in him, so convinced was he that the terms of the Bill would be found justified by the enquiry. 'This enquiry', he said, 'can convince no-one of the crime imputed to the Queen. We are sworn on our honour to judge that woman according to the evidence; we have to put aside our prejudices and any private opinions we may have. It is our duty to give judgement according to whatever conviction we may have arrived at from the evidence. There is no choice; nothing has been proved. Read the names of the minority and you will see what all honest and independent people think. A majority of 28 on a matter of State is tantamount to a defeat.' This is the general opinion; and goodness knows what the Ministers are going to do. . . .

The 8th

The Government and the Opposition have started a battle of wits that is interesting to watch. The first want to stay in power, the second to get into power – that is the explanation of their fantastic behavour. They are no more concerned with the Queen now than with me. The Opposition voted against the second reading of the Bill because, by doing so, they hoped to throw out the Government. The latter, on the other hand, saw that their honour as well as their political existence depended on getting the second reading passed as a justification of their action. Once that was achieved, they no longer cared whether the Bill passed; and, indeed, they did not want it to pass with the divorce clause, which they knew was distasteful to the people. Without that clause, the Bill might pass in the Commons; with it, never. So the Ministers are now siding against the divorce; at once, the Opposition insist on the divorce with the two-fold aim of imperiling the Bill in the Commons and of pleasing the King. The King finds himself deserted by his Ministers and supported by the Whigs in his dearest wish – the divorce. Yesterday, the majority in favour of that clause was made up of the enemies of the Government: isn't it extraordinary? Morality and the peace of the country go for nothing; thirst for power is the only thing that counts; I am a little disgusted by the spectacle and no longer find it amusing.

Talking of this, I attracted the attention of the mob yesterday. I was driving to Bond Street when I met the Queen in a State coach with six horses, being led at a walking pace, and escorted as usual by some hundreds of scallywags. As soon as they saw my carriage, they stopped it and ordered my servants to take off their hats, and me to let the window down. Neither I nor my servants obeyed. I was surrounded by people shouting abuse, whistling and booing. Meanwhile, the Queen passed by, throwing me a withering glance. I saw two enormous black eyebrows, as big as two of my fingers put together: the contents of two pots of rouge on her cheeks: and a veil over everything. She looks completely brazen. I broke up her escort, for half of them followed me with the same friendly demonstrations and did not leave me till I reached Lady Granville's door. They are decent people all the same; they carried off the honours in noise – that was all – and I held the honours in inflexibility.

You will hear by this post the decision about the fate of the Queen. Tomorrow, there will be a third reading; it looks like passing by a small majority. My letter will be handed over before the House adjourns. I could not find out anything from the Duke of York of what the King thinks of his nine Ministers voting against the divorce; he is extremely reticent on this subject. It was nicely done on his part, to vote for the divorce in his capacity as heir apparent to the Crown.

'Justice miraculously delivered from the voraciousness of her crying enemy' (November 1820). The King and the Lord Chancellor ride a crocodile which attempts to crush Justice in its jaws, but Caroline is supported by John Bull, a sailor, and a soldier, and protected by the eye of heaven

The 11th, 9 o'clock

I must begin my letter with the great topic of conversation in England, which has been occupying me ever since yesterday. The Bill against the Queen has been withdrawn. That is a great piece of good news. It may prevent incalculable harm. But who knows what evils and dangers the measure may yet bring in its train? Why, if you are going to finish by admitting yourself mistaken, allow such an affair to drag on so long? Was it worth the five months of disturbance we have just lived through? The throne has been degraded – what a mistake! Now come all the difficulties over details: what is to be done, what decision is to be taken about the woman? Everything still remains to be decided. However, there is general enthusiasm; all parties congratulate themselves on no longer being faced with the prospect of a revolution. That is the chief, the dominating feeling up to now. The Opposition have high hopes. The Ministers have been compromised in public opinion without satisfying their master – it is a position which offers natural opportunities to their opponents.

Do you know that the Queen had a protest ready in case she should have been convicted? It began like this: 'Carolina Regina in spite of you all.' It was not read; for Lord Liverpool withdrew the Bill as soon as the result of the division was announced. The Queen was waiting in the next room. When they came to tell her the news she burst into tears and cried: 'I am lost.' That convinces me that she is a woman of intelligence. What will you say and think of all this? The way the whole affair has been mismanaged! What does the King say now? I can think of a thousand questions and not a single answer. What I understand least of all is how the Ministers can remain after what has happened. I could not bring myself to send word to the Duke of Wellington; I don't know what to say to him, for I can imagine how upset he will be. Only two days ago, he said to me again and again: 'We must go on, we must persevere to the finish.' England will feel the ill effects of this miscarriage for a long time. . . .

The Times, *9 November*

DRURY-LANE THEATRE

We have frequently noticed, in our accounts of theatrical performances, the powerful interest shown by the audiences in the proceedings against her Majesty, and the quick sympathy with which every passage that could be deemed illustrative of her situation has been seized on and marked with loud expressions of applause. This interest has continued to deepen as the great national drama has approached its catastrophe, and never assumed as marked a character as it did last night during the representation of the tragedy of *Othello*, which indeed abounds with parallels that seem to have been conceived in a spirit prophetic of the present age. Nor were these alone selected by the audience, for scarcely a passage that ingenuity could wrest into an application was suffered to pass without the popular comment. Applause followed *Iago's* remark to *Othello* when commencing his deep-laid train of villainy:–

> Where's that palace, whereinto foul things
> Sometimes intrude not?

And still greater the well-known passage that succeeds it:–

> Good name in man or woman, dear, my love,
> Is the immediate jewel of their souls:
> Who steals my purse, steals trash – 'tis something, nothing;
> But he that filches from me my good name
> Robs me of that which not enriches him,
> And makes me poor indeed.

Though the tragedy was extremely well acted, the performers, in the midst of an interest of a higher nature, became a secondary object of attention. The susceptibility increased as the play proceeded, and reached its height in the scene where *Emilia*, indignant at the wrongs her mistress has received, brands the unknown villain with reproaches to which language can add no bitterness. They derived, too, their utmost force from the emphatic delivery of Mrs Glover. The repetition of *Othello's* accusation of *Desdemona*, and the enumeration of the injurious epithets bestowed on her by the jealous Moor, seemed to animate the pit with one spirit.
Then followed:

> Has she forsook so many noble matches,
> Her father, and her country, and her friends,
> To be called w—?

with applause so great that it was some time before the performance could proceed. The expression of *Emilia's* suspicion,

I will be hang'd if some eternal villain,
Some busy and insinuating rogue,
Some cogging, cozening slave, to get some office,
Have not devis'd this slander,

produced a more powerful and more durable effusion of the popular sentiment, accompanied with the waving of hats and handkerchiefs. Silence was again restored, and continued till Mrs Glover arrived at the following lines:–

The Moor's abused by some most villanous knave –
Some base notorious knave – some scurvy fellow:
O Heav'n, that such companion thou'dst unfold,
And put in every honest hand a whip,
To lash the rascal naked through the world!

We can compare the effect of this only to an electric shock, or a spark thrown on gunpowder. It seemed to put nearly the whole house in motion. The manner of testifying the feeling was the same as in the preceding instances; but more sudden, more vehement, and more durable. The strength of the impression was such as to create a scene which all who witnessed will long find stamped upon their recollection. We have little space left for the actors. Mr Cooper played *Othello* well, and Mrs Chester *Desdemona* in a style not without interest, but deficient in power. Booth was the *Iago*, whom he continued to transform into a *petit-maître*. For Bernard's *Cassio* we cannot say much. The remaining characters were filled as usual.

11 November

COVENT-GARDEN THEATRE

Joy at the result of the proceedings against the Queen was manifested last night at this theatre in the strongest and most marked manner. The play, which was *Twelfth Night*, with the recent alterations, had no sooner concluded, than a general cry arose from every part of the house for 'God save the Queen'. This call was frequently repeated, and completely drowned the sound of the music in the orchestra when a symphony was played between the acts. The curtain at last drew up for the farce of *A Rowland for an Oliver*, and the performers in the first scene came forward, but they endeavoured in vain to make themselves heard. The cries of 'Off, off,' and 'The Queen' were loud and incessant. The performers obeyed the order to retire, and Mr Abbot came on the stage and addressed the audience. It was, however, impossible to hear a word he said; but, in consequence of some communication which passed between him and part of the audience nearest him in the pit, a great number of the performers came on the stage, and the orchestra played 'Rule Britannia'. It appeared to have been expected that this would satisfy the demand of the audience, but it did not. The air was received with plaudits but the orchestra was no sooner silent than the call for 'God save the Queen' recommenced. The attempt to proceed with the farce was renewed, but it was reduced to a pantomime. After going on for a considerable time in this way, Fawcett, who was on the stage, came forward, and held another conference with some of the audience near enough the stage to hold converse with him.

The result was complete submission to the will of the audience. The air of 'God save the King' was then sung by the musical part of the company, but every stanza concluded with 'God save the Queen'. The return of these words was eagerly watched, and replied to with enthusiastic cheers. The whole of the audience stood up – gentlemen waving their hats, and ladies their handkerchiefs. The house in which this striking proof of public interest in the cause of the Queen, and of gladness at her triumph over her malignant but now defeated and humiliated enemies, was displayed, was exceedingly crowded. The company in some of the private boxes took an active part in the call for this tribute of respect to her Majesty, and in the applause which accompanied it.

Thomas Creevey to Miss Ord

Brooks's, Nov. 10, 3 o'clock

Three times three! if you please, before you read a word further. The Bill is gone, thank God! to the devil. Their majority was brought down to 9 – 108 to 99; and then the dolorous Liverpool came forward and *struck*. He moved that *his own* Bill be read this day six months. You may well suppose the state we are all in. The Queen was in the House at the time, but Brougham sent her off instantly. . . . The state of the town is beyond everything. I wish to God you could see Western. He is close by my side, but has not *uttered* yet – such is his surprise.

York Street, 11th Nov.

I was a bad boy *for the first time* last night, and drank an extra bottle of claret with Foley, Dundas, Western &c., &c., in the midst of our brilliant illuminations at Brooks's: not that I was the least *screwy*, but it has made me somewhat nervous. . . . We could distinctly see there were high words between Liverpool and Eldon before the former struck his colours, and when he moved the further consideration that day six months, Eldon answered with a very distinct and audible 'Not content'. It is quite impossible any human being could have disgraced himself more than the Duke of Clarence. When his name was called in the division on the 3rd reading, he leaned over the rail of the gallery as far into the House as he could, and then halloed – 'Content', with a yell that would quite have become a savage. The Duke of York followed with his 'Content' delivered with singular propriety. . . . It must always be remembered to the credit of our hereditary aristocracy that a decided majority voted against this wicked Bill. It was the two sets of Union Peers[1] and these villains of the Church[2] that nearly destroyed for ever the character of the House of Lords. However, thank God it is no worse. . . .

   . . . The people have learnt a great lesson from this wicked proceeding: they have learnt how to marshal and organise themselves, and they have learnt at the same time the success of their strength. Waithman,[3] who has just called upon me, tells me that the arrangements made in every parish in and about London on this occasion are perfectly miraculous – quite new in their nature – and that they will be of eternal application in all our public affairs. . . . They say the river below bridge to-day is the most beautiful sight in the world; every vessel is covered with colors, and at the head of the tallest mast in the river is the effigy of a Bishop, 20 or 30 feet in length, with his heels uppermost, hanging from the mast-head.

Lady Charlotte Lindsay to Miss Berry

Nov. 10th. – . . . I was in the House of Lords all this day, and in great anxiety as to the result, not only from wishing well to the poor Queen, but also from selfish motives: for, had the Bill passed into the House of Commons, what fresh examinations and renewed torments awaited me there, to say nothing of the grievous disappointment of not spending this winter with you at Rome. The Queen was also in one of the private rooms adjoining to the House of Lords, and when she went away, after it was known that the Bill was withdrawn, an immense crowd of people followed her carriage, hanging about the wheels, huzzaing, and congratulating her with every demonstration of delight; but there was no riot or attack of any sort upon the carriages of those Lords who had voted for the Bill. I went to the Queen's room to offer her my very sincere congratulations, but she was gone. I found there Mr Denman, who was in as high a state of excitement as myself; this sympathy united us. We embraced, and, according to the good 'John Bull' notions of friendship, he invited me to dinner; but I was engaged to dine with Mr Damer, at Twickenham. . . .

The manner in which I have been cried up and complimented by the Opposition, for having had sufficient presence of mind in some manner to defeat the designs of the counsel for the Bill, of drawing from me opinions that I conceived they had no right to extract, might have turned a head excitable as mine, and persuaded me that I am a female Solomon; while, on the other hand, the scurrilous and abominable attack upon my evidence in the ministerial papers, and the horrible anonymous letters with which I am daily persecuted, might, to a person of my nervous constitution, have frightened me into imagining myself a creature despised and contemned by all the honest part of the community! You know exactly all that I have thought and felt, and I trust that you will acquit me of any dishonourable or mean motives in all that I have done or said. I have suffered much uneasiness, terror, and perplexity during all this business.

I must not omit to tell you that Lord Liverpool, with much gentlemanlike good nature, put a stop to the abusive attacks upon me in those papers over which he had any influence.

Farewell, &c.

Charlotte Lindsay

Mrs Arbuthnot's journal, November 1820

10th. – Heard from Mr A. that the third reading of the Bill had been carried by a majority of nine & that, on that, Ld Liverpool had withdrawn the Bill. Mr A. was much pleased with the event of the Bill, for he had been most anxious not to have it in the Commons; and L^d L[iverpool] had declared that, if it was carried by 16, he w^d not give it up. The King was *delighted* when he heard the Bill was lost, that Bill which he had forced on the Ministers & the country. After this, what reliance can be placed on him!!

Mr A. proceeds to say, 'There was a terrible scene in the Cabinet last night. Three fourths of them were for getting rid of the Bill; but L^d L[iverpool] was in a phrenzy, & his rage got so high that for a time it stopped all deliberation. He abused the Chancellor. He complained of the ill usage he had received from several in the room, without particularising them, & ended by crying.'

The King has the folly to wish the Parliament sh^d meet immediately to settle her provision, but this will be resisted.

13th. – . . . Mr Arbuthnot seems to think the Government will not last long; that Ld Liverpool is tired of office & dying to resign; that Mr Peel's party (the Speaker at their head) abuse Ministers for not resigning; & that Mr. Canning's party, throughout the business of the Queen, has behaved shamefully. All this is certainly bad for the Government.

14th. – Had a letter from the Duke of Wellington, in which he says the King is still obstinate for the meeting of Parliament on the 23d, & that the Queen has sent to *demand a palace*!!, which will be refused. The King had talked of going to Hanover, but the Duke says there is not much chance of that unless we allow him to take his eating & drinking money, his money for buhl furniture & for buying horses, which we could not think of doing. There have been illuminations for the Queen's *triumph* as it is called, but Mr A. says the mob were not ill humoured. We had illuminations in all the neighbouring towns, but there was no ill humour. At the same time it is not a pleasant spirit, & it all arises from the King's great unpopularity.

17th. – They have had long & warm discussion with the King about the meeting of Parl^t, & he has at length given up & agreed to the prorogation. Mr Arburthnot saw him several times on the subject & says his language & manner were those of a Bedlamite; that he held forth for an hour and two hours at a time about not being able to *uphold the Ministers*, when in fact it is they who uphold him, & saying that all his unpopularity was gained from his standing by them.

'The bill thrown out, but the pains and penalties inflicted' (15 November 1820). The King and his attendants, in Chinese dress, receive the news of the withdrawal of the bill. The ladies are his mistresses, Lady Hertford, Lady Conyngham, and Mrs Quentin

Henry Brougham to his brother James

Friday, November 10, 1820

The bill is thrown out to-day. We run them to nine majority, so they gave in.

What will happen here God knows. The town is of course in a bustle. I should have been eaten up alive to-day, as I was near being yesterday at the Lord Mayor's Day, but I came away by a by-path. I walked quietly off therefore, and then got home unobserved; only I was recognised looking at something in a shop-window, so I got into a hackney-coach, and then went and dined as usual at the Bench table, Lincoln's Inn, and was all evening in chambers, and have been in court all to-day.

No business all day in the City, and now all is illuminated, even more than after Waterloo; and *it may be better* for the country, if it is well improved. If there is a change of system and an end of jobbing, it will be well. . . .

Lady Granville to Lady G. Morpeth

London: November 12, 1820

The Ministers found the King is a dreadfully nervous and irritable state, so much so that they had thought of sending the Archbishop of Canterbury to him to calm his mind. He shuts himself up, will see nobody, and is having new keys made to all the gates, to prevent the neighbourhood having access to the park and *alentours*. . . .

Princess Lieven to Prince Metternich

Monday evening, the 13th

At the moment I am writing to you, there is a terrific burst of firing in the street. That is the English way of rejoicing. They fire off cannons and muskets. . . . The whole city is illuminated, but we have held out, as well as our windows; I can see that the mob is pleased at the victory of the Queen only because it gives an excuse for all this tomfoolery. She will soon be forgotten. I am not so sure that the Opposition will forget its advantage as quickly. Many supporters of the Government will desert it. They cannot forgive the Cabinet for having led them into voting for the Bill and then left them in the lurch. I know three peers whom they will not get back on their side. The King is said to be resigned; I can't believe it.

London, the 14th

The mob is going on in the same way; the city is still illuminated. The people are mad with enthusiasm for the Queen, and, here and there, have indulged in looting and all kinds of brutality. I told my servants that they could take off their hats as much as they liked; when it is a question of being shot, I submit to the law of force; and, as I have no military escort, the mob is my master. They will never get it out of their heads now that it was they who triumphed over Parliament and the Ministers: and it is true up to a point. Cowardice influenced a large number of votes; and, in the end, it was that formidable minority which produced the result we have seen.

Letters from Thomas Babington Macaulay[4] to his father, Zachary Macaulay

13 November 1820 [Cambridge]

My dear Father,
All here is ecstasy. 'Thank God, the Country is saved!' were my first words when I caught a glimpse of the papers of Friday night. 'Thank God, the country is saved,' is written in every face and echoed by every voice. Even the symptoms of popular violence, three days ago so terrific, are now displayed with good humour and received with cheerfulness. Instead of curses on the Lords, on every post and every wall is written, 'All is as it should be' – 'Justice done at last.' – and similar mottoes expressive of the sudden turn of public feeling. How the case may stand in London I do not know, but here the public danger, like all dangers which depend merely on human opinons and feelings, has disappeared from our sight almost in the twinkling of an eye. . . .

Cambridge Nov. 21 1820

My Dear Father,
. . . Nothing can be more absurd than the reports of the London papers about our Cambridge tumults. The disturbance had nothing whatever to do with political feeling, but was merely an ebullition of insolence in the lower orders of the town and of high spirits and frolic among the gownsmen. Many men who look upon the Queen as an injured Saint, and the Milan Commission as an assembly more atrocious than the Council of Pandemonium, were concerned in the attack on the townspeople. Romilly for instance, a friend of mine who has inherited his father's politics as well as his warmth of heart and energy of character, after haranguing me for an hour in support of the Queens innnocence, got his gown torn and his head broken in attacking her champions. The disturbance was greater than I ever saw before in Cambridge, though both parties have overstated the number of the combatants. There might be four hundred gownsmen at the scene of the main battle, but certainly not more. I did not display so much heroism as you exhibited in Cadogan place. Indeed if my windows had been broken, I could neither have slept in my rooms that night nor sate in them next day. There was not, however, I believe, much danger; at least the injury done fell far short of the public apprehension. . . .

Anne Cobbett to James P. Cobbett, in New York

[11 Michael's Place] Brompton

November 15, 1820

My Dear James, – I suppose the same vessel which carries you this will convey to the Yankees the intelligence that even in an aristocratic country, a people under even a Kingly government may sometimes command and have their will; the greatest triumph has been gained by the people of England that ever was gained in this world. The Ministers had carried their Bill at the third reading by a majority of *nine*, but, fearing the vengeance of the people, they did not dare send it to the House of Commons, so they *gave it up*. The decision was known about *four* o'clock in the afternoon, and in less than half-an-hour afterwards, guns were firing in all directions, the church bells ringing in all parts of the town, and every street, and all the suburbs have been most brilliantly illuminated for the last *five* nights; everybody, whether the

Queen's friends or not, being compelled to light up, and the Ministers obliged to fly out of town and leave their houses filled with police officers. This is the triumph of the *people*, and they do enjoy it, I assure you. All the gentlemen's carriages are stopped and abused unless their servants have white bows in their hats, or laurel leaves. The Mail and other coaches that carried the news into the country spread it about very soon. At Winchester, where the Mail gets in at *three* in the morning, the parish officers were soon called up, all the Parsons were awaked before daylight by the ringing of the bells. Benbow (who lives opposite to where you may remember Mr Clement lived in the Strand), and from whence has issued that which has *caused* this triumph, has two fine emblematic and appropriate transparencies, and has the whole front of his house one mass of blaze. I think he ought to think *his* injuries avenged, for I assure you Govr. says *he* is satisfied, for his own part. Everybody gives *him* the credit for it, solely and undividedly. There will be a change of Ministers, but though the Whigs *want* to get in, still they seem *shy*, for they know they cannot get in unless the people help them, and in that case they know they must give *some* reform; and the Govr. says unless they do that they *shall not* come in, and if they give a *little*, the rest will soon follow. There will be another election, in that case, and then the Govr. will be got in by some means or another. At present the whole country is mad with rejoicing. It was the threat in the concluding part of the queen's letter which frightened them, and *her* triumph is *ours*, you know, my dear Jumpy. They have gone through the mockery of trapsing the Military through the streets every night, though they knew they could not trust them, and they actually *cheered* and *waved their caps* in passing Benbow's. Papa got a coach and took us all through the town two nights since, to see the illuminations, and the spectacle was fine beyond anything you can imagine. All the ships in the river lighted to the mast-heads, processions marching with bands of music carrying busts of the Queen with the crown on her head, covered with laurels, playing God save the Queen and bearing torches; altogether the sight was such as to overcome one, at the same time that it was most particularly gratifying to *us*.

John M. Cobbett to James P. Cobbett, in New York

[11 Michael's Place] Brompton

November 26, 1820

My Dear James,

. . . The Trial and all other *particulars* you will doubtless have seen from the papers. But you may not be able to extract from them the state of the public feeling and of the miserable plight of the two political factions: the Whigs and Tories. I will do what I can in drawing their cadaverous portraits.

In the first place, with one accord, the people, the whole of the people, Church people, Methodists and sectarians of all sorts, Tradesmen, *Farmers*, labourers, and *Soldiers* as much as any, had all long ago declared for the Queen, leaving for her enemies the King, Ministers, and all courtiers and all Parsons and Priests of every description. This, in the first place, was almost a Revolution; for the Queen is a Radical, and has consequently joined all together against the Government.

Seeing that the whole public had decided *prima facie* in her favour, the Ministers saw that they must find her guilty to save themselves from the odium of maltreating an *innocent* woman; therefore, until the last moment, they fully intended to pass the Bill. But the being *obliged* to drop it when it was on the eve of passing has been more to their disgrace than it would have been had they dropped it in an earlier stage of the proceedings. And if you read the debates immediately subsequent to the trial, you will see that it was at last thrown out merely from a fear of public vengeance, as a majority, certainly, of those who voted *against* the passing of the Bill declared the Queen guilty, but said 'it was dangerous, from the state of the public mind, to press the measure any further'. A confession of mob influence which must have stuck in their Lordships' throats sometime before they could give it utterance.

There is nothing now going on, the Parliament being prorogued for two months. But the whole Government is one universally hated monster! And the Ministers would willingly turn out, but those who come in must attend to the voice of the people, and all can plainly see that that voice would call, first, for the Trial of the Ministers as Criminals, and secondly, for Parliamentary Reform. The Ministers stay in to save their heads, and the Whigs stay out because they cannot perform what they *must* promise before they will be let in.

The state of things is, therefore, as you may conceive, delightful. The Governor's power is monstrous now, and they all feel it. He has pointed out their difficulties to them, and they plainly see that they can do nothing without giving the people all they want, and their stomachs are not quite brought to yet. We send you some papers giving account of the public rejoicings. Letters could not contain half.

Papa presented two or three addresses to the Q. one day, and has had many more every presenting day since, but he always sends a deputy.

F. Burton to Lord Colchester

Upper Brook Street, Nov. 15th

My Dear Lord, – . . . . Sure I am that on your own account you will not regret, though for the sake of the public many with me will have regretted, your absence from home. No doubt your curiosity must have been too much alive to rest satisfied without obtaining an ample detail of all the proceedings in this exhibition of national disgrace, which, though they have served to convict the offender, have not only failed of producing the sentence which ought to have followed, but have left her in a condition to gratify the worst of her bad passions, that of revenge.

She certainly is at this moment the rallying point and the tool of all the enemies of every description of the King, the Ministry, and the Constitution. Yet there is a time after which John Bull is able to distinguish black from white, and to return to his reason. It may be hoped, therefore, that this time is not so far distant as is generally feared, and the desire to give cooling time even to the House of Commons, is perhaps, one of the motives for the intended prorogation of the 23rd.

It is rumoured that Ministers do not mean either then or at any time, to propose *any allowance whatever*, but to leave that task to the Opposition; yet it is difficult beforehand to determine whether this would be the likeliest course to steer clear of the most dangerous rocks. It is easy to see now that, if the whole were to be done over again, many things might be done better, but among these I should not include Lord Liverpool's speeches, or his conduct in the House, which seem to have been quite unexceptionable, and becoming a judge as well as a statesman. They have accordingly raised him in the opinion of most men, and have extorted compliments from the chief of his opponents. To end this hateful subject, I shall not be content without some further parliamentary mark of degradation; but my first wish is that her Majesty will listen to the following address, which I heard yesterday.

Most Gracious Queen, we thee implore
To go away and sin no more;
But, if that effort be too great,
To go away, at any rate.

Yours very faithfully,
F. Burton

The Black Dwarf, *15 November 1820*

THE QUEEN'S TRIUMPH

O, let the bells of England
   Ring a right merry peal,
For our wronged royal lady,
   And for the common-weal!

No more shall petty greatness
   O'er tortured virtue reign –
The day of such dishonor
   May ne'er return again.

Sink, ye heartless Parasites!
   Sink low into the earth,
For little is your portion
   Of a glad people's mirth.

Go, court your wretched master,
   And teach him, if ye can,
To turn from crimes and folly,
   And be at last – a man.

And thou – accursed slanderer –
   The brand upon thy brow –
Where all are mean, the meanest –
   How beats thy base heart now?

Think not thy rank and title,
   Will guard thee from the hate,
The scorn and indignation
   Thy baseness must create.

Go, seek – some desert cavern,
   And waste thy life away;
From mortal vengeance hidden,
   And from the light of day!

Rejoice! ye happy millions,
  Who took the wronged one's part –
Let boundless joy and revelry
  Lighten each manly heart.

Your's is the noble triumph,
  As much as it is hers,
On whom the people's blessing
  Her greatest right confers.

To you – her first defenders
  That royal heart will turn,
In which the light of gratitude
  Will ever brightly burn.

On you – the brave and honest –
  The firm, altho' opprest,
Praise from all posterity
  Eternally shall rest!

Since crushed are the conspirers,
  The lofty and the low,
And since this hellish project
  Has met its mortal blow;

Since truth and justice conquer –
  The injured and opprest –
And since the base and mighty,
  No more the field contest;

O, let the bells of England
  Ring a right merry peal,
For our victorious lady,
  And for the common-weal.

Nov 11, 1820
J.W. Dalby

The dutiful and Loyal Address of the Inhabitant Householders of the City and Liberty of Westminster in Public Meeting Lawfully assembled this sixth day of December, One Thousand eight Hundred and twenty.

To the Queen's Most Excellent Majesty
  May it please your Majesty,
We his Majesty's subjects the Inhabitant Householders of the City and Liberty of Westminster in the discharge of the sacred duty we owe to your Majesty and to our Country, present to your Majesty this our Loyal and affectionate Address.
  When on the sixth day of July last we had the honour and the pleasure of addressing your Majesty, the infamous Bill of Pains and Penalties had not been

brought into the House of Peers. It was however anticipated by us as a probable measure and we could not but entertain the strongest apprehensions that whatever might be proposed by his Majesty's Ministers against your Majesty would be adopted by both the Houses of Parliament.

With the state of both the Houses of Parliament we were well acquainted and this knowledge left us no hope that your Majesty could be rescued from the impending danger but by the voice of the People. Your Majesty's most excellent letter to the King exposed that state and strongly impressed upon the minds of thousands the absolute necessity of raising their voices to save their Queen.

We know that the People are always backward to condemn and always forward to save, even their enemies from injustice; and we took the liberty to state to your Majesty our opinion that we should be supported by the People in our expressions of attachment and in our wish that your Majesty might triumph over your enemies, but we could not foresee, it was indeed impossible for any one to imagine, that just, and generous as the People are, they would have come forward as they have done spontaneously from one extremity of the land to the other to declare their confidence in your Majesty's innocence: to show their abhorrence of the injustice of your Majesty's enemies and to offer to your Majesty their best support. So universal has been this testimony, except indeed from the Aristocracy and the Clergy, that in the annals of the world it would be impossible to find its paralel [*sic*].

Your Majesty has proved that fair, open, candid conduct, on the part of those who govern will not only ensure safety to their persons; but that it will gain the confidence of the People, the best guards of Royalty. Your Majesty has seen what probably no Royal person ever before saw, a whole people lay aside their avocations to applaud and bless your Majesty; unsolicited, unpaid, either directly or indirectly; in the face of power exerted to repress them, in spite of menaces, and regardless of expense both of time, and of money.

To the wisdom, virtue and courage of the People, next to that of your Majesty; Your Majesty owes your deliverance from the most monstrous, most extended, and most powerful attempt, ever made to destroy an individual; and to the same causes are owing that an open despotism has not been attempted to be set up by Ministers.

So great indeed is the triumph of your Majesty, so complete the defeat of your enemies and so utterly degraded are your Majesty's persecutors, that to retain the power, now ready to fall from their hands, the most desperate efforts will no doubt be made. The very existence of your Majesty in this country as well as any, the smallest portion of Freedom among the People, is utterly incompatible with the existence of their mischievous power.

We owe to your Majesty a large debt of gratitude. Your Majesty's heroic conduct roused the People; your Majesty's Letter to the King and answers to the Addresses of the People, together with the open, barefaced, shameless conduct of your enemies, have caused millions to reflect upon the mal-administration of the affairs of the nation; and made them resolve to exert themselves to obtain such a Reform in what was designed to be and what ought to be their own House as while it shall restore to them their long lost Rights, shall also secure those of your Majesty; and we doubt not that with your Majesty's assistance that Reform will be obtained and those Rights secured. We contemplate with inexpressible delight the time when we shall have to hail your Majesty on your Throne, as the regenerator of our free forms of Government, a character which no King or Queen, with perhaps the exception of the immortal Alfred, ever truly merited.

Signed in the name, at the request, and on behalf of the Meeting,

High Bailiff

Benjamin Haydon's memoirs[5]

We brought by the mail the news of the Queen's triumph, and Edinburgh was in an uproar. I had gone to bed very fatigued, and had fallen sound asleep, when I was awakened by Mrs Farquharson screaming and thumping at my door 'to light up'. She had a candle in her hand. I got up, scarce awake, when bump came a stone against my bedroom window, and tinkle went the falling glass. The shout of the crowd was savage. They were coming out of the wynds of the old town with a hollow drum, just like the mob in the *Heart of Midlothian*. In my confusion I took the candle from Mrs Farquharson, who was screaming for her drawing-room glass, and put it against the place where the window had been broken. In came the wind and out went the candle, and bang came another shower from the roaring mob, so that I shut up the shutters, and they battered till there was not a pane left. . . . After smashing all the glass right and left of us, the drum beat, and away roared the mob into St Andrews's Square – certainly a more ferocious crowd than a London one.

Lady Erne to Lady Caroline Stuart Wortley[6]

November 12

. . . I hope it will rain plentifully this evening. Preparations are making for as general and as brilliant an illumination as possible, and it would very much lessen the crowd in the street, and perhaps a little cool the ardor of those who brav'd being wet to the skin. They might gain a few days for reflection *in their beds*. At this moment the lower classes are under a complete illusion (which every possible art is used to keep up), and believe their 'poor dear Good Queen' acquitted. . . . As I came along yesterday almost every one I met had laurel leaves stuck in their hats, and many had white cockades. A white flag had been flying on *the Church*, but the Magistrates had just had it removed, and I fancy they pretty seriously reprimanded the Church Wardens. I think that after this violent effervescence the feeling about Her Majesty will wholly subside, and many will discover their own folly and the imposition to which they have yielded. The circumstance of *her* drinking is already becoming pretty generally known. . . . I find *Brandy*bury is becoming a familiar name for Her Majesty's present residence. . . .

They say the Queen is really ill, and very impatient to get away, but that nevertheless she will not go as long as there is any thing further to be done to annoy the King. Of course I suppose she will wait for addresses of congratulation, and answer them in 'accents of triumph'. . . .

Nov. 15

I did not know of Lord Liverpool's intention to withdraw the bill, nor was that the result wish'd for by opposition. *They* meant it should go to the Commons, to give the Queen an opportunity of recriminating – at least so I have heard. She was prepared to do so to the widest extent, including the Women as well as Men of the Royal family. Mrs Brougham is on a visit here to her mother, & had a note from Mr Brougham yesterday, in which He tells her the Queen has demanded a Palace to reside in, & a suitable Household. How very audacious! I admire Mr Birnie for telling the people who were brought before him for riotous behaviour during the illumination, that he thought there had been more gallantry in England toward the sex, than to rejoice at the downfall of a Woman, & her being found guilty by a

'Moments of pleasure,' ?T. Lane (November 1820). The Queen, at Brandenburgh House, receives the news of the dropping of the bill. Alderman Wood capers with delight while Lady Anne Hamilton receives addresses of support from a crowd including J.C. Hobhouse (in profile). Over the doorway the King and Queen as puppets worked by politicians majority of the Peers. This should be repeated over & over, in all directions & on all possible occasions. Thousands at this moment have been made to believe that she is acquitted. There would be something quite laughable in all these illuminations, if it were not for the fears & dangers which accompany them. All the villages in this neighbourhood are to be illuminated. The Palace will of course be well guarded. . . .

Richard Rush's observations on the close of the 'trial'[7]

London was illuminated, more or less, for three successive nights, under edicts put forth by popular feeling, at the overthrow of the bill. The streets, the theatres, the highways, gave testimony of the popular joy at the Queen's triumph; for so her friends and partisans called it, notwithstanding the loud assertions to the contrary kept up by those who took part against her.

An impartial spectator of the whole scene, admonished by his public situation to side with neither party, may be allowed to say, (what he thought and felt,) that the Ministry showed great wisdom in surrendering up their measure as an offering to popular feeling, though they had carried the bill. Lord Rosslyn, in the course of his powerful speech, put their wisdom in a strong light by saying, amongst his other objections to the measure, that, had it passed, it would have become a formidable rallying point for disaffection throughout the kingdom, and have tended to bring the House of Lords into disrepute at a time when that branch of Parliament ought specially to desire and deserve popular approbation.

The trial exemplified striking characteristics of the English nation. A majority of the Peers held on to it with a firmness that the patricians of Rome could not have exceeded, until they carried their point by a conviction. Their sense of justice and pride satisfied, they allowed the popular part of the constitution to have play. The people, inflamed by wrongs done to a woman, as they viewed her cause, took it up with the unconquerable resolution of Roman plebeians, and would probably not have yielded. But that which was perhaps most remarkable throughout the fierce encounter, was the boundless range of the press, and liberty of speech. Every day produced its thousand fiery libels against the King and his adherents, and as many caricatures, that were hawked about all the streets. The Queen's counsel, Mr Denman, addressing himself to the assembled Peerage of the Realm, denounced, in thundering tones, one of the brothers of the King,[8] as a slanderer:– 'Come forth,' said he, 'THOU SLANDERER;' a denunciation the more severe, from the sarcasm with which it was done, and the turn of his eye towards its object; and even after the whole trial had ended, Sir Francis Burdett, just out of prison for one libel, proclaimed aloud to his constituents, and had it printed in all the papers, that the Ministers ALL DESERVED TO BE HANGED! This tempest of abuse, incessantly directed against the King, and all who stood by him, was borne, during several months, without the slightest attempt to check or punish it; and it is too prominent a fact to be left unnoticed, that the same advocate who so fearlessly uttered the above denunciation, was made Attorney-General when the Prince of the Blood who was the OBJECT OF IT, sat upon the Throne; and was subsequently raised to the still higher dignity of Lord Chief Justice, where he still remains – an honor to the kingdom.

Robert Plumer Ward's diary[9]

Nov. 17th. – Another Cabinet. I hear the Queen has written to Ld. Liverpool to *demand* a Palace, as if she was an innocent person. This the Cabinet have resolved to refuse, being determined, at all hazards, to act upon their conviction of her guilt. They have, therefore, resolved to stand or fall upon this and her restoration to the Liturgy. They do not mean by this to oppose a liberal allowance for her comfort, and had accordingly told her that she might have what money she chose to provide herself a house; but I am not prepared to say the refusal of the Palace is a proper measure. I am at least much swayed with the notion that not to enhance her consequence, by opposing her in trifles, would be the wisest way to let the subject dwindle.

November 20th, 1820. – Heard from Lord Kenyon,[10] who had got to Gridlington. He gave a ludicrous account of his distresses on the way. The mob, it seems, at . . . , not understanding his real sentiments of the Queen, and taking him (as well they might) for one of her partisans *de bon coeur*, like Alderman Wood or Sir R. Wilson, had attempted to draw him through the town, and prepared flags, with 'The Queen and Kenyon for ever!' Nothing on earth could have annoyed him more, and he was forced to run for it through the town and escape. We were much amused. He implores peace, and that this bad woman, by being no more noticed, may be allowed to drop with her infamy into oblivion.

November 21st. – . . . Sir Colin Campbell, who commands at the Tower, told us the mob insulted, and had even beaten some of the soldiers who were out on leave. Six of the mob against two soldiers. They began by asking if they were the King's men or Queen's men. They not answering, the mob thrashed them. The soldiers complained to their comrades, who conferred together, and said, if this was to be, they would come out in parties and see who would have the worst.

'John Bull the judge – or the conspirators at the bar' (November 1820). The prosecutors and witnesses against the Queen (including Majocci and one of the naval lieutenants on the left) are condemned by John Bull

Mrs Arbuthnot's journal, November 1820

18th. . . . The Queen's *demand* of a Palace has been refused. She means now to make a mockery of religion by going to St Paul's to *return thanks* for her *escape from a conspiracy*! She who has never been within a church since she came to England & used to *go to mass abroad with Bergami*. The Duke [of Wellington] writes me word that she is in league with the Opposition & that she had sent word to the King that she was ready to do any thing he wished if he would dismiss his present Ministers, but that she w^d do her utmost to torment him if he retained his present Ministers.

Henry Brougham's memoirs

I have often been asked what I should have done had the bill passed the Lords, instead of being withdrawn after the second reading. I have said, as I did while it was going on, that I should certainly stop it in the Commons. It must, according to the rules of proceeding, have been brought down by two judges, as a royal family bill, and not by Masters in Chancery; and I used to say that these judges would pass a great part of their lives in the lobby of the House of Commons; for I should assuredly debate night after night, and prevent it being brought up to the table. With a large portion of the House in our favour by their votes, almost the whole in their hearts against the bill, possibly a majority even voting against it – but at all events a very large minority, and nearly the whole country agreeing with that minority – its making any progress was absolutely impossible.

Much has been said of the feeling of the troops. Of this we had remarkable proofs. The soldiers, like many of the people, considered that the Queen as well as the King was entitled to their allegiance. Indeed, '*God save the King and Queen*' was in former days a very common form of expression; for instance, it was at the foot of all the play-bills. I recollect a letter of my mother telling me with some alarm of a regiment of cavalry stopping on its march at Penrith, and hearing they were in my neighbourhood, they drank my health, but the Queen's, of course, with much more enthusiasm; and vowed 'they would fight up to their knees in blood for their Queen'. At one time the evidence against her appeared to be strong, and the impression unfavourable for a day, as on Majocchi's examination in chief. The Guards, in their undress trousers and foraging-caps, came at night to where they supposed the Queen was, or her family and friends, and they said, 'Never mind; it may be going badly, but, better or worse, we are all with you'. I was exceedingly alarmed at such things, and peremptorily desired that not only no encouragement should be given to these men, but that no communication whatever should be had with any soldiers. I was quite certain that it only required a single instance of such language being used in the presence of any one connected with our case, not only to destroy it at once in both Houses of Parliament, but in a week's time with all rational and reflecting persons, and in less than a month with the rest of the community, whom the respectable and reflecting class never fails to influence sooner or later. . . .

Independent of our support from the people, and even upon the supposition of the case appearing against us, I had a sure resource – a course which could not have failed, even if the bill had actually passed the Lords. The threat which I held out in opening the defence was supposed to mean recrimination; and no doubt it included that. We had abundant evidence of the most unexceptionable kind, which would have proved a strong case against the King; indeed, an unquestionable one of that description. But we never could be certain of this proving decisive with both Houses; and it assuredly never would have been sufficient to make the King give up the bill. He knew that all the facts of his conduct with Lady Jersey and others were universally known in society, and he cared little for their being proved at the bar of the Lords. When I said that it might be my painful duty to bring forward what would involve the country in confusion, I was astonished that everybody should have conceived recrimination to be *all* I intended. Possibly their attention was confined to this from nothing but recrimination having ever been hinted at, either by us or our supporters in either House, or by the writers who discussed the case in the newspapers; and I was very well satisfied with the mistake, because it was of the last importance that the real ground of defence should be brought forward by surprise; or, at all events, that it should be presented at once in its full proportions, and by a short and clear statement. The ground, then, was neither more nor less than impeaching the King's own title, by proving that he had forfeited the crown. He had married a Roman Catholic (Mrs Fitzherbert) while heir-apparent, and this is declared by the Act of Settlement to be a forfeiture of the crown, '*as if he were naturally dead*'. We were not in possession of all the circumstances as I have since ascertained them, but we had enough to prove the fact. Mrs Fitzherbert's uncle, Mr Errington, who was present at the marriage – indeed it was performed in his house – was still alive; and though, no doubt, he would have had a right to refuse answering a question to which an affirmative answer exposed him to the pains and penalties of a *premunire*, denounced against any person present at such a marriage, it was almost certain that, on Mrs Fitzherbert's behalf, he would have waived the protection, and given his testimony to prove the marriage; but even his refusal would have left the conviction in all men's minds that the marriage had taken place. However, there existed ample evidence, which Errington would undoubtedly have enabled us to produce without the possibility of incurring any penalty whatever. Mrs Fitzherbert was possessed of a will of the Prince in her favour, signed with his own hand, if not written entirely by himself, and in which he calls her his dear wife. I had a copy of this, if not the original, given me by her favourite, and adopted child, Mrs Dawson Damer, who naturally took a warm interest in defending the memory of her friend and protectress. . . .

The bringing forward therefore, the marriage with Mrs Fitzherbert, was of necessity the announcement either that the King had ceased to be King, or that the other branches of the Legislature must immediately inquire into the fact of the prohibited marriage, or that there must be a disputed succession, or, in other words, that civil war was inevitable. The bringing forward this case, therefore, must at once have put an end to the bill; and whether that would suffice, depended upon the Duke of York; but the very best that could happen was the abandonment of the bill peaceably, and the King being left with a doubtful title, which his adversaries would not fail to represent as no title at all. . . .

The end of the bill, though it terminated the greatest risks, did not by any means put an end to all ferment, either in Parliament or in the country. The Queen's treatment, and especially the late proceedings, formed the main subjects of discussion in the Commons, and agitation at all public meetings. Wetherall's motion on the omission of her name in the Liturgy – Archibald Hamilton's opposition to the Address – had a great effect in the Queen's favour; and I can answer for constant resolutions of thanks in various parts of the country, and applications to attend meetings, which all her counsel of course refused. It was with great difficulty that, happening to be at Raby on my way from Brougham at Christmas, I escaped a concourse assembled to congratulate upon the fate of the bill. Grey had the same reception among the Newcastle people. So had Denman and Williams at different places. Carlton House now took the course of filling the press with libels to deter all ladies from visiting the Queen. Papers were established with the avowed purpose of attacking every woman of rank who accepted her invitations. Carlton House was thrown open at the same time to such as refused to visit the Queen; and I hesitate not to declare that this course was perfectly successful, not merely with the women, but also with their male relations, so as, to my certain knowledge, to influence their votes in both Houses. They both were unwilling to expose their wives and sisters to a slanderous press, and averse to losing for them the balls at Carlton House. The queen bore it all with great patience, and even good-humour. She used to say, 'Oh, it is all in the common course. People go to different inns: one goes to the King's Head, another to the Angel.' It must be admitted, however, that she did not act with discretion. Difficult as it would have been to avoid all errors in her peculiarly hard position, she was far too free of access, and invited persons to her table who came there for no other purpose than to gossip and laugh at her. Against this she was warned; but, indeed, the reports carefully circulated by her enemies, that she had formed an acquaintance with certain individuals, should have been warning enough. . . . She passed her time very uncomfortably, in consequence of constant vexations arising from the scandalous newspapers and the reports in society, most of which were purposely brought to her knowledge, in the hope of wearing her out, and making her again go abroad. Among the tricks practised, there were thefts of her papers and letters, as well as of letters in other people's possession. I recollect one instance of a person in the Duke of York's service, who had been in that of Sir James Graham, and had there picked up a letter of mine giving an account of the difficulty we had in prevailing upon her to attend the great ceremony of her going to St Paul's to return thanks on the bill being defeated. I had observed how false the belief was that she was so fond of popular demonstrations; and I said it was with great difficulty that we could get her to St Paul's. This was put into some person's hands for the purpose of being printed, and of showing how disrespectfully her lawyers talked of her. I do not recollect what the letter called her, but the slander-monger who used it thought it would be the better if a word were added, and he put in 'sober', it being one of the many lies told about her that she was given to drink – a thing which had at no time of her life the shadow of foundation. Lady Charlotte Lindsay was beset by persons to find out the fact respecting this ridiculous charge, and always gave the same answer, as did all her ladies, and Mrs Damer, who lived a great deal with her. It is undeniable that all these vexatious proceedings tended to make her turn her thoughts toward once more travelling; and she had some intentions of visiting Scotland, but upon the whole her thoughts were turned more towards Switzerland and the north of Italy.

On 29 November the Queen went to St Paul's to attend a service of thanksgiving organized by her Radical supporters.

Princess Lieven to Prince Metternich

November 30

Yesterday, I saw the Queen going in procession to St Paul's. There was a crowd of at least 50,000 people. It was beautiful, absurd, frightening, all at once. Not a single soldier, and perfect order, enthusiasm and good humour. On the first banner in the procession was written: 'The Queen's Guard – the People.' You could see nothing but laurels and white ribbons. They cheered twice as loud when the Queen's coach passed in front of the King's palace. No doubt, he was there, hidden in some corner. She was in an open carriage. It will be a strange memory for me, that procession. I don't know what is going to happen here; it is more of a muddle than ever. Mr Canning is at daggers drawn with all his colleagues. He says they are fools; the King says so too; but the colleagues do not budge. . . .

Henry Crabb Robinson's diary

November 29th [1820]

Being engaged all day in court, I saw nothing of the show of the day – the Queen's visit to St Paul's. A great crowd were assembled, which the *Times* represents as an effusion of public feeling echoed by the whole nation in favour of injured innocence. The same thing was represented by the Ministerial papers as a mere rabble. I think the Government journals on this occasion are nearer the truth than their adversaries; for though the popular delusion has spread widely, embracing all the lowest classes, and a large proportion of the middling orders, yet the great majority of the educated, and nearly all the impartial, keep aloof.

The disgraceful end of the disgraceful process against the Queen took place while the Wordsworths were in town. Whilst the trial was going on, and the issue still uncertain, I met Coleridge, who said, 'Well, Robinson, you are a Queenite, I hope?' – 'Indeed, I am not.' – 'How is that possible?' – 'I am only an anti-Kingite.' – 'That's just what I mean.'

Anne Cobbett to James P. Cobbett, in New York

Brompton, December 6, 1820

My Dear James, – . . . This day week our Gracious lady the Queen went in state to St Paul's to return thanks for her escape from the fangs of the Government; when I say *in state*, I mean that her intention of going had been announced a week before, and that the City authorities had been notified to meet her at Temple Bar and accompany her to the Church, for she had none of the usual appendanges of *state* to attend upon her, no soldiers, constables, civil officers, or anything of the kind, not one of the nobility; and it was the finest sight ever beheld. About a *thousand* gentlemen mounted on horseback formed themselves into a guard of honour, and riding four abreast, five hundred rode before and five hundred behind her carriage. She was from ten o'clock till half-past twelve going from Hyde Park corner to St Paul's, owing to the immense mob, and yet it was wonderful to see how well the people behaved; all seemed actuated by one common feeling, and, strange to say, not one accident happened during the whole day. It was a very fine dry cold day, and all together it was a most gratifying concern. As she went to the Church the Queen's carriage was shut, but in returning she had it thrown open, that the people might see her, and this, you know, considering the weather, was very kind and condescending. I assure you, my dear Jumpy, we all wished for you that day, as, indeed, we do every day, but then in particular, for it was *our* triumph as well as the Queen's, and it was a great damper to us that you were not here to participate in the pleasure with us. In short, we begin to be very impatient about your coming home now. . . .

'The triumph of Innocence over Perjury, Persecution and Ministerial Oppression,' W. Heath (6 November 1820). The Queen in the coronation chair, with Justice on her right and Truth on her left. Among the hydra heads are Eldon, Castlereagh (on the left), Liverpool and Sidmouth (right). Two demons carry off the King to Hanover

The Times, *30 November 1820*

PROCESSION OF HER MAJESTY TO ST PAUL'S

Yesterday being the day appointed by her Majesty for public thanks, at St Paul's Cathedral, for the defeat of the late conspiracy against her honour; the metropolis and its vicinity, in every direction, presented such scenes of active bustle, and splendour, as we believe its oldest inhabitants never before witnessed, and such as will not be forgotten by the youngest who did witness it. Certainly on no public occasion within our memory has the interest or the enthusiasm of the metropolis been so unanimously evinced as on the present. The feeling was natural, and it was general. The scene which yesterday presented would, even if there were no other circumstances in their favour, be sufficient to acquit Englishmen generally of any participation in the late nefarious attempt to degrade their Queen, and, through her, the illustrious house of Brunswick. We apprehend that the hirelings who daily amuse themselves and disgust the public by declaring that only the Radicals or rabble (as they usually term the working classes of the community) have evinced any feeling for her Majesty under her manifold persecutions, must now alter their tone, if indeed they have any respect for truth yet remaining; for such a practical disproof of their daily slanders was yesterday given as must convince even their masters. . . . At a very early hour in the morning every street and avenue leading to Hyde-park-corner began to be thronged with an unusual concourse of spectators on horseback and on foot. . . . At about a quarter past 9 o'clock about 150 gentlemen on horseback assembled at Hammersmith, from whence they proceeded in a body to the field in front of Brandenburg-house: there they were formed three abreast, according to the arrangement which had been previously made. In this manner one body, of about fifty horsemen, which was to precede her Majesty's carriage, proceeded to the avenue before the house, the remaining body, whose numbers by this time had considerably increased, forming in like manner in the rear. Her Majesty's state carriage, drawn by six chestnut horses, was at the door by half-past nine; and at a little before ten her Majesty was handed in to it, followed by Lady Anne Hamilton. . . . Before the cavalcade left the grounds it was joined by a barouch and four, which took its station about fifty paces in the rear of her Majesty's carriage. The barouch was occupied by the churchwardens and some other officers of the parish of Hammersmith. At a few minutes before ten o'clock the procession moved off in very excellent order towards Hammersmith. In passing the parish church her Majesty was very warmly greeted by the cheers of the charity-children, who were drawn up in front, dressed in their holyday-gear; but their juvenile plaudits were almost drowned in the louder shouts of the older inhabitants of the village, who seemed to vie with each other in expressing their feelings of gratitude and veneration for their benefactress and Queen. Many of the houses in the village were decorated with handsome flags, with various devices and mottoes, expressive of a conviction of her Majesty's innocence, and of the injustice of her persecutors; and there were few houses which were not ornamented with laurel-leaves, intermixed with knots of white riband, as emblematic of the late victory of injured innocence over powerful oppression. The windows were thronged with well-dressed females, who, by waving of handkerchiefs, and occasionally of streamers of white riband, evinced their warm concurrence in the general feeling. We ought not to omit that, from a very early hour a large flag waved from the church-top, and the bells continued ringing 'merry peals' until her Majesty passed through. After the cavalcade had passed Hammersmith very considerable accessions were made to its numbers. . . . Viewed from any station on the road's side, between that and Kensington, it presented a most pleasing spectacle. The richness of the royal liveries, the number and respectability of the equestrian escort, the handsome decorations of the horses, and the tasteful knots of white favours (added, in very many instances, to medallions of her Majesty, suspended from the neck by blue ribands), gave to the entire spectacle a splendid and interesting appearance. On the arrival of the procession at Kensington her Majesty was received with most enthusiastic cheers. Every aperture of every house, through which even a glimpse could be had, had been occupied by 'eager and enquiring eyes' long before her Majesty's arrival. Flags and banners of various descriptions floated from many houses, and in others their place was supplied by the waving of less costly emblems – handkerchiefs and ribands. All, however, were equally significant of the same feelings – the heartfelt satisfaction of the inhabitants at the triumph of their much-injured Queen. . . . [At Knightsbridge] her Majesty was met by Sir Robert Wilson, and a deputation from the large body of horsemen who waited on horseback for her at Hyde-park-corner. The gallant officer headed (we believe) the procession until it joined the main body from which he had been deputed. At Knightsbridge, also, her Majesty was loudly and warmly cheered. The barrack gates were shut, but a number of troopers were in the streets (unarmed), and were the only apparently passive spectators of the scene. From Knightsbridge to Hyde Park-corner the crowd was immense, and at both sides of the road. . . . Thousands and thousands of spectators occupied the walls and trees in the Park, and every other eminence from which even an indistinct view of the scene might be obtained. The shouts, cheers, and loud huzzas which rent the air on every side at this period, might have been heard for more than a mile around. . . . The procession was followed by an immense number of carriages of every description , from the barouch to the taxed cart, thronged with spectators of every class, all equally eager to partake in the general jubilee. Many of these carriages and carts went no further than Hyde-Park-corner, owing to the immense pressure of the crowd from thence to the other end of Piccadilly. . . .

[The Queen was escorted from Temple Bar to St Paul's by the Mayor and members of the Corporation of the City.]

About half-past eleven the Lord-Mayor, the Sheriffs of London, Alderman Wood, Mr Favell, and other members of the Common Council, in their respective coaches, with horses splendidly decorated, and with all the pomp and state of the metropolitan corporation, proceeded towards Temple-bar to receive her Majesty. They were loudly cheered by the immense multitudes on every side, as they advanced. At Temple-bar they inverted the order for the return, the Lord-Mayor, who had advanced first, now taking his station last. Her Majesty . . . took her station immediately after the Lord-Mayor. . . . The multitudes along the streets now ranged themselves in the closest phalanx, and cleared a passage for the procession to advance with perfect ease and safety. It is quite impossible to imagine any gratification to the eye or ear of man more magnificently sublime than this scene presented. Above, below, on every side, nothing was to be seen but eager and continued waving of hats and handkerchiefs; the shouts of congratulation and heart-felt blessings that resounded along were at once awful and animating. When the preservation of order made it necessary to halt occasionally, those who had a view of her Majesty raised a shout of redoubled enthusiasm: this was invariably a signal to all who heard the shout or saw the agitation of white handkerchiefs to join in the triumphant cry of 'God bless our Queen' and to wave their white handkerchiefs in token of their conviction of her innocence. Her Majesty on these occasions acknowledged, with every symptom of feeling and condescension, the ardent expressions of sympathy or admiration which she called forth. The eagerness to get a near view of her Majesty was extreme, and must have caused considerable annoyance to many gentlemen in the procession; but no interruption to perfect good humour was anywhere offered. We heard of but one attempt at picking pockets, and the attempt was scarcely made when the miscreant found himself in society that would not harbour him for a moment [and] he was instantly apprehended. We believe we may safely affirm that so numerous a concourse of human beings was never before seen on the face of the earth. It is proudly peculiar to the Queen of England and the City of London that this immense assemblage should be seen within the barriers of London, to celebrate the triumph of a Queen, the greatest triumph ever obtained over the worst passions that ever disgraced human nature – without one emblem of military control, or one instrument of war, and without the slightest cause to regret their absence. . . .

[The scene in St Paul's:]

. . . By half-past eleven o'clock the choir contained a great number of beautiful Ladies, dressed in a manner as tasteful and elegant as was consistent with a prudent regard for their health at the present season of the year. Among them we observed Mrs Alderman Wood, and her two lovely and elegant daughters, occupying a seat nearly opposite to that set out for her Majesty. The Bishop's throne and the Dean's seat were not occupied at all, both these reverend dignitaries having written to the Lord Mayor, prohibiting them from being used. The seat appropriated to her Majesty's use on this occasion was the one uniformly occupied by members of the Royal Family, and called the Bishop's seat: it is situated in the middle of the choir, on the south side. The corresponding seat on the opposite side of the choir was set apart for the Lord-Mayor. . . .

At a quarter before 12 o'clock the committee of sixty ladies, who were in attendance to receive her Majesty, entered the choir, and took their seats on the forms placed in front of the communion-table. They were all, with two exceptions, dressed in white, their hair decorated with white ribands, and white veils hanging gracefully on their shoulders and bosoms. The effect produced by seeing so many beautiful and elegant females uniformly dressed, and seated together, was peculiarly striking and pleasing. . . .

At thirty minutes past twelve her Majesty approached St Paul's, and the west centre doors, fronting Ludgate-hill, were thrown open. The vast pile resounded with murmurs of gratulation; and the distant shouts of the multitude without continued to increase in loudness as her Majesty drew nearer to the majestic temple. Notice of the Queen's approach having been given to Dr Hughes, he proceeded with the choir, to the west door, to receive her Majesty. The committee advanced and joined the choir, and in a few seconds her Majesty entered the Cathedral amidst loud shouts. The west door was then closed, and her Majesty advanced thus attended:–

Two Marshalmen
Members of the Committee, two and two
The Officers of the Corporation
Mr Sheriff Waithman and Mr Sheriff Williams
Her Majesty, resting on the arm of the Lord-Mayor
Alderman Wood, and the members of her Majesty's suite
Lady Hamilton, resting on the arm of Mr Flavell
Members of the Committee

Her Majesty was also attended by the Hon. Keppel Craven, Sir Robert Wilson, Mr Hume, MP, Mr Hobhouse, MP, and several other persons of distinction.

As her Majesty approached, Mr Attwood, the organist, performed a voluntary, and one of Mozart's fugues. . . .

Her Majesty wore a white silk pelisse, with deep trimmings of white fur, and a close turban head-dress, covered with a white veil. As soon as she was placed in her seat, she turned round, and, kneeling slowly down, offered up the usual silent prayer.

The usual morning service was then read. . . . It is impossible not to remark how strikingly applicable the psalms appointed for the morning service of yesterday are to her Majesty's situation. . . .

PSALM CXL *Eripe me, domine*
1. Deliver me, O Lord, from the evil man. . . .

Notes

1. The Representative Peers of Scotland and Ireland, who were notoriously subservient to the government of the day.
2. The bishops.
3. Robert Waithman (1764–1833), linen draper, Alderman of London, MP 1818–20, a leader of the metropolitan Radical movement.
4. Thomas Babington Macaulay (1800–59), later Lord Macaulay, politician and historian.
5. Benjamin Robert Haydon (1786–1846), the painter.
6. Mary, wife of John, 1st Earl Erne, brother of the 1st Marquess of Bristol. Her daughter Caroline married James Archibald Stuart-Wortley, MP for Yorkshire, later 1st Baron Wharncliffe.
7. Richard Rush, American ambassador to London.
8. The Duke of Clarence, later William IV, under whom Brougham became Lord Chancellor in 1830 and Denman Attorney-General (1830) and Lord Chief Justice (1832).
9. Robert Plumer Ward (1765–1846), novelist and politician, Clerk of the Ordnance 1811–23.
10. George, 2nd Baron Kenyon (1776–1855), a Tory.

CHAPTER NINE

The Queen Rejected

The Queen's triumph was short-lived. Its height was reached with the thanksgiving service at St Paul's. After that there was nowhere for the movement to go. The dropping of the bill and the end of the proceedings in Parliament took the affair out of the daily attention of the newspapers and ended the pretext for processions and demonstrations, while the government's steadfast refusal to make any concessions to her meant that she had in fact gained nothing. She was back in the position she had occupied in June on her arrival in England: Queen in name only, she was still omitted from the Anglican liturgy and the continued refusal to give her an official residence and an income, unless she left the country, left her without resources. The Whig opposition had supported her cause against the bill but they were no more anxious than the government to endorse or encourage the Radicals by using the affair to discredit the political system and achieve parliamentary reform. Lord Grey and the Radical leaders detested each other as heartily as their monarch and his queen disliked each other. Caroline's value even to the Radicals had been only symbolic: she was no asset to their political cause, for, whatever the Cobbetts might claim, she was no Radical herself.

At the same time, the loyalist reaction began to set in. Lady Erne noted that even in Alderman Wood's London stronghold loyal addresses were being voted as early as the beginning of December, and when the King visited Brighton at Christmas there were demonstrations in his favour, though *The Times* tried to play down the extent of the popular enthusiasm. In fact, the English were attached to their monarchy even in the person of George IV, and whether in his presence or in the evenings at the theatres displays of loyal enthusiasm soon replaced the hostile demonstrations of the past months. In Parliament the mood reflected that of the public. Attempts by the Queen's partisans to have her name restored to the prayer book were blocked by large majorities in both Houses and her personal demands were repulsed. She was also unsuccessful in her attempts to be crowned with the King in July, when the coronation, postponed from the previous year, was held. She was bluntly informed that she had no right of attendance and that the King alone had the right to decide whether or not his consort should be crowned. This decision was upheld by a unanimous vote of the Privy Council after thorough discussion – it remains the rule to this day. The spectacle of the Queen, refused admittance to the abbey, running from one door to another in a vain attempt to gain entrance, aroused the derision rather than the sympathy of the crowd which only seven months before had hailed her triumph over the King. The coronation was the most splendid – and expensive – ever staged in modern times, George's love of pageantry and theatre being fully indulged at the enormous cost of £240,000. The public responded with acclamations, for the King and not the Queen; as J.W. Croker wrote, the incident was designed to demonstrate her strength but it only showed her weakness. She retired to Hammersmith a defeated, dejected, and, it soon appeared, a sick woman. She at first refused, but finally accepted, the government's offer of an annuity of £50,000 on condition that she should leave England and live permanently abroad; but her health deteriorated so rapidly that she was never able to do so.

Letters from Lady Erne to Lady Caroline Stuart Wortley

December 5

. . . I can hear nothing of the Queen since St. Paul's, addresses excepted. I suppose she and her advisers are brewing some more mischief. They say she looked very cross on Wednesday, & was very much annoy'd by their making her open her carriage on Her return from the Church; in all that raw fog it must have been disagreeable enough, & rather perilous to her precious health. . . .

December 6

. . . There is at present a strong reaction, the loyal addresses [to the King] are pouring in fast – that from Cripplegate Ward is a tremendous blow on Alderman

Wood. If [the King] was any thing almost but what He is, I think there would be a rapid change.

The Queen was certainly very much disappointed & put out the day of her visit to St Paul's, & burst into a violent passion of Tears when she got home. It was a poor cortège for a Queen going to the Cathedral of the Metropolis, & the cheering was flat. She is longing to be gone, but they will not let her go. Ministers are no doubt right to be stout about the Liturgy, but I do dread all the violence with which the subject will be treated in both Houses. . . .

Lady Cowper to Frederick Lamb

George St. Decr. 18 [1820]

. . . The Ministers and the King all quarrel, but he is in their hands and cannot help himself. He insisted upon Par[liamen]t meeting and having the thing settled. They said if so they would resign, upon which he gave way. I believe this is certain. They say if she is restored to the Liturgy or has a palace, they must go out and without these concessions the popular ferment never will be allayed. Nothing, in my opinion, is so foolish as the Ministers' conduct, it even beats the Opposition's. In their place, having gone so far, I would certainly have forced the Bill thro', or having once given it up, they should now give up everything, give her an income, Hampton Court and her name in the Liturgy. She would then have nothing to ask for and soon get tired of the thing, as people would get tired of her. Now the battle keeps her alive, and she is wise enough to know (as Archibald Hamilton says) that if she was to go she would go hissed out of the country, and never be able to set foot in it again. Now (tho [she] might prefer being abroad) her time passes well. She has a dozen Italians about her, plenty of society, and always fresh events to interest her. She is in very good spirits, he says. . . .

Princess Lieven to Prince Metternich

The 22nd [December]

Mr Canning's resignation from the Ministry is ostensibly regretted by his colleagues; personally, I cannot help thinking that they are very glad. Considering the terms they were on, it must have been much more inconvenient to keep him than to lose him. Wellington told me that quite recently he had been deputed to urge him to stay and that he had had a very strange conversation with him in this context. The immediate cause of the split is the question of the Prayer-Book. The Ministers will not consent to have the Queen's name put back into the prayers, and he wanted it to be; here is the reason. He told the Duke of Wellington that he was with the Princess of Wales when, after the first year of their marriage, she received the famous letter from the Prince of Wales giving her her freedom and taking back his. She consulted Canning as to how she was to take this document. He decided peremptorily that it was a letter giving her permission to do as she liked, and they took advantage of it on the spot. I rather fancy that might have happened even before the letter. However that may be, he regards himself as the first to incite the Queen to the course of action she has since followed; and, making it a question of conscience, he declared that he could not pronounce her unworthy to occupy the throne on grounds for which he considered himself responsible; and a split with his colleagues has resulted. He will be out of England by January 1.

Lord Holland's memoirs

The Queen's advisers and partizans, miscalling the cessation of all proceedings an acquittal, were busily endeavouring to set up her Court in rivalry to that of her husband. She gave dinners and had parties; but she had neither a case, a character, nor friends, to enable her to play that game with success; and some ladies of rank and character wrote their names at her door, or even on invitation dined at Brandenburg House, but none took office in her household. It was manifest that her station in fashionable society could never be made either brilliant or comfortable to herself or her visitors.

Whatever might be her failure in London society the agitation in the country continued. Numberless meetings were held, which passed petitions for the introduction of her name in the Liturgy, and pointed more or less directly to the removal of Ministers who advised the prosecution. If I may judge from the two which I was prevailed upon to attend – those of Bedfordshire and Oxfordshire – the enthusiasm in her cause had not abated in the country for several months after the failure of the bill. Yet perhaps in the course of the winter, and yet more manifestly during the early part of the ensuing year, the tide of popularity was on the turn. Her exhibition at St Paul's and the King's re-appearance at the public theatres had very opposite effects. The first weakened the interest engaged in her cause, and the latter softened in some degree the displeasure felt against him. She, on November 29, proceeded to St Paul's to return thanks and take the Sacrament. She thereby scandalized many religious persons, who deemed it a profanation of a holy rite, and she disgusted the indifferent, who regarded it as a piece of needless hypocrisy. The King, three months afterwards, mustered courage to show himself in public, and his reception at the theatres in February, though neither brilliant nor striking, indicated plainly enough that the popular frenzy was subsiding.

All this preceded and accounted for the comparative flatness with which her subsequent endeavours to revive popular feeling at the Coronation, and even her death and funeral, with all their exciting circumstances, were received in the course of a short year from the period of her prosecution. The King's asperity was not so speedily mitigated as the people's disrelish of it; for when in the ensuing year the intelligence of the death of Napoleon, which arrived before the Queen was taken ill, was announced to him in the ambiguous terms – 'I have, Sir, to congratulate you: your greatest enemy is dead,' he unguardedly exclaimed, 'Is *she*, by God?' thus betraying the gradation in which personal spite ranged above political enmity in his narrow and pitiful mind.

Two accounts of the King's visit to Brighton, 23 December:

The Times, *26 December*

TO THE EDITOR OF THE TIMES

Sir – His Majesty having been graciously pleased to honour this town with his presence at this festive season of the year, it may prove interesting to your readers (if not an intrusion on your valuable journal) to hear a detail of the enthusiasm displayed on that occasion.

His Majesty, since his accession to the throne, having, in his previous visits, entered the town in private, and with his usual rapidity, it was determined by some of the inhabitants, when he again visited the Pavilion (or palace), to request he would condescend to permit them to hail his approach with public expressions of their unalterable attachment to his person. These manifestations of loyalty being approved, and information having been received on the 21st that his Majesty proposed to enter Brighton on Saturday, the 23rd inst., at three o'clock, a requisition numerously and respectably signed was transmitted to the High Constable to convene a meeting, and which being held on Friday morning, at the Old Ship Tavern, it was resolved 'that a public and loyal testimony of affectionate respect should be paid to their gracious Sovereign and patron'. A committee being formed 'to carry this desirable object into effect', and a printed circular distributed by the parish beadles, communicating the result of the meeting, stating the order of procession appointed to meet his Majesty, with an invitation to the inhabitants and visitors of Brighton to join therein, announcing also that in the evening of Saturday a general illumination would take place, sub-committees were also formed, with orders to sit late on Friday evenings and early on Saturday morning, to afford information, provide and fix the price of carriages, &c., and determine the best means to ensure a numerous and well-regulated procession. Four gentlemen were appointed to place the horsemen 'on the road towards Preston beyond the carriages;' the same number were selected to 'place the carriages in a line, commencing from the (King's) Dairy toward London', and the High Constable and his assistants were to marshal 'the pedestrians' on each side the road as far as the carriages; the horsemen and carriages to take their station at one o'clock, and the pedestrians at two o'clock, his Majesty being expected by three o'clock, and that each person in the procession do wear a dark blue favour on the left breast. These arrangements being determined, the respective committees assembled, in the expectation of full employ; but it appears the committee for conducting the carriages, after waiting at the Old Ship with much anxiety on Friday evening from 7 to near 11 o'clock, and from 9 o'clock Saturday morning, were only favoured with the names of only a few gentlemen from London, two of whom have recently become inhabitants of the town. It was anticipated that many ladies would have volunteered to join the procession in carriages, as the seats were fixed at the very small charge of 2s. 6d. each; but as none offered, the committee broke up in disgust, and left those who wished for carriages to hire for themselves. About 2 o'clock 20 horsemen assembled opposite the pavilion in conformity to the general order; all others – horses, carriages, and pedestrians – followed the bent of their inclinations, without at all consulting the regularity necessary to make the procession appear truly respectable. At half past two o'clock his Majesty approached the environs of the town, in his travelling carriage, and was greeted with loud and reiterated applause; but all seemed to be in confusion, and particularly the carriages, uncertain as to the course they were to pursue. The horsemen appeared to be under some kind of order, though not such as ought to have been observed. About 50 or 60 were present, a party of whom preceded his Majesty; the remainder formed a body guard on each side the carriage, and a few followed in the rear. The carriages (chiefly belonging to visitors) then closed in the best manner they were able, and would have appeared respectable had they been subject to proper regulations. As soon as his Majesty had alighted, the horsemen and carriages drew up in lines (the former in front) near to Marlborough-row. At this moment the High

Constable and his assistants, on horseback, embellished with red staffs, and accompanied by two trumpeters on foot, and a band of music in a caravan, with a pair of regimental colours, made their appearance; the music playing *God save the King*; after which the public gave three times three cheers. His Majesty (who we were happy to observe looked well) appeared at the drawing room window and tried several times to force the window up, but not being able, he made several respectful bows, and seemed to feel grateful for the public expression in his favour.

The procession after this took a circuit through the principal part of the town, and, after giving three cheers at the Pavilion, dismissed. His Majesty, not making his appearance the second time, disappointed many that had assembled to greet him. In the evening an illumination took place, and, with the exception of a few houses, it may be said to have been general. The notice having been short, there was not much preparation. There were some tasteful variegated lamps in different parts of the town, forming G.IV.R. In North-street we observed two gas-light stars, and two G.R.'s, with crowns; these would have had a very pleasing effect, but for the current of air preventing the splendour they would otherwise have emitted. We observed also in the same street a transparency neatly executed, representing a pedestal with G.R. on the left, and C.R. on the right side, and the following mottos; 'Liberty of the press', 'Trial by jury', in the centre, 'The Constitution', and at the bottom, 'Public Opinion'. On the Steine a barrel of lighted pitch was rolled about, accompanied by fire-works, to the terror and dismay of female spectators. A circumstance in reference to some sailors is worthy of observation: they had 3 or 4 middling-size cannon mounted in a cart, with 2 flags, which they intended to discharge from an eminence, on his Majesty's approach; but, as this was earlier than expected, the tars were not able to fire a salute until his Majesty had nearly reached his palace.

Brighton, Dec. 23

The following is another account, from a ministerial paper:

ENTHUSIASTIC RECEPTION OF HIS MAJESTY AT BRIGHTON

BRIGHTON, DEC. 25

We have this week the satisfaction of announcing the arrival of our illustrious benefactor, the King. His Majesty was met on the road, near Preston, and thence followed to the Palace, by a numerous confluence of the inhabitants of this place, on horseback and in carriages; and immense was the number of pedestrians extending from the Palace northward. The string of carriages, in which were many elegant females with purple favours on their bosoms – the gentlemen with similar symbols of loyalty and affection attached to their dresses – occupied much of the road between the extremity of this town and the place above named, and still more lengthened was the line of horsemen. The loyal fishermen here, anxious to evince their attachment to their beloved Sovereign on the occasion, manned a large tilted waggon, having hoisted the national flag, upon a suitable support, at the stern of it, and placed three pieces of mounted cannon in the body of the roomy vehicle, the muzzles of which appearing through the tilt had somewhat the resemblance of great guns projecting from the broadside of a ship of war. This seamanlike contrivance had a novel but pleasing appearance, and the weighty machine, drawn by three or four strong horses, at length took its station on the slope of the hill on this side of Preston, commanding

'John Bull's little darling,' ?T. Lane (25 January 1821). One of a growing number of loyalist satirical prints attacking the Queen in the winter of 1820–1

a full view of the turnpike. A band of music, colours, &c., gave harmony, military show, and brilliance, to the scene generally, while pleasure beamed in every eye, and made known the actual qualities of every heart. One soul of enthusiasm animated all present; and if ever there appeared a loyal accordance in sentiment, without any the slightest alloy of a different character, it may truly be said to have existed in this instance. The arrival of the sovereign at the earliest had not been expected before three o'clock in the afternoon; and as the probability was that it would be much later, flambeaux were provided to be at hand, should they be needed. Contrary to this expectation, however, his Majesty and suite appeared on the road about fifteen minutes after two o'clock, before the order of the procession had been arranged, and though comparatively confused to what had been intended, most ardent, animated, and enthusiastic, was the scene which ensued. The band struck up the national anthem, the colours were raised, then lowered to the ground, the huzzas were simultaneous and inspiriting, while the great guns from the seaman's car mingled their loyal thunder with the joyous roar predominant. The Monarch, with dignified condescension, bowed to the delighted populace, and 'Long live George the Fourth, God bless our King', was 'floated in air from all points of the compass'. From this time the horses and carriages of the gratified throng were mixed, though the original design was that they should be separate; but the cause mentioned prevented it, and nothing could stay the unanimous crowd when their Sovereign was in the midst of them, or check the prevalent ecstacy of the moment. As the royal suite moved on, impetuous as the descent of a mountain torrent, the congregated body moved with it, and, in the end, collecting their scattered companions, formed themselves into one immense and almost impenetrable phalanx, covering the Grand Parade in front of Marlborough-row, at one of which houses his Majesty had alighted. 'God Save the King' was again played by the band, and a simultaneous, but regular burst of huzzas, four times four, succeeded, and which echo, as if enraptured also, repeated. The King at this time witnessed the exhilarating process without, from the window of the drawing-room of the house he had entered; which window, to render the apartment less pervious to the wintry blast, had been made fast with iron instruments and screws; but these, by royal mandate, were presently removed, and in a few minutes after his Majesty presented himself to the people on the balcony. We cannot do justice to the scene that followed. the Monarch seemed fully to appreciate its character, placing his hand upon his breast, he several times bowed: there was an affection in his manner that struck home to the hearts of the spectators; and many, in the restless acumen of their feelings, burst into tears. As his Majesty withdrew, huzzas and loyal acclamations once more rent the welkin, and the assemblage gradually disappeared.

In the evening the illuminations in the town were most general: the residences of all ranks and descriptions of people partook of the splendid blaze, from the mansions of the nobility down to the meanest cottage in which an ignited symbol of loyalty could be placed. Many well-executed transparent paintings were displayed; blazing tapers shed their radiance in all directions, variegated lamps, in the shape of crowns, stars, &c., were innumerable, and most effulgent was the aggregate and glittering effect produced.

Anne Cobbett to Frederick Cobbett, 17 January 1821

. . . The Queen has bought a house in Pall Mall, a large house fit for her to live in, the gardens of which communicate with Carlton House, and she says she will have a hole cut in the wall and be in with her spouse in a trice. How she will worry them to be sure, and she is resolved not to give up an inch. . . .

Anne Cobbett to James Cobbett, 31 January 1821

. . . The Whigs have been talking very big indeed at Public Meetings about Reform, and they have tried to shake the Ministers in the House of Commons upon the question of whether the Queen's name should be restored to the Liturgy, but they are beaten, and so much the better, for P. does not want the Whigs to come in *yet*. Neither has the Queen any great dependence in them. She says she owes all to the Govr. and as for the letter she says if it had not been for *that* her head would have been upon Temple Bar long before this. We are *told* that she says that if ever she possesses the power she will feel bound in gratitude to show the Govr. that she fully appreciates the great services he has rendered her, and I make no doubt but she means it for she is a truly good hearted woman. . . .

Lady Cowper to Frederick Lamb

Thursday, Feby. 1st [1821]

. . . Politics are fallen very flat, high expectations have been disappointed. The Whigs are low and out of temper; the Ministers are abused and consequently peevish; the landholders are all poor and get only two-thirds of their rents. In short, every body has a grievance, and I alone am in spirits, for I am glad to find myself *perfectly* well. . . The Peers, who all came to town exulting and triumphant from their country meetings, cheered and drawn and huzza'd, found the scene in London horribly flat. . . . This Queen's subject is detestable, for one thing that it moves the calmest people to choler; nobody's temper can stand it. One party thinks the other fools, idiots, and madmen, and the compliment is returned with the epithet of base, ungenerous and time serving. Nobody is allowed an inbiassed [*sic*] opinion. There never was such an Apple of Discord as that Woman has been to the public and private families. As for me, I think it all fun, for I am in spirits and that makes all the difference of one's view of events.

. . . There is certainly a change in popular feeling about the Queen, the Theater shows it, and the difference is remarkable. On the Accession Day 'God Save the King' was received with rapture and waving of hats and encored, a few hisses quite drowned and when they called for 'God Save the Queen' they were hissed down directly. . . .

Charles Greville's memoirs, 1821

London, February 7th. – The King went to the play last night (Drury Lane) for the first time, the Dukes of York and Clarence and a great suite with him. He was received with immense acclamations, the whole pit standing up, hurrahing and waving their hats. The boxes were very empty at first, for the mob occupied the avenues to the theatre, and those who had engaged boxes could not get to them. The crowd on the outside was very great. Lord Hertford dropped one of the candles as he was lighting the King in, and made a great confusion in the box. The King sat in Lady Bessborough's box, which was fitted up for him. He goes to Covent Garden to-night. A few people called 'The Queen', but very few. A man in the gallery called out, 'Where's your wife, Georgy?'

Thomas Creevey to Miss Ord

Feb. 11th

. . . I was at Brougham's by half-past two, and found Craven waiting. As soon as Brougham was ready, we set off to pick up Mrs Damer, who was to dine also with the Queen. . . . Well – when we reached Brandenburg House, we were ushered up a very indifferent staircase and through an ante-room into a very handsome, well-proportioned room from 40 to 50 feet long, very lofty, with a fine coved ceiling, painted with gods and goddesses in their very best clothes. The room looks upon the Thames, and is not a hundred yards from it. Upon our entrance, the Queen came directly to Mrs Damer, then to Brougham, and then to me. I am not sure whether I did not commit the outrage of putting out my hand without her doing the same first; be it as it may, however, we did shake hands. She then asked me if I had not forgotten her, and I can't help thinking she considered my visit as somewhat *late*, or otherwise she would have said something civil about my uniform support. She is not much altered in face or figure, but very much in manner. She is much more stately and much more agreeable. She was occasionally very grave. . . . She took me aside twice after dinner, and talked to me of her situation. She is evidently uneasy about money. . . . She mentioned no women, but the Duke of Wellington did not escape an observation from her, as to the surprise it occasioned in her that he should be so violent against her. . . .

Lady Cowper to Frederick Lamb

[Tuesday, February 27th, 1821]

. . . Ld Gower tells me a report today that the Queen had seen some Physician, I think Baillie, and that he said hers was a dangerous time of life, and that he thought she ought to take care of herself, and had advised her going *to Spa*. This looks to me like a preparation, I believe you will have her at Frankfort before long. . . .

Correspondence on the Queen's request to have her name restored to the liturgy.

Queen Caroline to Lord Liverpool (original spelling and grammar)

Brandenbourgh House, 3the of March, 1821

The Queen having been informed through the midium of Lord Liverpool, namely, that Parlement had voted a Provision for the Queen, and that the sum agreed to by the two Houses of Parlement would be ready for the immediate use of the Queen, she find herself under the necessity of accepting it, with a sense of gratitude towards the King, having been proposed by His Majesty himself at the opening of Parlement; and the Queen is only anxious to show to the King that She wishesse to Received from Him, and not from a mere Party Spirit. The Queen at the same time thinks herself authorised to look upon this messure as the first act of Justice of His Majesty toward's the Queen. She also add that she most entertains the flattering expectation that the same sentimens of Justice which has prevailed in her favour will also effect upon the Heart of the King, by plaicing her name in the Liturgi as Queen, as such having been the Rights and custum of Her Predecessors. The Queen can never forget what difficulties, and a great deal of troubles She has undergone on that account upon the Continant by having her Name been omitted in the Liturgi, and in consequence She deed not Received the Honour which where due to the Queen, as the Consort to the King of England.

Justice is the basis of happiness for King's, and the good judgment of His Majesty will point it out to him the Methods by which he will accelerate the wish of his People, and the satisfaction of the Queen on this subject, and the Queen has not the least doubt but that the King will, taking into his consideration the Queen's situation, and to act accordinly with that generosity which Characterises a great Mind. Under such circumstances the Queen submit herself intierly to his Majesty's dicesion.

Caroline R.

Bandenbourgh House, 18th March, 1821

The Queen communicates to Lord Liverpool that in consequence of not having Receved a answer of her last letter which she wrot on the 3the of March, the Queen requests Lord Liverpool to inform His Majesty of the Queen's intentions to present herself next Thursday in Person at the King's Drawing Room, to have the opportunity of Presenting a Petition to his Majesty of obtaining her Rights that the Queen's Name should be restored to the Liturgi as her Predecessorie's.

Caroline R.

Fife House, 19th March, 1821

Lord Liverpool has the honour to inform the Queen that the letter which he received on the 3d inst. was immediately laid before the King; but as His Majesty saw no reason for altering his determination upon the principal question of the Liturgy referred to in it, and as the Queen concluded her letter by saying that 'she submitted herself entirely to his Majesty's decision', the King did not consider any answer requisite.

Lord Liverpool is now commanded to state that the King must decline receiving the Queen at his drawing-room; but he will be ready to receive any petition or representation the Queen may be desirous of bringing before him through Lord Liverpool or through the Secretary of State.

Brandenbourg House, 19th of March, 1821

The Queen is much surprised at the contents of Lord Liverpool's letter, and is anxious to know from Lord Liverpool if his Majesty has commanded him to forbid the Queen appearing at his drawing-room, or merely to prevent her Majesty presenting her petition in person to the King.

The restoration of the Queen's name to the Liturgy, being the first and only favour the Queen has ever solicited from his Majesty, she trusts he will be graciously pleased to acquiesce in, and she most earnestly prays his Majesty to grant.

Caroline R.

'Carrying coals to Newcastle!!' ?T. Lane (16 February 1821). An anti-Queen satire on the procession of the brassfounders to present addresses to her at the end of January 1821

Minute of Cabinet

19th of March, 1821

It is not probable that, after receiving the proposed answer, the Queen should make any attempt to come to court on Thursday.

It appears to be proper, however, to be prepared for such an event, in case it should occur. The King's confidential servants are unanimously and decidedly of opinion that in such case no attempt should be made to obstruct the Queen on her way to Buckingham House. Such obstruction could not be made without the risk of creating general confusion in the metropolis, and of shedding quantities of blood.

It is proposed therefore that if the Queen should arrive at Buckingham House she should be immediately shown into a room on the ground floor, and that the Lord Chamberlain, Vice-Chamberlain, or some other officer of his Majesty's household, should be sent to her to receive her petition.

If she should decline delivering it into any hands but the King's, the King should not be advised to permit her to come up to the drawing-room, but should himself go down to the room where the Queen is, attended by such of his household and his ministers as may be there, and receive the petition.

It is conceived that there can be no difficulty, by previous arrangements such as those which have been recently adopted, to prevent the Queen from coming up the stairs, without incurring any of the inconveniences which must arise from a conflict in the streets or in the park.

The Queen submitted her petition to Liverpool.

TO THE KING'S MOST EXCELLENT MAJESTY

THE PETITION OF CAROLINE, QUEEN CONSORT

Brandenbourg House, March 21st, 1821

Her Majesty seeks to lay before the King this representation of the grievance to which she has been subjected by the continued omission of her name in the Liturgy. The privilege of being prayed for by name in the Church service has been enjoyed by her predecessors Queens Consort of England from the time of the Reformation, and has been ever highly esteemed as a mark of honour and dignity.

Her Majesty has always been impressed with the strongest feelings of regret that the King should have yielded to any advice by which she should be excluded, and thereby degraded in the estimation both of his Majesty's subjects and of foreign nations. All further proceedings against her Majesty being now finally abandoned, the Queen solicits your Majesty as an act of justice and grace to permit her the enjoyment of that privilege now so long withheld.

The Queen with reluctance makes this her appeal to your Majesty, and earnestly prays that this, her only request, may be granted.

Caroline R.

Carlton House, Wednesday, March 21st, 1821

The King has the pleasure to return to Lord Liverpool the Queen's note and petition, and has no doubt that his lordship will return a proper answer to each.

The King congratulates Lord Liverpool upon the prospect of his being relieved from a disagreeable duty to-morrow.

Lady Cowper to Frederick Lamb

Friday March 9th [1821]

. . . Everybody is here talking of . . . the Queen's letter. The Ladies are coming down from their High Horses. The Queen's letter is quite ridiculous and absurd, as far as I hear stated, for a copy I have not yet been able to see. They say it is not at all of a piece with her late proceedings, all low and thankful, obliged to the King for the money, obliged to the people and, *by the way*, hopes he will put her name back in the Liturgy. In short, the substance comes out much to this. Her friends look blank, and it's all her own doing and writing, ill-spelt and without help or consultation; *elle est folle voilà tout!!!*

Correspondence on the Queen's demand to be crowned

29the of april

The Queen, after having been a considerable time of receiving a answer from Lord Liverpool, in consequence of the last conversation that passed between his Lordship and Doctor Lushington:

Her Majesty feels herself under the necessity to establish herself in England, and communicates to Lord Liverpool that the Queen intends to be present at the Coronation, and requests him to present the inclosed letter to his Majesty.

Caroline R.

Brandenbourgh House, Sunday, 29the of April, 1821

The Queen from circumstances being obliged to remain in England, she requests the King will be pleased to command those Ladies of the first Rank his Majesty may think the most proper in this Realms, to attend the Queen on the day of the Coronation, of which Her Majesty is informed is now fixed, and also to name such Ladies which will be required to bear Her Majesty's Train on that day.

The Queen being particularly anxious to submit to the good Taste of his Majesty most earnestly entreate the King to informe the Queen in what Dresse the King wishes the Queen to appear in, on that day, at the Coronation.

Caroline R.

Most private
Brighton, May 1st, 1821

The King has just received the box from Lord Liverpool containing the copy of a letter from the Queen to Lord Liverpool, and Lord Liverpool's account of a conversation which took place a short time since between Lord Liverpool and Dr Lushington, referred to in the Queen's letter to Lord Liverpool, and a letter from the Queen addressed to the King.

The King highly approves of the line and of the tone taken by Lord Liverpool in his conversation with Dr Lushington. The King, however, entertains considerable doubts whether some decided notice should not be taken of the 'threat' (as Lord Liverpool justly terms it) held out by the Queen in her letter to Lord Liverpool, 'of her intention of being present at the coronation'. Had such an intimation reached Lord Liverpool merely in the shape of an idle report or of a fabrication, such as almost every day produces, the King would then entirely concur with Lord Liverpool's opinion that it would not justify any direct notice being taken of it.

The matter here, however, stands widely different, as the Queen has decidedly and pointedly specified to Lord Liverpool 'that it is her intention to obtrude herself at the King's coronation'. If, therefore, the subject were suffered to pass over in *utter silence* after this express and positive declaration on the part of the Queen, officially communicated by her under her own hand to Lord Liverpool as the King's first minister, the Queen, on the one hand, might have some sort of colour to assume that it had never been formally notified to her, as it is now the King's intention that it shall be, that she should *never* be suffered by the King, under any circumstances, to appear at that most solemn ceremony, the law having placed the entire control upon that head in the hands and at the pleasure of the King; while, on the other hand, she might attribute such silence to an unworthy timidity on the part of the King and of his Government, as well as invidiously pretend that her intimation upon this point had not only not been treated with common civility, but had been contemptuously disregarded.

Lord Liverpool will observe that the King returns *unopened* the letter addressed by the Queen to the King. This is only in conformity to a resolution adopted more than twenty years ago, and since invariably adhered to by the King (but which must have escaped Lord Liverpool's recollection) that the King would *never again* receive or open any letter or paper addressed to him personally by the Queen.

The King will only further suggest to Lord Liverpool the propriety of postponing any reply or communication whatsoever upon this subject to the Queen until after the Court at Buckingham House on Thursday next. From what so recently occurred with respect to the last drawing-room, the King thinks that Lord Liverpool will clearly perceive the wisdom of this precaution.

Fife House, May 4th, 1821

Lord Liverpool has the honour to inform the Queen that, as it has been his Majesty's invariable determination for some years to receive no communication from the Queen except through his Government, the King directed Lord Liverpool to open the Queen's letter; and, Lord Liverpool having laid the substance of it before his Majesty, the King has commanded Lord Liverpool to say in answer that it is his Majesty's prerogative to regulate the ceremonial of his coronation in such manner as he may think fit; that the Queen can form no part of that ceremonial, except in consequence of a distinct authority from the King, and that it is not his Majesty's intention under the present circumstances to give any such authority.

Lord Liverpool thinks it must be unnecessary, in consequence of this communication, to notice the other points in the Queen's letter, but he will further add that the King has dispensed with the attendance of all ladies upon his coronation.

Brandenbourgh House, Saturday, 5th of May

The Queen is much surprised at Lord Liverpool's answer, and assures the Earl that her Majesty is determined to attend at the coronation; the Queen considering it as one of her rights and privileges, which her Majesty is resolved ever to maintain.

The Queen requests Lord Liverpool to communicate the above to his Majesty.

Caroline R.

Fife House, May 5th, 1821

Lord Liverpool has the honour to send your Majesty the answer which he has received from the Queen. Lord Liverpool humbly submits that the correspondence would better end here, at least for the present. The threat is an empty threat, which the Queen has evidently not the power of carrying into execution, and must appear to have been made solely with a view to extorting money.

Lord Liverpool will request your Majesty to be pleased to return the Queen's letter. Lord Liverpool has directed a copy to be prepared for your Majesty of the whole correspondence.

Fife House, 7th May, 1821

Lord Liverpool has received the King's commands, in consequence of the last communication of the Queen to Lord Liverpool of the 5th inst., to inform the Queen that his Majesty having determined that the Queen shall form no part of the cermonial of his coronation, it is therefore the Royal pleasure that the Queen shall not attend the said ceremony.

Mrs Arbuthnot's journal

May 6th. – The Queen has written to Lord Liverpool to say she means to go to the Coronation, desires to have ladies of high rank appointed to hold her train, & wishes to know *what dress* His Majesty w^d desire her to wear!! The impudence of this woman is beyond belief. It w^d have been well to have sent her word to appear in a white sheet. Ld Liverpool wrote her word that it was the King's prerogative to order the ceremonial as he pleased, & that it was not his intention that she sh^d assist at the ceremony. However, she has written another letter to say she is determined to go.

11th. – I dined at Lord Westmorland's, where Lord Duncannon told me the Duke of Norfolk, as Earl Marshal, meant to offer his seats at the Coronation to the Queen. I said I did not believe the Duke capable of such indecorous behaviour & that, whatever he might do, I thought the Queen would have too much pride to appear as a common spectator at a ceremony in which she had been judged unfit to assist as a principal. He said he did not know what she might do, but he knew the D. of Norfolk w^d give her the places. To which I replied that he might then, I thought, consider the Catholic question settled during this King's reign, for that such an offensive insult w^d not be readily forgiven the head of the Catholic body.[1] I asked Lord Londonderry what he thought of this & he said he could not believe it, that it w^d be utter ruin to the hopes of the Catholics & of no use, for he thought the King w^d have legal power to forbid the presence of any one obnoxious to him.

Henry Brougham's memoirs

It was now determined that the coronation should take place, and till that was over she could not quit London. Her claim was made to be crowned as a right; and the claim being referred to the Privy Council, we were heard before a very crowded meeting, Lord Harrowby, as President, in the chair. The Attorney and Solicitor General attended as assessors to the Council; and there were present to assist, the Chancellor, the Chief Justices, and Chief Baron, and all the other judges who were privy councillors. Denman and I argued the case at the bar for the claim, the Attorney and Solicitor General (Gifford and Copley) against it; and the decision was, that as the Queen was living separate from the King, she had no right to be crowned; and thus it was left to the King to refuse it. This was manifestly a political judgment, entirely influenced by what had taken place the year before; for we showed, by the clearest proofs, that there was no instance whatever of a queen not being crowned, except one, when she was abroad; and another, where there was a difference of religion, and she declined it; but none whatever of a queen-consort not being crowned when she was within the realm, of the same religion with the king, and willing to be crowned. My own impression was that the lay Lords, not being in office – and even Lord Harrowby, though in office – were inclined to our case; but that the law Lords, including the judges, were against us – those judges who had taken a very decided part against us in the Lords as assessors to the House, and had done themselves as little credit as possible in their answers to the legal questions put to them, the most important of which has been disapproved by all lawyers since, and declared to be erroneous by late statutes – so much so that 'the rule in the Queen's case' has been a strong topic of ridicule in the profession.

The Queen to the Lord President of the Council

Brandenburgh-House, July 11, 1821

My Lord, – Your Lordship's letter of yesterday to Lord Hood, conveying to me the report of the Committee of Council, on my Memorial to the King in council, claiming my right to be crowned, and as I find the Committee positively denies the right which I have claimed, and which all Queens-consort have enjoyed (without one exception arising from the will of the Sovereign), I consider it necessary to inform your Lordship, that it is my intention to be present at the ceremony on the 19th, the day fixed for his Majesty's coronation, and I therefore demand that a suitable place may be appointed for me.

Caroline R.

To the Right Hon. Lord Viscount Sidmouth.

The Times, 13 July

Affairs remain at present in a state of tranquillity with respect to The QUEEN, her rights, and claims. What a pity it is that this perverse obstinate woman, being innocent, cannot be prevailed upon to feel all the timidity and abashment of guilt. What insolence in her, that, being of a rank equal to the highest, she will put herself forward, assume her station, and act as if she had never been persecuted, slandered, and insulted, in every conceivable way. 'Why are you not depressed? Why do you not crouch? Why are you not sunk into the earth by the incessant assaults of so potent antagonists?' Such is the language of her enemies; while her MAJESTY holds on the tenour of her way, and that a high one also, apparently unconscious of the important part which she is acting, and doing what she does with noble simplicity as matter of course. Kings fume – counsellors consult – Cabinets assemble – Ministers plot, while this lady smiles, and orders her own course as she will. If she cannot obtain her right, she can make known that the right is hers, and that she is unjustly deprived of it: and afterwards she takes what she can get – much more than her enemies would allow her if they had their own way – and then she smiles again and goes on, living down the slanders which have been circulated against her, but still provoking her enemies to invent more by the innocence of her life and the habitual ease of her conversation and habits. A box, it is now said, is to be assigned to her to witness the ensuing spectacle. Thither will millions of kind wishes attend her. How different would have been her present state and condition, if she had in any degree yielded or given way to the atrocious attacks on her royal dignity; or if she had listened to the hollow proposals of her adversaries. She would now have been an exile, wandering no one knows where, and exposed to the insults of the vilest of mankind, – the native retainers of foreign courts, and runagate Englishmen hanging about those courts, some with and some without missions or employments. And yet we are told that her MAJESTY is ill-advised, misled, exposed, and all the rest!

Sarah Lyttelton to Captain the Hon. F. Spencer

Putney, July 4, 1821

. . . All the circle are vastly well; my Father is in such good spirits about himself that he means to *walk* among the other Peers in the Procession at the Coronation, if it takes place. Nobody, however, seriously seems to expect that festivity to take place at all: the mob are rather too cross, and too fond of the Queen to be allowed to witness a pomp and ceremony in which she is *not* to take a part; and they will make some bustle on the occasion; we are all in a fright about it. As it is they make bustle enough; every day there is a gathering on some account or other. And Her Gracious Majesty takes care to keep it up, by showing herself all about London in a shabby post-chaise and pair of *post-horses*, and living in the scrubbiest house she could think of, to *show* she is kept out of the Palaces. Nothing ever was like the absurdity of the Ministers' conduct towards her – that is, they have complied with every wild fancy of the King's; he has certainly lost his head on the subject, and rather than *go out* they do everything he orders when he is in a real fury and rage. . . .

Henry Brougham on the coronation

The coronation then went on; and finding the Queen inclined to appear in the Abbey, we very strongly advised her against any such proceeding. A letter was addressed to her by Denman and myself, protesting against such a step, although she had got a ticket of admission through a friend, who had obtained the Duke of Wellington's order; and the using this was an additional imprudence, which gave rise to much obloquy, not unnaturally. The King, being apprised of her intention, was beyond measure alarmed; and every precaution was taken to prevent her from getting into the Abbey. She was stopped at one gate, and then went to another, where she was again refused admittance; and those very foolish persons who had set her upon this most unwise proceeding now saw that even the mob were against them; for they confined their feeling against the King to a little hissing as he passed, and received the Queen very coldly. The difference between her reception then and on that wonderful day when she went to St Paul's was very striking. But it must be added that much of the difference and all the failure was owing to herself. We had all told her that she ought not by any means to attempt to enter the Abbey, and gave her many good reasons against it – among others, that the public feeling would not go along with her. But we distinctly said that if she made the attempt, she must do it with her wonted firmness, and that she must make her way into the Abbey if she chose to try it, because, having an order she could not be stopt when she insisted upon it. Had I known whose order it was, I certainly should have made it an additional ground of refusing my consent to her proceeding. But I only knew it was a valid order, and joined with Denman and one or two of her ladies in saying she must either not make the attempt at all, or must make it so as to succeed. On the contrary, she flinched – I verily believe, for the first time in her life; and instead of insisting on admission at the great gate, she drew back on the refusal, which was made known to those at the other door, and she was entirely defeated. There was some talk of allowing her to enter Westminster Hall and see the banquet, but that she of course refused.

The consequence of this unfortunate day was a severe illness, which she made worse by taking opiates to relieve the great pain she suffered; and it was soon found that there was a most dangerous obstruction. There were hopes, however, of it yielding to the treatment employed, and when I left town for York the prospect of her recovery was favourable. I saw her the day on which I set out, and was with her half an hour. She spoke very calmly of her case; and when I told her of the satisfactory opinion which I had just heard from her medical men, she said, 'Oh no, my dear Mr Brougham, I shall not recover; and I am much better dead, for I be tired of this life.'

Letters from Henry Brougham to Thomas Creevey

London, 19 July, 1821

. . . To-day the Q's being allowed to enter the Abbey is doubted . . . but I still think it possible the Big Man may have gout and not be up to it.

Yours,
H.B.

20th July

. . . The paroxysm rather encreases than diminishes, and literally extends to all classes. There never was a more humbling sight in this world. The Ministers are still sitting and squabbling; nor have they to this hour (5) [a.m.] made up their minds whether to stop her or not. My belief is they will let her pass, and also admit her at the Abbey if she persists. She is quite resolved to do so, and comes to sleep at Cambridge House for the purpose. But she is sure to blunder about the hour, and to give them excuses for turning her back by being late. . . . We [Brougham and Denman] thought at one time she meant to command our attendance, which we had resolved, of course, to refuse, as no more in our department than going to Astley's; but she did not venture. . . .

Thursday

Dear C.,

The Qn. (as I found on going to her house at 20 minutes before six this morning) started at a quarter past five, and drove down Constitution Hill in the mulberry – Lady A[nne] H[amilton] and Lady Hood sitting opposite. Hesse (in uniform) and Lord H[ood] in another carriage went before. I followed on foot and found she had swept the crowd after her: it was very great, even at that hour. She passed thro' Storey's Gate, and then round Dean's Yard, where she was separated from the crowd by the gates being closed. The refusal was peremptory at all the doors of the Abbey when she tried, and one was banged in her face. . . . She was saluted by all the soldiery, and even the people in the seats, who had paid 10 and 5 guineas down, and might be expected to hiss most at the untimely interruption, hissed very little and applauded loudly in most places. In some they were silent, but the applause and waving handkerchiefs prevailed. I speak from hearsay of various persons of different parties, having been obliged to leave it speedily, being recognised and threatened with honors.

About ½ past six [a.m.] she had finished her walks and calls at the doors, and got into the carriage to return. She came by Whitehall, Pall Mall and Piccadilly. The crowd in the Broad Street of Whitehall was immense (the barriers being across Parlt. St. and King St.). All, or nearly all followed her and risked losing their places. They crammed Cockspur Street and Pall Mall, &c., hooting and cursing the King and his friends, and huzzaing her. A vast multitude followed her home, and then broke windows. But they soon (in two or three hours) dispersed or went back.

I had just got home and she sent for me, so I went and breakfasted with her, and am now going to dine, which makes me break off; but I must add that the King was *not* well received at all – silence in many places, and a mixture of hisses and groans in others. However, there were some bounds kept with him. For Wood and Waithman –

a division of hissing and shouting – for the Atty. and Solr. Gen. an unmixed hissing of the loudest kind. *This* verdict is really of some moment, when you consider that the jury was very much a special, if not a packed, one. The general feeling, even of her own partisans, was very much agt. her going; but far more agt. their behaviour to her. I still can't see it in that light; and as she will go quietly back to B[randenburg] House, avoiding all mob most carefully, she gains more than she loses, and I think her very lucky in being excluded. They put it on not being at liberty to recognise her or any one, except as ticket-bearers. Lord H[ood] shewed me one which they said of course would pass *any one* of the party, but she refused to go in except as Q. and without a ticket. . . .

Mrs Arbuthnot's journal, July 1821

19th. – Coronation of the King. We had seats in the Lord High Constable's box which, in the Hall, was immediately over the Royal Family, an excellent place; in the Abbey, not quite so good. We went to Battersea Bridge & there got on board the Ordnance barge, which landed us at some stairs which took us into the Speaker's House & from there into the Hall. We set off at ½ past six & were seated in the Hall in less than an hour. Those who went in carriages were, some of them, three hours in getting up. The King came into the Hall at ten o'clock, the procession having been previously partly arranged. He looked at first excessively pale & tired but soon recovered &, after giving the Regalia to the different persons who were to carry it, the procession moved to the Abbey. While it proceeded by the platform to the north door of the Abbey, we went by a narrow passage erected from the door of the House of Lords to Poets' Corner & were seated in the Abbey before the procession arrived. On the King's entrance into the Abbey he was received with the loudest cheers, which were repeated with increased vehemence when the crown was placed on his head &, particularly, when the D. of York did homage & kissed him. It was a magnificent sight, that fine building full of people as it could possibly hold, all magnificently dressed, peers, heroes & statesmen all joining in one unanimous hurra. The ceremony occupied till towards three o'clock when the King returned to the Hall & passing thro' it, retired to a private room to rest till dinner.

The Duke of Wellington & Mr Arbuthnot then came to where we were & took us to Mr Bankes' in Old Palace Yard, where we had some thing to eat. They then told us that the procession along the platform had been much finer than the sight either in the Hall or Abbey, that every spot in sight to the very tops of the houses was crowded with people who had rent the air with their acclamations, . . . I wish I could have seen the procession along the platform; it must have been so fine to have seen the nobles & *sages* of the land decked out in velvet & satin, gold & jewellery, passing in procession amongst countless thousands, the sun shining without a cloud, & all uniting to do homage to that constitution under which we have so flourished!

The King returned to the Hall about 5 o'clock, when the Earl Marshal, the D. of Wellington (High Constable) & Ld Anglesea (High Steward) rode up the Hall with the first course & backed out again. They came in again with the second course, & the two latter with the Champion. It was very well done; the Duke of Wellington rode a white Arabian who backed most perfectly. There were a great many services done, caps given & returned, falcons presented by the D. of Atholl. The peers drank to the King, & he in return to the peers & his good people, & the whole concluded with 'God save the King,' sung by the choristers & chorused by the whole assembly. After the riding was over, the people had been allowed to crowd into the body of the Hall & only a small space was kept open at the foot of the steps, & it is not possible to describe any thing finer than the scene was, the galleries all standing up waving their hats & handkerchiefs & shouting, 'God bless the King!' Altogether it was a scene I w^d not have missed seeing for the world, & shall never again see so fine a one.

The King behaved very indecently; he was continually nodding & winking at L^y Conyngham & sighing & making eyes at her. At one time in the Abbey he took a diamond brooch from his breast &, looking at her, kissed it, on which she took off her glove & kissed a ring she had on!!! Any body who could have seen his disgusting figure, with a wig the curls of which hung down his back, & quite bending beneath the weight of his robes & his 60 years w^d have been quite sick. All his pages were chosen from Opposition families such as the D. of Bedford & Lord Jersey, & all selected by Lady Conyngham, who met with some rebuffs upon the occasion. Lady Jersey w^d not allow her sons to go till the King himself asked it in writing; & Ld Manvers, to whom she made a similar offer, sent her word that, had the King asked it, he sh^d have considered his son most highly honoured, but he w^d not for an instant listen to such a proposal from any woman whatever & rejected it with the utmost indignation. The King paid great attention during the ceremony to the Opposition, by whom, in fact, he was surrounded. The ceremony was ended by eight o'clock, & we changed our dresses at the Speaker's & walked home. Some people were detained till twelve o'clock, waiting for their carriages.

The Times' *account of the coronation, 20 July*

THE QUEEN

A considerable crowd assembled about her Majesty's house in South Audley-street, soon after 4 o'clock. As soon as it was ascertained that her Majesty's coach was making ready in the yard, the crowd . . . became very great. The wall opposite to her Majesty's house in Hill-street, was soon covered with spectators, who announced to the crowd below each successive step of preparation. 'The horses are to'; 'everything is quite ready'; 'the Queen has entered the coach', were the gradual communications, and they were received with the loudest cheers. Lady Anne Hamilton arrived a few minutes before 5, and was most cordially and respectfully greeted. Soon after 5, the gate was thrown open, and a shout was raised – 'The Queen!' 'The Queen!' The Queen immediately appeared in her coach of state drawn by six bays. Lady Hood and Lady Anne Hamilton sat opposite to her Majesty. . . . . Her Majesty looked extraordinarily well; and acknowledged, with great dignity and composure, the gratulations of the people on each side of her coach. The course taken was, through Great Stanhope-street, Park-lane, Hyde-park-corner, the Green-park, St James's-park, Birdcage-walk, and by Storey's-gate, along Princes-street, to Dean's-yard – a way, it must be observed, the least likely to attract notice, or to gather crowds. The crowd accumulated immensely along this line; the soldiers everywhere presented arms with the utmost promptitude and respect; and a thousand voices kept up a constant cry of 'The Queen', 'The Queen for ever'. The *coup d'oeil* from the road along the Green-park, was the most striking which can be imagined; the whole space presented one mass of well-dressed males and females hurrying with every possible rapidity to accompany the Queen, and shouting their attachment and admiration. The two torrents that poured along the south side of the park and the eastern end occasioned the greatest conflux at Storey's-gate. As soon as the Queen's arrival was known in the scene of the King's coronation, shouts of – 'The Queen', at once arose from all the booths, and hats and handkerchiefs were everywhere waved in token of respect. As soon as her Majesty came in sight of the coronation platform and Westminster-abbey, the coach stopt for a few minutes. The cheering of the crowd all the while was cordial and incessant. When the coach advanced towards Dean's-yard a person in the box behind, who from the colour of his countenance ought to be a tar, but whose long sunned coat eloquently prayed for promotion, attempted to utter some hisses. But this unmanly and most unnaval effort was sneakily covered from general observation by a filthy handkerchief held over the mouth. The cowardly act of servility was, however, detected, and the loud demand of the multitude below, happily aided by the general and decisive approbation of the respectable spectators in the booths, obliged the solitary hisser to desist. We were prevented from observing the mode in which her Majesty demanded and was refused admission into the Abbey. . . . The cheers of the spectators soon announced her Majesty's return through Tothill-street. . . . Her Majesty next demanded admission at Westminster-hall and the House of Peers. The consternation occasioned by the demand at the former place was exceedingly great. The gate was barricaded as against a hostile power; but her Majesty . . . rode slowly along the whole line of the procession, receiving and acknowledging the plaudits and various signals of respect which all the spectators liberally bestowed. The coach was at this time thrown open, and her Majesty was seen to great advantage looking at all objects around with great attention and composure, acknowledging the gratulations of the people with peculiar courteousness, and expressing in all her countenance a proud consciousness of 'injured merit', and a cheerful resignation to her unmerited lot. . . . Through Delahay-street, Charles-street, and Whitehall, the applauses from the multitudes at windows and in the streets was not unlike those which marked her Majesty's procession to St Paul's. Her Majesty had entered Storey's-gate some minutes before 6, and it was considerably past 7 when she returned by Whitehall. In the course of that hour she enjoyed in the highest degree those gratifications which can give any value to a coronation in the estimation of those whose judgment is sound, and whose taste is uncorrupted. She received every demonstration of respect and homage from multitudes whom no influence could induce to withhold the honest expressions of their feelings. Her Majesty returned through Pall-mall, St James's-street, and Piccadilly, followed all along by a great concourse of people, and every where greeted with spontaneous and ardent plaudits. In St James's-street the water had previously created abundance of mud, and this material the crowd bestowed upon some public offices which were prepared for illumination. During the whole course of her Majesty's progress not the slightest accident occurred to occasion the smallest pain or even inconvenience. . . .

from The Traveller

Her Majesty set out from her house in South Audley-street, and proceeding through the Parks to Westminster-abbey, went to Dean's-yard, where her Majesty got out of her carriage, in expectation of being allowed to enter, but was refused at

'The grand coronation of her most graceless majesty C-r-l-e Columbina, the first Queen of all the Radicals,' T. Lane (5 August 1821). A burlesque coronation of the Queen, with Bergami on her right and Wood as her champion, mounted on an ass. Brougham and Denman, in wigs and gowns, applaud. The naval officers represent Flynn and Hownam, who gave evidence for the Queen at her 'trial'

two doors of entrance; and her carriage having drawn off, her Majesty was obliged to wait in the passage till it was called back, when her Majesty proceeded towards Poets' Corner, and again got out of her carriage in Old Palace-yard, and sought admittance by two temporary doors, which upon her Majesty's approach, were shut in her face: after which, some of the people pointed out the entrance to the platform. Upon ascending this, her Majesty was again obstructed by the police-officers, till an officer, it is believed of the Guards, politely allowed her Majesty to cross the platform; and her Majesty walked from thence to Old Palace-yard, and entered first the passage to Cotton-garden; after which her Majesty proceeded along the covered way to Poets'-corner, and when arrived at the door was refused admittance without ticket, upon which Lord Hood produced one, and was informed it would only admit one person; upon which Lord Hood observed, he did not suppose the Queen required a ticket of admission; to which one of the persons appointed for the admission of the company observed, he did not know the Queen, and positively forbade her Majesty from entering; and one of the Poor Knights of Windsor came up and said there was no place for her Majesty. Finding every effort to gain admittance ineffectual, her Majesty returned to her carriage, and proceeded through Whitehall, Pall-mall, and St James's-street, Piccadilly, to her house, attended by an immense concourse of people, manifesting their respect to their Queen, and expressing their indignation at the unexampled treatment experienced by her Majesty. . . .

Lady Cowper to Frederick Lamb

Friday, 20th [July 1821]

The Coronation was yesterday and we are all delighted with it. We found it very
fatigueing and the whole might very easily have been curtailed one half; but,
however, we have outlived it and so has the King, but he looked more like the
Victim than the Hero of the Fete. I really pitied him from my heart, several times
he was at the last Gasp, but then came a cheering draught in the shape of a look
from Ly C[onyngha]m who sat near me, and it revived him like Magic or Ether. I
was in the line of fire so I had a full view. When he put on the Ruby ring he cast up
a most significant look at her, but I could not well make out whether the look
meant, I will wear it for your sake, or, after the Ceremony I will give it you *pour
tenir Compagnie au Saphir*, which was in full display, and must have nearly put out
Leopold's eye when the sun shone upon it. I rather imagine this last was the true
interpretation.

The great sight was truly beautiful both in the Hall and Abbey, perhaps more from
the brilliancy of the Spectators than from the sight itself, but the whole thing was
indeed very handsome in the Procession and the variety and beauty of the dresses had
a very fine effect. Much of the Ceremony in the Abbey was Monkish and twaddling
and foolish and spun out, but the music and applause had a grand effect. He was very
well received everywhere, and seemed much gratified and had a complete victory over
the Queen, who if she could have been lower than she was before would have made
herself so by her miserable attempt of yesterday. Even the Mob and Spectators hooted
her away after she had been refused at every door and had walked thro' the mob with
only Ly Anne [Hamilton] and jostled by all the lowest rabble. Think what a
degradation for a Queen, if Queen she can be called. Even Ly Jersey has left her, and
the King, who wishes to make an end of all feuds and perhaps from a less fine motive
to slap his Ministers' faces by his civility to their enemies, took Ld Jersey's two boys
into his train of Pages. So there is a reconciliation. . . .

Anne Cobbett to her brother James, 25 July 1821

. . . We have got an engraving of the Queen framed, to send to Mrs Tredwell. It is a
very good likeness, and she is represented holding the celebrated letter in her hand,
which is esteemed as a great compliment paid to the *author*. Her lawyers have been
betraying her again. The King had his coronation on the 19th of this month, and the
Queen was excluded from all participation in the ceremony. A person that you and I
know[2] did not take any part in the discussion at all, which all the world I dare say
wonder at. But in the first place the stupid Alderman, thinking I suppose that *he*
could manage the affair without us, did not *come* to *ask* for assistance, in the next
place if he had Papa would have declined being *under* Watson again, and lastly we had
a mind to let the lawyers have it all their own way for once, in order that the Queen
and the country might see what a mess they would make of it. If Papa had taken the
thing up, the man would no more have been crowned without her than he would have
swam across the Atlantic to take you by the nose. We none of us went to witness any
part of the show, though Papa approved of the King's being crowned, but as the
Queen was not there, we were not there, neither did we illuminate. – They said it was
a sumptuously grand affair, as far as the King and the Court were concerned, but

there were very few people as spectators. This was in great degree to dislike of the King, and because the Queen was not there, but much more it was owing to apprehension. The tremendous military preparations, thirty thousand men in the metropolis, a man of war and armed boats in the Thames, all this struck such a terror that every body expected a row of some sort or other, and so all staid away from the scene. At which I should think the King must be highly incensed. Many people that erected gallery's in front of the houses by which the procession passed, expecting to let a single seat for *thirty guineas* and upwards, will be entirely ruined; for we have heard of one man who had laid out *five thousand* pounds in erecting and fitting up these places, and within two days of the coronation he had not let *two seats*. So that it has gone off very poorly indeed. The *mobility* hissed the King most terribly it is said.

J. W. Croker to Robert Peel

July 24th, 1821

My Dear Peel,
You can have no idea either of the splendour of the pageant or of the good order and good luck which accompanied the ceremony of the coronation. . . . I assure you it was not only worth seeing, but, according to Dr Johnson's distinction, worth going to see, particularly the procession on the platform and the fête in Hyde Park. . . .

The Queen and Wood were hooted by the spectators. She went off in a rage of disappointment. She, no doubt, came down not to get in, for she took care to have but one ticket, and that one irregular, although she might have had fifty good ones, and would have been let in if she had produced a proper ticket. The attempt to get admission was therefore only a pretence for the parade through the streets, and that I firmly believe was *calculated* to try her strength, and it only proved her weakness. And from eight o'clock on Thursday morning we heard not a word more of her till about the same hour yesterday morning when the *Morning Post* and all the town had it she had fled, some said to Italy, and others to Scotland. In fact she was in the dumps at Brandenburgh House, and we hear to-day intends, like the Duke of Monmouth of old, to make a progress in the West. . . .

Notes

1. The Duke of Norfolk, hereditary Earl Marshal of England, was a Roman Catholic. Agitation for the removal of civil disabilities on Roman Catholics was to achieve its object (Catholic Emancipation) in 1829.
2. i.e. William Cobbett, their father.

The End of the Affair

In February 1821 Lady Cowper recorded that the Queen's doctor had warned her about her health and suggested a visit to Spa. Five months later, Brougham noted that her rejection at the coronation brought on an illness which she made worse by taking heavy doses of opiates. She appeared to develop an intestinal obstruction. Within three weeks of the coronation she lay dying, talking incessantly and feverishly until the final loss of consciousness. The King had left for a state visit to Ireland, and received the news of his wife's death on board the packet in St George's Channel. He had the decency not to appear overjoyed at the event, and in fact toned down the celebration of his birthday the following day as a gesture of respect. *The Times*, loyal to her to the last, published a final eulogy which spoke of her last moments as 'soothed by the consolations of religion . . . she died as she had lived, a Christian heroine, and a martyr', though she was not attended by any clergyman. Her friend Lord Hood wrote of her firmness and courage at the last.

The government quickly decided that her body should be sent to Brunswick for burial, and that there should be no public ceremonial in this country, and no official recognition of her status as Queen. However, the plan to send her cortège round London to Harwich, avoiding the danger of demonstrations in the city, was thwarted by a crowd at Hyde Park Corner who broke through the cordon of troops stationed to divert the procession and carried the coffin through the centre of London. The discipline of the soldiers broke down, shots were fired, and two men were fatally wounded and several injured. The manner of the Queen's departure from the country in which she had suffered such indignities was of a piece with her experiences when alive. The cortège eventually embarked from Harwich and on 24 August the body was interred in the Burg church in Brunswick in the presence of her English friends, Alderman Wood, Lady Anne Hamilton, Lord Hood, and the young William Austin whom she had made her legatee. Sixty young ladies dressed in white with black sashes and carrying wax tapers accompanied the coffin to the vault where the remains of Caroline, Queen of England, still rest.

The affair of Queen Caroline was at an end. It was one of the most sensational events of the nineteenth century, and one which might have brought the country to the verge of revolution. Yet it left remarkably few permanent traces. Economic recovery in the early 1820s was a major factor in quietening agitation; but even in the later stages of the crisis there was evidence that the basic fabric of English society and institutions was still strong. Not for the first nor for the last time, Englishmen, and women, showed themselves tenacious of their rights and liberties, disrespectful of authority when wrongly asserted, and unafraid of violence in pursuit of what they believed fair and just; but they also showed themselves to be fundamentally law-abiding, deferential, and even conservative in believing that their freedoms were rooted in their existing institutions and in the traditions of their history.

Some historians have suggested that the Queen Caroline affair had lasting effects on the development of English Radicalism, particularly in giving ordinary people experience of political organization and in developing the power of the Press. It was not unique in these respects, however, and eleven years later the agitation over the Great Reform Bill brought out some of the same features of popular political activity, without building specifically on the experience of 1820. Perhaps the most remarkable feature of this crisis was the way in which women came forward in defence of their rights and identified themselves with a political cause; yet even here, there was no immediate change in the status of women in society, no easing of the disadvantages faced by married women as regards divorce or subjection to the legal power of their husbands, and no permanent enhancement of the role of women in political life. It was to be many years before women began to claim or achieve any advance in their legal, social, or domestic status, and almost a century before they acquired the right to participate in political life through the vote. If the Queen Caroline affair awakened a sense of injustice in the hearts of the women of England it failed to mould this into a positive and continuing feminist movement. The women of England may have identified Caroline with their aspirations and feelings but, like her, they were no better off at the end than in the beginning. The affair of Queen Caroline illustrated, but did little to change, the fundamental conditions of English life and society in the early nineteenth century.

Lady Anne Hamilton on the Queen's last illness

. . . Upon her Majesty's arrival at Brandenburgh House, after being refused admittance to the coronation, she took a cup of tea, and then retired to her room for nearly four hours. In this interval, the queen resolved to visit Scotland; she wrote to Lord Liverpool on the subject, and requested his lordship to apprise the king of her intention. This letter was received by his lordship, and answered in the usual strain, 'that he (Lord Liverpool) had laid her Majesty's letter before the king, but had not received his Majesty's commands thereon'. In the intermediate time, it was announced, the king would visit Ireland; and his Majesty left Carlton House at half-past eleven o'clock, on the 31st of July, on his way to Portsmouth for Dublin.

On the 30th of July, the evening previous to the king's departure, her Majesty visited the theatre, and was much indisposed, but would not be persuaded to retire before the performance was concluded; indeed, it was the queen's usual line of conduct not to disturb any public assembly by retiring earlier than was positively needful. Before her Majesty went to the theatre she felt indisposed, but declined remaining at home, for fear of disappointing the people. When her Majesty returned from the theatre, she was very sick, and had much pain in her bowels the next day. In the afternoon of this day, Doctor Holland called, apparently by chance, and, on feeling her pulse, said she must have further advice. She objected, as having most confidence in him, who had travelled with her; but to satisfy his mind, her Majesty said he might bring whom he liked. Next day (Wednesday) he brought Doctor Ainslie, who desired to have more assistance called in; and on Thursday morning Doctor Warren accompanied the other two, both king's physicians, according to etiquette, we believe. Previous to this, she seemed much surprised herself at her illness, and said to Doctor Holland, 'Do you think I am poisoned?' This day, she was told, they hoped things would end well; but if she had any papers of consequence, she had better dispose of them, as, in the event of her decease, everything must go to the king, or the ministers, – we forget which. At this, she astonished them all by her greatness of mind; for her Majesty did not betray the slightest agitation, but immediately and coolly answered, 'Oh, yes, I understand you; it shall be done'. She sat up almost the whole of that night with her maid Brunette only, burning letters, papers, and MS. books. She then called Hyronemus (her *maître d'hôtel*) and made him swear to burn everything she gave him in the kitchen fire. More letters, papers, and MS. books were then given him, besides a large folio book, full, or nearly so, of her own writing. It was about two feet long, and five or six inches thick, and bound. This book she always said contained the whole history of her life ever since she came to this country, together with the characters of the different persons she had been intimate with. Besides papers, she sorted all her little trinkets, wrapped them in separate papers, and wrote herself the names of all her different friends who were to have them, charging Brunette to dispose of them after her death according to the directions; but these presents never reached their destination.

From Thursday, her Majesty seemed regularly to get worse, and the inquiries after her health by the people at large were equal to the interest she had raised in her country. It was pretty generally said that her Majesty's danger arose from a stoppage in the bowels. . . .

No one was suffered to approach the queen but the king's physicians, except in their presence, though her Majesty most anxiously asked for William Austin, saying, 'How odd it is that he never comes near me;' in the meanwhile, he was weeping bitterly outside the door, but was always told, either 'the queen is asleep', or else, 'too ill to see him'. Her Majesty's sufferings must have been dreadful, and they seemed to come on periodically, when her cries could be heard in all the adjacent rooms, and then it appeared that the doctors dosed her with laudanum, which, of course, added to the constipation of her bowels, as well rendered her quite insensible when her friends did see her. . . .

On the Sunday before her death, her Majesty said, 'I should much like to take the sacrament; and I desire that the clergyman who does the duty at Hammersmith may be sent for to administer it.' Application was immediately made; but the gentleman said, 'I cannot administer it without leave from the rector, who is now at Richmond.' A messenger went to Richmond, and found that the rector had gone to dine in London, and that the clergyman must either go there to him, or solicit permission from the king's ministers. Notwithstanding this unfeeling piece of tyranny, her Majesty said, 'I do not doubt but my intentions will be accepted by God, the same as if I had been permitted to receive it.' The queen was truly an example of patience and resignation, for she never repined, not even in her most agonising moments. Her Majesty, alas! too well knew she must eventually be the victim of tyranny. . . .

Her Majesty, in her agony, frequently exclaimed, 'I know I am dying, – they have killed me at last! but I forgive all my enemies, even Dumont,' her maid Brunette's sister, who had done her Majesty the greatest injury, – 'I charge you (turning to her maid Brunette) to tell her so.' Brunette and her Majesty's *maître d'hôtel*, Hyronemus, wished to marry. Her Majesty called them to her, and joined their hands over her body (one standing on each side of the couch), and charged Hyronemus to be kind to Brunette. Her Majesty then told them she had left them all her linen (by right belonging to her lady in waiting) and two of her carriages. On Tuesday, her Majesty became much worse, and moaned terribly with pain from four o'clock till ten at night, when she rapidly grew weaker, till Doctor Holland, with the awful watch in his hand, feeling her pulse, at last closed her Majesty's eyelids, and declared 'All is over!'

Malice and crime had now done their worst: the fatal blow had been struck, and Caroline, the injured and innocent Queen of England, was for ever relieved from her despicable and heartless persecutors!

'O, what a noble mind was here o'erthrown!'

Henry Brougham to Lord Grey

Grantham, August 5, 1821

My Dear Lord Grey, – As you may be desirous of knowing really how the Queen is, I write this to say that, though she was still in great danger when I left Brandenburgh House yesterday at four o'clock, yet she was better, and had several favourable symptoms. The day before there seemed hardly a chance, but the inflammation had not returned; the pulse was good, both strong and moderate; she had had refreshing sleep, and the stomach quiet. The obstruction still continued in spite of 35 grains of calomel in her, besides twenty more *supposed* to have been rejected, and castor-oil and jalap, &c., enough to physic a hundred people.

The two risks she runs are, the obstruction continuing, and inflammation coming on when it is removed; but the pulse is now such that they can easily bleed her again. She lost sixty-four ounces altogether.

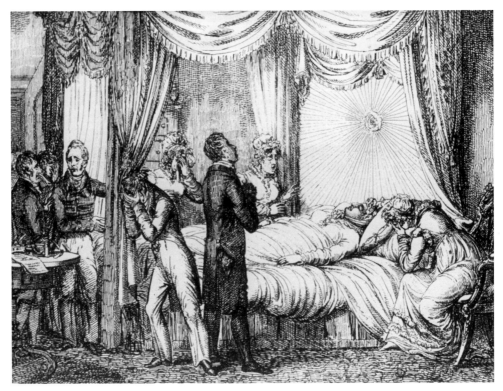

'The last moments of Queen Caroline, Queen of England,' a frontispiece of a verse satire on the Queen's death

I saw her on Friday night, when she signed her will, and she *seemed* not to be very ill, and her voice and hand were as firm as I ever saw any person's. She said to me that she was quite sure she should die, but did not mind it. However, there was something made me believe she did not at all think so.

All London was in the greatest hubbub about it, as I learn. – Yours ever,

H.B.

I suppose the King would at first be very glad at her death; but he would soon find how odious it made him.

Brougham's memoirs

Two days after I arrived at York I had a letter announcing her death. Indeed the favourable symptoms had disappeared the morning after I saw her, and the first letter I received at York appeared to preclude all hope.

I returned to London to attend the funeral, and I found that Lushington and Wilde, whom she had appointed her executors, had a long interview with her the day before she died. She was then in no pain, mortification having commenced, and she had altogether lost her head. She talked incessantly on every subject for three hours; and it is very remarkable that the only persons she mentioned were the 'Petite Victorine', Bergami's child, and the child of Parson Wood,[1] which she had taken one of her fancies for. While at Hammersmith she had made him her chaplain, and caused Lord and Lady Hood to quit their places of Lord of the Bedchamber and Mistress of the Robes in order to appoint Wood and his wife, who had not the proper rank, and indeed were in all respects unfit for the situation. This is the only bad thing I can recollect of her doing in the management of her household or other affairs, for the Hoods had been most invaluable friends and servants, standing by her through all her troubles, and behaving on every occasion with the most admirable delicacy, as well as tact. But she could not control her fancy for Wood's child, which amounted almost to a craze. She would have it brought to play with her, not only at all hours of the day, but even of the night, as she often sat up till a very late hour. This was the cause of her making way for the Woods, just as the Petite Victorine had been the cause of her taking Bergami into her service, and the sailmaker's child at Deptford, who was called Billy Austin, but for whom another was substituted after a few years, the child of one of her ladies in Germany, by Prince Louis of Prussia. She had often mentioned this to Lady Charlotte Lindsay and Mrs Damer, but they supposed it was a jest. However, when Lushington and Wilde went with the funeral to Germany, and one of them presented the other to the general who came to receive the body, and then said, 'And here is Mr Austin, of whom you have often heard;' he said, 'Yes, I have often heard of Billy Austin, but this is not he: this is the son of my old general, Prince William, and so like him that I at once knew him before you named him.' This poor lad, to whom Leach, by his decision in the affair of the Queen's estate, gave a considerable legacy, became a good-for-nothing person, and after going to Italy, where he lived near Victorine, then respectably married to an Italian count, became deranged, and died in a lunatic asylum.

The funeral was attended by most of those in town who had been the Queen's friends. I took Sir Robert Wilson to Hammersmith, where she lay in state, and from where the procession took place. His son Henry, who had been one of her equerries, was in the carriage with us. The King had gone to Ireland, and ministers, having no orders, except to prevent all honour being paid, and if possible to prevent the procession from marching through the City, acted upon their own notions of fulfilling his intentions, and turned out the troops to obstruct our passage. An attempt was made by us at Kensington to move round the Palace, and so reach Oxford Street, as we were told that we must not go by Piccadilly. But they prevented us, and obliged us to go through Hyde Park, intending to turn us at Apsley House, and so oblige us to go by the New Road. We told them distinctly that the funeral must pass through the City. Nothing occurred till we got near Apsley House, where the crowd was very great. The hearse was allowed to pass, and turned into the Park Lane direction by the soldiery. They then tried to stop us, but we went on notwithstanding: I heard firing, and one or two bullets whistled past us. On the first noise I asked Wilson what it was: 'Oh,' said he, 'it is a noise you are not used to; we are in fire.' Then said I, 'We must get out of it; but perhaps we should do so as soon by going on.' He said, 'Certainly we should not be one whit worse than if we turned round.' So we went forward. Only Wilson got out and told the officer commanding who we were, and that we belonged to the procession. After a shot or two more, this was effectual, and we escaped without hurt, though one of the bullets struck the carriage. We then got into Oxford Street, and found it crowded by troops, who made us turn into one of the streets leading to the New Road, the great object being to prevent us from getting into the City. However, we made the procession go at a round pace, so as to be there before the soldiery could come up; and this was the more easy because the New Road was nearly empty, while the parallel streets were extremely crowded. We then got down the street that slants towards St Paul's, and were soon in the Churchyard. The crowd was enormous, and furious at the appearance of the soldiery. As we moved slowly through it, several officers, not much liking their situation in the crowd, came up to our carriage and entered into conversation with us, manifestly thinking that their being seen to be friends would make things easier with the mob, which it did; for those officers were not at all maltreated, as many of the others were. We at length got clear of the City, and went as far as Ilford in Essex, on the Harwich road. We then returned to London, and I can answer for Wilson having been at no meeting, or indeed anywhere but at Brookes's and his own house. For whatever meetings there were, all were over long before he left me at Brookes's, where he remained till midnight. His dismissal from the army was grounded, therefore, on an utterly false pretence. I was to start early next morning, to overtake the funeral before it arrived at Chelmsford. I found it had just arrived, and it was deemed proper that the coffin should be conveyed to the church; but the authorities there objected, and Lushington had to call for the interposition of the magistrates to overcome the religious scruples of the clergy. Next morning it proceeded to Harwich at a continued rapid rate, there being the strictest orders sent from Dublin that the embarkation must be over before the arrival of the King, which was fixed for the next day. On arriving at Harwich we found everything ready prepared for immediate embarkation. The scene was such as I never can forget, or reflect upon without emotion. The multitudes assembled from all parts of the country were immense, and the pier crowded with them, as the sea was covered with boats of every size and kind, and the colours of the vessels were half-mast high, as on days of mourning. The contrast of a bright sun with the gloom on every face was striking, and the guns firing at intervals made a solemn impression. One of the sights, however, which most struck me, was a captain in the royal navy, who sat on the pier, and could not be persuaded to leave it; he was deeply affected, and wept exceedingly. Having been in her service, and employed then, and ever since, in dispensing her charities, he could not tear himself away; but being refused his earnest request of accompanying her remains to Brunswick, he was resolved to witness the embarkation. The crimson coffin slowly descended from the pier, and the barge that conveyed it bore the flag of England, floating over '*Caroline of Brunswick, the murdered Queen of England*', the inscription directed by herself, and the justice of which was felt by the thousands who had indignantly seen the indecent haste of the funeral procession from London, and who felt their share in a kind of national remorse, as well as commiseration, for all that had passed.

J. W. Croker's diary

August 11th. – The Queen died on Tuesday evening. Her will is tolerably expressive of her feelings. She mentions neither Brougham, Denman, nor Wood, and leaves Billy Austin residuary legatee. She desires that on her coffin may be inscribed 'Caroline, the *injured* Queen of England'. Lord Liverpool writes to Lord Sidmouth that this inscription no authority can place, but that her servants may do as they like. It is observed that she says *injured*, not *innocent*, and that no clergyman attended her in her last moments.

August 12th. – The King came over in the steam-packet, and landed at Howth at about half-past four. His birthday. Dined with the equerries. The King was uncommonly well during his passage, and gayer than it might be proper to tell; but he did not appear upon deck after he heard of the Queen's death, and, though it would be absurd to think that he was afflicted, he certainly was affected at the first accounts of this event. He walked about the cabin the greater part of the night on which the news reached him.

The Times, 8 August 1821

The tragedy of the persecutions and death of a QUEEN is at length brought to its awful close; and thousands – we may say millions – of eyes will be suffused in tears, when they shall read in this column that CAROLINE OF BRUNSWICK is no more. The greatest, perhaps the best woman of her day, sunk by what may be called a premature death, at twenty-five minutes past ten yesterday evening.

Her illustrious daughter – the only object, in truth, for which the mother wished to live – died three years and nine months before her; and, in their persons, a branch the most illustrious of the reigning house of England, and the closest to the royal stem, which, under happier auspices and more kindly treatment, might have given future EDWARDS and HENRIES, and ELIZABETHS, to the country, is for ever and for ever cut off. How the surviving members of the Royal Family may feel on this portentious occurrence, we know not; but the nation, which, during the sufferings of the QUEEN, evinced its loyalty to her person and its admiration of her character, feels now widowed by her decease; and politicians must perceive with some anxiety that the destinies of the monarchy are now transferred to, and wound up with, the life of an infant girl.[2] Sound be her frame, and lengthened be her days! But the nation has once already too fondly indulged hopes resting on such a basis, to repose implicit confidence in that which a sorrowful experience, as well as reason, hath taught it to be so frail.

. . . Her Majesty was sustained by the consciousness of innocence; she was soothed by the consolations of religion; and that firm courage which a benevolent Providence had so amply supplied to her, and all the members of her suffering race, did not desert her when she came to struggle with the last enemy of our nature. She died as she had lived, a Christian heroine, and a martyr. . . . No kindred hand was near to close her eyes; no mitred prelate to receive, amidst the impressive ceremonials of his office, and to publish to the world her solemn declarations of innocence. But peace was there, smiling like a cherub and the life which had been spent amidst clouds and tempests was blest with one last moment of serenity and joy. . . .

Thomas Creevey to Miss Ord

Cantley, Aug. 8

. . . Brougham was here for a very short time on Sunday night. . . . As to his Royal Mistress, his account was most curious. On Friday last she lost sixty-four ounces of blood; took first of all 15 grains of calomel, which they think she threw up again in the whole or in part; and then she took 40 grains more of calomel which she kept entirely in her stomach; add to this a quantity of castor oil that would have turned the stomach of a horse. Nevertheless, on Friday night the inflammation had subsided, tho' not the obstruction on the liver.

Her will and certain deeds had been got all ready by Friday night according to her own instructions. Brougham asked her if it was her pleasure then to execute them; to which she said – 'Yes, Mr Brougham; where is Mr Denman?' in the tone of voice of a person in perfect health. Denman then opened the curtain of her bed, there being likewise Lushington, Wilde and two Proctors from the Commons. The will and papers being read to her, she put her hand out of bed, and signed her name four different times in the steadiest manner possible. In doing so she said with great firmness – 'I am going to die, Mr Brougham; but it does not signify.' – Brougham said – 'Your Majesty's physicians are quite of a different opinion.' – 'Ah,' she said, 'I know better than them. I tell you I shall die, but I don't mind it.'. . .

Viscount Hood to Henry Brougham

Brandenburgh House, 8th Aug., 1821

. . . The melancholy event took place at 25 minutes past 10 o'clock last night, when our dear Queen breathed her last. Her Majesty has quitted a scene of uninterrupted persecution, and for herself I think her death is not to be regretted. . . . She died in peace with all her enemies. *Je ne mourrai sans douleur, mais je mourrai sans regret* – was frequently expressed by her Majesty. I never beheld a firmer mind, or any one with less feelings at the thought of dying, which she spoke of without the least agitation, and at different periods of her illness, even to very few hours of her dissolution, arranged her worldly concerns. . . .

Dr Lushington to Henry Brougham

Carlton, near Newmarket, 9 Aug., 1821

My Dear B.,
. . . I arrived just before 4 on Tuesday, and the Queen immediately desired to see me. . . . Baillie soon after assured me she was dying, but that the event would not take place for some hours. I went away for a short time, and then remained in the room till death closed the scene. . . . On her death happening, Wilde and myself secured all the repositories as well as we could. This occupied us till between 2 and 3 in the morning. . . . My situation was truly painful. You know I was to be married that very morning – Wednesday. I could not, for various reasons, postpone it; so, having taken 2 hours rest, I went to Hampstead, was married, and immediately returned to town. I had, on the death taking place, sent an express to Lord Liverpool. He came to town. I saw him with Wilde. He behaved extremely well – said Government would defray the expense of the funeral, and that he issued orders from the Chamberlain's office. He readily assented that the body should not be opened, and that the funeral should take place at Brunswick. By his desire I went over to Lord Melville, and he arranged that two frigates should be sent to Harwich and convey it to Cuxhaven. . . .

Thomas Creevey to Miss Ord

Cantley, Aug. 11

. . . The death of this poor woman under all its circumstances is a most striking event and gave me an infernal lump in my throat most part of Thursday. . . . There is one subject which gives me some uneasiness – in the making of her will, the Queen wished to leave some diamonds to Victorine, the child of Bergami, of whom she was so fond. This was not liked by Brougham and her other lawyers, so the bequest does not appear in the will; but the jewels are neverthelesss to be conveyed to Victorine. This, you know, is most delicate matter – to be employed on her deathbed in sending her jewels from Lady Anne Hamilton and Lady Hood to Bergami's child appears to me truly alarming. I mean, should it be known, and one is sure it will be so, for Taylor had a letter from Denison last night mentioning such a report, and being quite horrified at it. On the other hand, when I expressed the same sentiment to Brougham, he thought nothing of it. His creed is that she was a *child-fancier*: that Bergami's elevation was all owing to her attachment to Victorine, and he says his conviction is strengthened every day of her entire innocence as to Bergami. This, from Brougham, is a great deal, because I think it is not going too far to say that he absolutely *hated* her; nor do I think her love for her Attorney General was very great.

Henry Brougham to Thomas Creevey

Aug. 14, 1821

Dear C.,

I have seen Lushington and Wilde repeatedly. They are at this moment in negociation with the Govt.; or rather throwing up all concern with the funeral on account of this indecent hurry. Their ground is a clear one: they won't take charge of it from Stade – the port in Hanover – to Brunswick without knowing that arrangements are ready to receive them. . . . The Govt., only wishing the speedy embarkation, *as they avow*, for the sake of not delaying the dinner at Dublin, insist on getting it on board as quick as possible, and don't mind what happens afterwards. . . . I shall, I think, be satisfied with going to Harwich with it, and not go, as I had intended, to Brunswick.

Mrs Arbuthnot's journal, August 1821

15th. – Most disgraceful riots have taken place in London at the Queen's funeral. The people were dissatisfied at the procession being settled not to go thro' the City & actually, by force & violence, by breaking up the roads & blocking them with carts & carriages, forced it into the City. One man was killed & many wounded, & nothing prevented a dreadful slaughter but the exemplary patience & forbearance of the military. . . .

21st. – Mr Arbuthnot writes me word from London that he thinks all the mischiefs at the Queen's funeral were caused by Sir Robert Baker's[3] folly & cowardice, that the Riot Act was not read & the soldiers fired without orders; but, after all, men with arms in their hands cannot be expected to stand & be pelted to death without retaliating. Inquests are sitting upon the two men who were killed, & nothing ever was so absurd as the proceedings. Sheriff Waithman acts as Counsel for the dead man & treats the Coroner & every body with the utmost impertinence; the Life Guards were paraded today that the witnesses might try & identify the man who fired, but all picked out different people & most of them men who were not on duty, so that it is quite a farce. . . .

'The funeral procession of Queen Caroline, 14 August 1821, at Cumberland Gate, Hyde Park,' ?I.R.
Cruikshank (August 1821), depicting the clash between the Life Guards and the crowd when the funeral
cortège was forcibly diverted into the city

30th. – I returned to Woodford, where Mr A. had arrived in the morning. He told me
that Ld Liverpool was persuaded the King meant to turn us out when he returned to
town. It seems he is exceedingly displeased at all the proceedings about the Queen's
funeral, & very angry that the Ministers sent him no accounts of her illness, which
certainly seems strange neglect; all the accounts he received were from his private
secretary. I dare say, however, all this will blow over, the more particularly as a change
of government now w^d prevent his going to Hanover. He returns to London about
the 15th & talks of being only five days in London.

There was a great riot at the Knightsbridge barracks at the funeral of the two men
who were killed on the day of the Queen's funeral. The people hissed & hooted the
soldiers & at last attacked one who was amongst them unarmed. His comrades
defended him, & a general battle ensued. Nobody was much hurt. . . .

Lord Liverpool to the Marquess of Londonderry

Private
Coombe Wood, August 12th, 1821

My Dear Londonderry,
I have this moment read your letters of Friday.

I must just say, in justification of myself, that I had given directions for the Queen's
body being embarked in the river, but the Admiralty made so strong a representation

of the difficulties and eventual delay which might take place before the frigate could leave the British shore, that at a small cabinet, at which the Lord Chancellor, Lord Westmoreland, Lord Melville, and myself attended, and to which Sir George Cockburn was called, we felt ourselves obliged to agree that the embarkation should take place at Harwich.

It has been so arranged that the funeral will not pass through the town, but go round by the New Road. I regret very much the objections of the King to the Order from the Lord Marshal's office, as this Order is made, not only in the cases of the demise of the king or queen, but in those of brothers and royal progeny.

Whether the funeral is public or private, I think the reason suggested (the omission of the Queen's name in the Liturgy) would be still more unfortunate, considering all the circumstances under which that omission took place, and I cannot but wish that you and Lord Sidmouth would bring this matter again under the King's consideration. . . .

With respect to the duration of the mourning, . . . I think three weeks decidedly too short a time. I should recommend the usual short period, particularly at this season of the year, when no comparative inconvenience arises from mourning; but, at all events, I think six weeks the shortest time that could decently be fixed.

In considering all these questions, the object ought to be to do all that is right, and nothing that would offend decent and serious people.

As long as the Queen lived it might not unreasonably have been apprehended that every concession would be followed by some fresh demand; now all her demands are at an end, and the only consideration should be how we can close the business most quietly and without offence.

I will communicate with the Lord Chancellor on the other points in the Queen's will; but, as the executors must attend the funeral, nothing can, I conceive, be done upon them till they return.

Believe me, &c.
Liverpool

Lord Liverpool to Lord Sidmouth

Fife House, 8th August, 1821

My dear Lord,

I think it right to send you a copy of the letter which I had the honour of addressing to the King upon receiving intelligence of her Majesty's death. I have since seen Dr Lushington, who has communicated to me a copy of the Queen's will, with the codicils annexed to it, and I shall send them by the same conveyance to the King.

We are fortunately relieved from any difficulty about the funeral, as her Majesty has directed that she shall be buried at Brunswick, and that the body shall be sent off within three days, if possible, after her decease.

The inscription which the Queen has directed to be placed upon her coffin cannot obviously be put on by any authority or consent of government, nor be permitted whilst the coffin is in the possession of the officers of government. What her Majesty's executors may do afterwards, it is not our business to inquire. . . .

Thomas Creevey to Miss Ord

Cantley, Aug. 18th

. . . Here is Brougham again. He has been at Harwich, where he saw the body of the Queen embarked about 3 o'clock on Thursday; and then immediately came across the country, and, after travelling all night, got here to dinner yesterday, and proceeds to Durham to-night to join the circuit there. I wish very much I had been at Harwich: according to Brougham's account it must have been the most touching spectacle that can be imagined – the day magnificently beautiful – the sea as smooth as glass – our officers by land and sea all full dressed – soldiers and sailors all behaving themselves with the most touching solemnity – the yards of the four ships of war all manned – the Royal Standard drooping over the coffin and the Queen's attendants in the centre boat – every officer with his hat off the whole time – minute guns firing from the ships and shore, and thousands of people on the beach sobbing out aloud. . . . It was as it should be – and the only thing that was so during the six and twenty years' connection of this unhappy woman with this country. . . .

And now what do you think Brougham said to me not an hour ago? – that if he had gone with the Queen's body to Brunswick, it would have been going too far – it would have been over-acting his part; '*it being very well known that through the whole of this business he had never been very much for the Queen!*' Now upon my soul, this is quite true, and, being so, did you ever know anything at all to equal it?. . . .

Lady Anne Hamilton on the Queen's funeral

. . . It is well known that the queen, in her jocular moments, used to say, 'They did not like my young bones, so they shall not have my old ones;' and, in her last illness, her Majesty unfortunately added, 'and that as soon as possible'. This formed an excuse for the tools of George the Fourth to hurry her funeral beyond all decorum; as, in one single week after her Majesty's death, did Lord Liverpool order that all the cavalcade should be ready. The route was chalked out, and strict order given that, on no account, was the procession to go through the city; but every avenue was so choked up and barricaded by overturned coaches, carts, and rubbish, that they were obliged, at Piccadilly, to turn through Hyde Park; and, at Cumberland Gate, the scene of bloodshed commenced. We observed a pool of blood in the gateway, and a woman with her face all over blood, and two men lying dead. The people had pulled down the wall and railing for a hundred yards opposite Connaught Place; and the horse-soldiers (the Blues, we think) were pursuing the unarmed multitude down the park. A spent ball had fallen very near the hearse, and a gentleman in the retinue got off his horse, picked it up, and said, 'This will be proof against them'. At last Sir Robert Wilson, being a military man, rode up to the soldiers, and contrived to end the combat. The procession was then suffered to pass quietly along Edgeware and the New Roads till it came opposite to Portland Road, when the same obstructions of overturned carts, wagons, etc., prevented the cavalcade from continuing along the City Road or turning into any street eastward, until it arrived at Temple Bar, when it turned into the city, to the great joy and acclamations of the millions of people who had followed and who had lined the streets, windows, and tops of houses, although it rained in torrents, and the well-dressed women who attended were ankle deep in mud; nor did the people gradually drop away till the procession had entirely left the suburbs of London. . . .

The procession arrived at Harwich, on Thursday, at half-past eleven, at which place not even a single hour was allowed for retirement or repose; for the order was almost immediately given, that the coffin should be taken to the quay, and from thence lowered by a crane into a small barge. This was not accomplished without great difficulty, the coffin being extremely heavy. Four men rowed the boat to the side of the *Glasgow*, which was waiting to receive the remains of England's injured queen. Sir G. Naylor and his secretary, with Mr Bailey, accompanied it, and added the sad mockery of laying a paltry crown upon the coffin. The ladies and the rest of the suite followed in boats. At this moment, the first gun was fired from the fort. Such was the indelicate hurry and rude touch of the persons engaged in the removal of the royal coffin, that before it was received on board the *Glasgow*, the crimson velvet was torn in many places, and hung in slips. When the boat reached the *Pioneer* schooner, the coffin was hoisted on board, the crown and cushion were laid upon it, and the pall was thrown out of the boat to a sailor on deck, by one of the three gentlemen who had it in charge, with no more ceremony than if it had been his cloak. Before it could possibly be announced that the corpse was safe on deck, the sailors were busily employed in unfurling the sails, and in less than ten minutes the *Pioneer* was under sail, to join the *Glasgow* frigate. The body and the mourners were at length received on board the *Glasgow*, and here followed perplexity upon perplexity. The captain had not been informed of the probable number in this melancholy procession, and was incompetent to set before them sufficient food, or furnish them with suitable accommodation. Corn beef was therefore their daily fare; and hammocks, slung under the guns, were the beds assigned to the gentlemen, while the ladies were very little better provided for in the confined cabins. The coffin was placed in a separate cabin, guarded by soldiers, and with lights continually burning. On the 19th of August, the *Glasgow* appeared before the port at Cuxhaven; and, as she drew too much water to get up the Stade, she resigned her charge to the *Wye*, commanded by Captain Fisher.

On Monday evening, the 20th, the remains of the Queen of England were landed at Stade. The coffin, without pall, or covering of any kind, was brought up the creek, a distance of three miles, the mourners following in boats. On their arrival at the quay, no preparation had been made for receiving the body on shore, and had it not been for the sympathy of the inhabitants of the place, the coffin must have been laid upon the earth; but they were so impressed with the necessity of paying regard to decency, and so incensed against the heartless and abominable conduct manifested toward the queen, that they, as if by one consent, brought out their tables and chairs, to afford an elevation for the coffin from the ground; and thus a kind of platform was raised, on which it was protected from further injury. After a short delay, arising from want of due notice having been given of the arrival of the procession, the citizens of the town, headed by the magistrates and priests, proceeded to meet it. The coffin was then taken up, and carried into the church, which was lighted, and partially hung with black. A solemn anthem was sung, accompanied by the deep-toned organ; after which the numberless crowd retired, leaving the royal corpse to the care of those who were appointed to watch over it. Early the next day the procession departed for Buxtehude. About a quarter of a mile from this town it was met by the citizens and magistrates, who attended it, bareheaded, to the church, where the royal remains were deposited for the night. On the ensuing day, the 22d, the procession was met on its entrance into Saltan by the authorities, in the same manner as before named. On the 23d, it reached Celle, where the coffin was carried into the great church of the city, and placed upon the tomb of the unfortunate sister of George the Third, Matilda, Queen of Denmark.[4] On the 24th, the procession was met at Offau, by count Aldenslaben, the grand chamberlain of the court, and arrangements were made, that the funeral should take place at midnight. The mourners were immediately to proceed to Brunswick, and the funeral procession to follow, so as to arrive by ten the same night at the gates of the city, there to be met by the mourners; but further delay of interment than this was strictly forbidden. At the appointed hour, the last stage of the cavalcade commenced. On a near approach to the church, whose vaults were to receive the remains of this royal victim, the children of a school (founded and supported by a lady of truly patriotic principles) walked before the hearse strewing flowers on the road. Arriving at the church, the Brunswick soldiers demanded the privilege to bear the remains of their beloved princess through the church to the vault, in which were deposited those of her illustrious ancestors. This being granted, the corpse was borne, by as many of them as could stand under the coffin, into the abode of death. It was then placed upon an elevation in the centre of the vault, which had previously been prepared for its reception, and where it will remain until another occupy its place; her Majesty's coffin will then be removed to the space appointed for it. After an oration had been delivered in German, the curtain was drawn over our persecuted and destroyed queen. The mourners retired, and the assembled crowds dispersed, shortly after two o'clock.

The Times, *5 September, from Hamburgh papers, Brunswick, 25 August*

Yesterday was performed here the funeral ceremony of the entrance and depositing of the body of the late Queen of England, with all the solemnity and attachment to the House of their Princes which characterises the brave Brunswickers.

The royal corpse, the conveyance of which from England by way of Stade, Celle, &c., had been directed by Sir George Naylor and Mr Calvert, of the Lord Chamberlain's office, was received at Steinhoft, about a league from this city. Eight post horses and three postilions were sent to that place. These brought the body, which was accompanied by a detachment of Brunswick hussars to the White Horse, a short English mile from the city; and four postilions with torches rode beside it. At the White Horse the funeral car, with eight horses from the Prince's stables, was ready to receive the body and convey it to the vault in the Burg church. The citizens of Brunswick, however, would not allow of this, and drew the car to the church themselves. The houses and gardens before the gates, and the streets through which the procession passed, were illuminated. The funeral car was surrounded by a great number of wax tapers. Immediately behind it followed several hundred merchants and citizens with torches. Behind the train of the citizens followed the carriages of the English, Alderman Wood, Lord Hood, Lady Hamilton, Austin, &c., and several carriages belonging to persons of this city, attached to the House of Brunswick. A signal was given by sky-rockets for tolling of the bells of all the churches in the city, which continued from half past eleven to half past twelve o'clock, when the processions terminated. There were certainly 20,000 persons who followed the royal corpse, and the greatest tranquillity and order prevailed during the whole of the funeral solemnity.

The church was hung with black, and 60 young ladies, all dressed in white with black sashes, received the corpse, and accompanied it, with wax tapers, to the vault. The Reverend Mr Wolf delivered an excellent discourse, adapted to the occasion, as was to be expected from this celebrated preacher.

Notes

1. The son of Alderman Wood.
2. The future Queen Victoria (b. 1819).
3. The chief metropolitan magistrate.
4. Caroline-Matilda, b. 1751, married the unstable and profligate Christian VII of Denmark in 1765. He became insane and she became the mistress of the Danish chief minister, Struensee, who was arrested and executed in 1772. She and her child were imprisoned at Elsinore, from whence George III forcibly secured her release. She died in 1775 at Celle.

List of Sources

Unpublished papers

Broughton papers (J.C. Hobhouse's diary), British Library
Cobbett papers, Nuffield College, Oxford
Francis Place papers, British Library

Printed works

(the place of publication is London unless otherwise stated)

The Autobiography and Memoirs of Benjamin Robert Haydon, 1786–1846, A.P.D. Penrose (ed.), 1927
Bagot, Josceline, *George Canning and his Friends*, vol. 2, 1909
The Black Dwarf, 1820–1
Chronicles of Holland House 1820–1900, Earl of Ilchester (ed.), 1937
Correspondence and Diaries of Rt. Hon. John Wilson Croker, vol. 1, L.J. Jennings (ed.), 1884
Correspondence of Sarah Lady Lyttelton 1787–1870, the Hon. Mrs Hugh Wyndham (ed.), 1912
The Creevey Papers, Sir Herbert Maxwell (ed.), 2 vols, 1903
Despatches, Correspondence, and Memoranda of Arthur, Duke of Wellington, vol. 1, 1819–22, Duke of Wellington (ed.), 1867
The Diaries and Correspondence of James Harris, 1st Earl of Malmesbury, vol. 3, 3rd Earl of Malmesbury (ed.), 2nd edn 1845
Diary and Correspondence of Charles Abbot, Lord Colchester, vol. 3, Lord Colchester (ed.), 1861
Diary, Reminiscences, and Correspondence of Henry Crabb Robinson, vol. 1, T. Sadler (ed.), 1872
Extracts of the Journals and Correspondence of Miss Berry, vol. 3, Lady Theresa Lewis (ed.), 1865 (incorporating Lady Charlotte Lindsay's journal)
The Farington Diary, vol. 8, J. Greig (ed.), 1928
The First Lady Wharncliffe and her Family (1779–1856), vol. 1, Caroline Grosvenor and Lord Stuart of Wortley (eds), 1927
Greville, C.C.F, *A Journal of the Reigns of King George IV and King William IV*, vol. 1, H. Reeve (ed.), 1874
Hansard's *Parliamentary Debates*
Holland, Lord, *Further Memoirs of the Whig Party, 1807–21*, Lord Stavordale (ed.), 1905
Journal of the Hon. Henry Edward Fox, 1818–30, Earl of Ilchester (ed.), 1923
The Journal of Mrs Arbuthnot, 1820–1832, vol. 1, F. Bamford and the Duke of Wellington (eds), 1950

Letters of Harriet, Countess Granville 1810–1845, vol. 1, Hon. F. Leveson Gower (ed.), 1894

Letters of Lady Palmerston, Tresham Lever (ed.), 1957

Letters of T.B. Macaulay, vol. 1, T. Pinney (ed.), Cambridge, 1974

Life and Letters of William Cobbett in England and America, vol. 2, L. Melville (ed.), 1913

The Life and Times of Henry Lord Brougham written by himself, vol. 2, 1871

Memoirs of the Court of George IV, 1820–1830, vol. 1, Duke of Buckingham and Chandos (ed.), 1859

Memoirs of . . . Plumer Ward, vol. 2, Hon. E. Phipps (ed.), 1850

Pellew, G., *Life and Correspondence of . . . first Viscount Sidmouth*, vol. 3, 1847

The Private Letters of Princess Lieven to Prince Metternich 1820–1826, P. Quennell (ed.), 1937

The Republican, 1819–20

Rush, R., *A Residence at the Court of London . . . 1819–1825*, vol. 1, 2nd ser. 1845

Sir Thomas Lawrence's Letter-bag, G.S. Layard (ed.), 1906

The Times, 1820–1

Twiss, H., *The Life of Lord Chancellor Eldon*, vol. 2, 1844

Yonge, C.D., *The Life and Administration of Robert Banks, 2nd Earl of Liverpool*, vol. 2, 1868

Index